In this study Gillian Brown draws on a wide range of examples of discourse analysis to explore the ways in which speakers and listeners use language collaboratively to talk about what they can see in front of them and about a series of events. She examines the conditions under which communication is successful, and the conditions under which it sometimes fails. The focus of her attention is upon the listener's role, as the listener tries to make sense of what the speaker says in a highly constrained context; and her cognitive/pragmatic approach to discourse analysis both complements and challenges the sociological/anthropological perspectives on the subject which currently predominate.

Speakers, listeners and communication

Speakers, listeners and communication

Explorations in discourse analysis

GILLIAN BROWN
University of Cambridge

Published by the Press Syndicate of the University of Cambridge
The Pitt Building, Trumpington Street, Cambridge CB2 1RP
40 West 20th Street, New York, NY 10011–4211, USA
10 Stamford Road, Oakleigh, Melbourne 3166, Australia

First published 1995

Printed in Great Britain at the University Press, Cambridge

A catalogue record for this book is available from the British Library

Library of Congress cataloguing in publication data
Brown, Gillian.
    Speakers, listeners, and communication: explorations in discourse
analysis / Gillian Brown.
        p.   cm.
    Includes bibliographical references and index.
    ISBN 0 521 48157 0 (hardback)
    1. Oral communication.   2. Discourse analysis.   3. Reference
(Linguistics)   4. Grammar, Comparative and general–Deixis.
I. Title.
P95.B77   1995
302.2'24–dc20   95–48079
ISBN 0 521 48157 0 hardback

SE

Contents

Acknowledgements

Many individuals and institutions have contributed in various ways to this book. I must thank the ESRC for supporting the projects 'Maintaining Comprehension' (grant number C00232060) and 'Learning listening skills' (grant number C00232377) as well as the Leverhulme Trust for supporting the project 'Learning to listen', and the Scottish Education Department (SED) for supporting the project 'Listening comprehension'.

The original design of the Map task evolved during a conversation in my room in Edinburgh on a November afternoon in 1982 where crucial contributions were made by Anne Anderson, Nigel Shadbolt and Richard Shillcock, who were working on the SED grant. They were responsible for the collection of the Scottish data which is cited here. We acknowledge the generous help of a number of Edinburgh headteachers, English teachers and, crucially, over four hundred pupils.

The Map task evolved further during the first ESRC grant, held at the University of Essex, where major developments were designed by Barry Smith and Peter Wright. They were also responsible for the development of the temporally structured video task, the Stolen letter task, whose character-istics in some significant respects resemble those of the Map task. A valuable contribution was also made by Gordon Brown, Amanda Sharkey and Lee Humphries who worked on the Leverhulme grant. Barry Smith and Peter Wright were responsible for collecting the Essex data cited here, from a number of schools and a large number of co-operative pupils.

I must also thank John Lyons, who read and commented on drafts of the first three chapters, and my colleagues Kirsten Malmkjaer and John Williams who read much of the preliminary draft. An anonymous reviewer wrote a valuable constructive report on a partial draft, and Peter Matthews made particularly helpful comments on the final version. Finally I must thank my husband, Keith Brown, for consistent illumination on syntactic issues, and Susan Rolfe, without whose unfailing support the time to write the book would not have been created.

Transcription conventions

The initials of members of the pairs of subjects who produced the dialogue from which each extract has been taken are indicated at the top of each dialogue taken from the Map task data. Similarly the number of the relevant quartet or of the undergraduate (ug) pair is indicated at the top of extracts from the Stolen letter task.

The transcription conventions have been kept to a minimum. The following conventions are used:

–	a very brief pause
+	a pause of about half a second
++	a pause of about a second
?	high rising intonation
(...)	indecipherable speech
...	some portion of the text is omitted
[	overlap between speakers
(*laughs*)	italicised comments in brackets indicate relevant non-verbal behaviour by the speaker

Introduction

This book is primarily concerned to give an account of how listeners behave as they participate in dialogues in which information is exchanged. What listeners have understood from what a previous speaker has said is frequently revealed in what listeners say themselves when they next take a turn at speaking. We shall examine what listeners say in their turn as speakers, looking for evidence of what they have understood previous speakers as saying. Detailed knowledge of such behaviour is fundamental to the development of our understanding of the cognitive basis of language use.

If we want to make claims about the nature of comprehension processes, we had better be sure that such claims will be widely applicable within the population. The subjects who participated in the dialogues illustrated here are drawn from a wide range of backgrounds and are diverse in their academic ability. They are drawn from Edinburgh schools and the University of Edinburgh, as well as from schools in the county of Essex and Essex University. They include young adults and adolescents of demonstrated intellectual ability, as well as 14–16 year-olds who are deemed by their schools to be in the bottom third of the academic ability range.

I am not concerned here to make quantitative claims. Rather, I draw attention to patterns of behaviour which occur repetitively in the data. The intention is to seek to explore the nature of the behaviour rather than to examine its detailed distribution. Even if only a handful of subjects manifests a problem of understanding at a point in the exchange of information where others have apparently no difficulty, this itself may illuminate the process as a whole.

1

The dialogues which form the data emerge from tasks where different participants had access to different but related information, which needed to be shared in order for the task to be achieved. The participants spoke freely and as much as they felt that they needed to; thus some groups completed a task in ten minutes which others took forty minutes to fail to complete. All of the dialogues were audio-taped and transcribed. The value of the task structure is that the analyst can identify what is being spoken of, knowing what information was potentially available to the participants, and can compare treatments of the same point of information by different individuals and different groups.

It seems reasonable to suggest that a basic requirement of understanding is the ability to understand reference to persons and things, to understand how they are disposed in space, and to understand how they interact over time. The tasks described here explore these abilities.

The tasks fall into two groups. The first group, called the Map task, is concerned with the identification and spatial relationships of features on maps, where one speaker describes a route to the listener. How much listeners have understood of what the speaker says is to a considerable extent revealed in what the listeners draw on their maps, by what questions they ask, and by the comments that they make as the task proceeds. There are easier and more difficult versions of these spatially structured tasks, which make different cognitive demands on the subjects, differences which are reflected in the language speakers use and the consequent changed demands on the listeners. Of particular interest is the way in which subjects set about constructing the context required to interpret a given utterance.

In the second set of tasks, the Stolen letter tasks, different participants in the same dialogue watch different stretches of the video-recording of a temporally structured series of events, in which it is necessary to distinguish between three characters and to track each of them through the series of events. The participants narrate to each other the action which they have witnessed, and then together try to work out the sequence of the events which they have (a) watched and (b) heard about. The narrative genre requires subjects to retain in memory what they have witnessed and listened to, and to attempt to construct a coherent account of the input from two different modes. This genre elicits a much wider variety of linguistic forms from speakers, which in turn requires enhanced strategies of interpretation as compared to those which were used in the Map task. In particular, this shift of genre makes it necessary to reformulate the notion of context to accommodate how an utterance must be understood in the narrative mode.

In this study, the listener's role in conversation is emphasised. In chapter 1, I discuss the nature of communication and the notion of the correct interpretation of an utterance. While not denying that there are types of utterance which can demonstrably be correctly or incorrectly interpreted, I suggest that, for most utterances, particularly those which form part of extended discourse, the most we can hope for is adequate interpretation – adequate as seen from the listener's point of view rather than from that of the speaker.

In chapter 2, I consider the range of ways which are currently used to explore the nature of the processes of comprehension and suggest that an additional, complementary, method is required, which would permit an account of fully successful communication and allow us to distinguish this from partially successful, or wholly unsuccessful, communication and would yield, in part at least, an account of the reasons for this range of behaviour. I suggest that the Map task method performs this function, at least for the genres of data examined here, since it obliges participants to cope with combining dissonant information, from an auditory linguistic source and from a visual source, in a plausibly ecological environment (in the sense of Neisser 1976).

Chapter 3 explores the ways in which participants construct and interpret expressions which refer to landscape features in a range of different spatial domains, in the context of considering what it might mean for speaker and listener to think of a referent in a 'pretty similar' way (Evans 1982:316). It shows how listeners who are successful in understanding referring expressions appear to construct a restricted search field within the general context of the Map task. I also show how vague expressions, intended by the speaker to refer, may be taken by the listener, in the absence of a referent, as constitutive of new information.

In chapter 4, I turn to the issue of how, in a spatial domain, the speaker, by the use of deictic (or indexical) expressions, can construct for the listener a particular viewpoint, yielding a perspective on what is spoken of which the listener must share with the speaker in order to understand the speaker's utterance.

Chapters 5 and 6 retrace some of the ground covered in chapters 3 and 4, but this time in the context of a temporally structured task, the Stolen letter task. These chapters draw attention to the different demands made upon the listener as soon as we move away from a stable, external representation of the sort that we see in the spatially structured maps, to demand from the listener an ability to combine the memory of episodes watched on a video with a verbal account of a different episode in the same narrative.

In the final chapter, the listener's various roles are the focus of attention, as, using data from both types of tasks, we analyse the way in which a listener behaves in a two-person dialogue as opposed to a four-person dialogue, and show how differently listeners behave when they listen to information which is new to them, rather than overhearing information which they already know. We explore the part played in information exchanges by the establishment of mutual beliefs and we then address, once again, the issue of sentence meaning and speaker intention.

I have focussed in this study on the time/place/person parameters. The data I discuss, particularly that in the Stolen letter task, where subjects attempt to work out the order in which two scenes must have occurred and ascribe intentions to characters in the narrative, offers a rich source of evidence on the types of inferences which listeners draw from what other speakers say in conjunction with what they themselves already know. I had intended to include in this volume a chapter on this topic, but the contents of this putative chapter have grown out of all proportion to the rest of the volume and, it is now clear, must constitute a separate book.

The discourse analyst sits, rather uneasily perhaps, between the semanticist who attempts to give an account of what sentences mean, and the cognitive psychologist who attempts to give an account of how listeners process utterances and texts. The discourse analyst draws on a range of more-or-less well understood theoretical models to attempt to describe listeners' behaviour as they listen to spontaneously produced language which they try to make sense of while attempting to put that understanding to immediate use. The data presented here is, in an obvious sense, artificial and highly restricted in type, and should be extrapolated from with caution, since it seems likely that each newly examined genre will throw up characteristics of behaviour which were not manifested in the relatively simple tasks which we investigate here. Nonetheless a careful, qualitative, analysis of the behaviour of listeners, even in banal tasks, should contribute to a better understanding of how listeners actually go about the process of constructing an interpretation, of how they sometimes fail, and why they fail.

1 · Speakers, listeners and communication

1.1 The nature of communication

How do people use language to communicate with each other? For centuries the commonsense view has been that articulated by Locke: 'Unless a man's words excite the same ideas in the hearer which he makes them stand for in speaking he does not speak intelligibly' ([1689] 1971:262). Locke was himself fully aware of the difficulties of achieving such an ideal, guaranteed, form of communication, but it still claims its adherents in the twentieth century. In the simplest version of this view, the speaker has a thought which is encoded into words and transmitted through the air by sound-waves so that it reaches the listener, who decodes the words and then has the speaker's thought. Such an account of communication would have little more to say than that it consists of speakers exchanging thoughts (see for instance Shannon & Weaver's account of signal-information in Information Theory, 1949).

Swift parodies such a simplistic view in *Gulliver's Travels*, where Gulliver describes an even more direct method of ensuring the passage of the same thought. The mathematics master in the Grand Academy of Lagado (Swift's splenetic version of the Royal Society) requires his students to eat each idea, so that it may progress directly to the brain without any distorting mediation arising from the student's own contemplation of the idea:'the proposition and demonstration were fairly written on a thin wafer, with ink composed of a cephalic tincture. This the student was to swallow upon a fasting stomach, and for three days following eat nothing but bread and water. As the wafer digested, the tincture mounted to his brain, bearing the proposition along with it' ([1726] 1960:224). Despite the ingenuity of the method, at the time of writing Gulliver was unable to account the method a success, because of persistent failure on the part of the students to carry out the specified procedures.

Although direct passage of thoughts might seem to offer an ideal system of communication, where sets of expressions with fixed meanings are passed from one mind to another, thus guaranteeing the preservation of the identity of the thoughts associated with the expressions, the problems of such an account have often been pointed out, though rarely more effectively than by Swift. The only systems of human communication which can be described as operating through fixed meanings are relatively limited systems like those used in arithmetic or, to choose a simpler example, like traffic lights. Locke himself observed that, since different individuals had different experiences, they used and understood words in different ways ([1689] 1971:300) – Locke's own use of the term *idea* is a good example of this). He suggested that, as our ideas become more complex and more abstract, the meaning intended by the speaker (which may not be fully clear even to the speaker) is increasingly less likely to be understood in exactly the same way by the hearer.

The traditional response to what was seen as the danger of inefficient communication was to talk of the 'imperfections' of language, as Locke sometimes did ([1689] 1971:299–301). This was a view widely held at the inception of the Royal Society, which was intended to remedy such deficiencies. It is a view still expressed by some scholars today: Herskovitz (1986:192), acknowledging vagueness and inconsistency in the semantics of prepositions in English, speaks of the 'design defects' of language. The difficulties confronting any effort to rationalise the structure or to fix the possible meaning of language, appear to be, in principle, insoluble (and indeed such an outcome, we shall argue, would be undesirable). Nonetheless, throughout the last three hundred years at least, the failure to ensure the passage between minds of an identical thought has been seen as fundamentally dangerous to the basis of human knowledge and, in particular, to scientific knowledge. Frege, for instance, insisted that in order to understand an utterance by person A, which refers to an object, person B must not only identify the same object but must think of it in a particular way – in the same way as A, since if B thinks of it in some private way we lose the notion of a public language, and without a public language which conveys meanings which are guaranteed to be interpreted identically by everyone, science is impossible (an issue discussed in Evans 1982:15).

Today, there still remain those who believe that a guaranteed system of communication is possible in a human community, even where individuals have a diversity of experiences, though this view has been extensively challenged in recent years (see the discussion in 1.3). One of the functions of a system of education, which is extended over ten or more years of adolescent life, must be to provide repeated experiences of using particular technical terms in restricted ways within particular subject areas, to ensure, as far as possible, a common usage of such terms for those who are participating in a meaningful discourse, shaping their utterances for others who, they believe, are at that moment thinking of what they are thinking of. As a result of this extended education, we may rely on a commonality of usage among educated laymen of such terms as *stanza, molecule, tributary, multiplication, treaty, germination, convection,* and *clause.* But for the purposes of everyday life, where technical terminology is not at issue, the language available to each of us to describe the great variety of changing experience has hourly to be stretched in new ways, with its potential meanings subtly modified. Ziff (1969:233) writes on the importance of recognising the fact that a natural language 'does not ever have, not even at an arbitrary moment of time, a static fixed store of word-senses'. Rather, the vocabulary of a natural language is continually being recreated, and the range of senses which are available to a particular word is constantly being modified and, at the same time, the range of possible interpretations of each of those senses is itself being modified.

It is important to remember that apparently satisfactory communication may often take place without the listener arriving at a full interpretation of the words used. We would expect that this must be a frequent experience for young children learning the language. A 3 year-old boy listened with apparent enjoyment and comprehension, on several occasions, to a story about 'an enormous turnip'. Some weeks later, in a friend's garden, he pointed to a large acanthus plant which was a good deal taller than he was, and asked *Is that an enormous turnip?* Note that he had understood enough of the meaning of the phrase – that it was a very large plant with big leaves which grows in the garden – to make sense of the story, which did not hinge on 'the turnip-ness' of turnips, whatever that may be. He may or may not have understood that turnips have edible roots below the ground. What he was apparently seeking to do was to relate the meaning of this unanchored, partially understood phrase which he had retained in memory, to the real world containing this plant, whose strikingly large size had brought to mind the familiar phrase.

It is not only small children who carry partial information about the relationship between quite familiar words and the objects that these words may appropriately be used to describe. Quine (1960:125) remarks that 'Vagueness is a natural consequence of the basic mechanism of word learning' and he goes on to suggest that a general term which denotes physical objects 'will be vague in two ways: as to the several boundaries of all its objects and as to the inclusion or exclusion of marginal objects' (ibid.:126). He takes as an example the term *mountain* and points out, as an example of the first kind of vagueness, that it will generally be unclear where a mountain begins and ends. He goes on to suggest that it will be difficult to determine a cut-off point between what is called *a mountain* and what is called *a hill*, a difficulty which exemplifies the second kind of vagueness.

In addition to the types of vagueness of which Quine writes, which appear to be inherent in categorisation, listeners are sometimes able to interpret a given expression in one context of use which, on another occasion, they cannot adequately interpret. Many adults are able to understand utterances containing expressions such as *beech, elm, sycamore* or *aspen* quite adequately in many contexts, but would be embarrassed if they were asked to pick out the photograph of 'a sycamore' from a set of ten photographs of different trees. Putnam (1975) remarks that since he cannot distinguish between an instance of 'elm' and an instance of 'beech', his personal conceptualisation of both of them must be identical, as either of the expressions will call to mind some sort of undifferentiated deciduous tree. (But Jackendoff (1983:145) points out that if Putnam were told that a particular tree was a beech, he would at least know that it could not also be an elm.) It certainly seems to be the case that, for large areas of experience, many of us must operate with words related to vague prototypes which bear only an insecure relation to things in the world. I know many pairs of quite familiar words whose senses are (I think) similar but distinct, where I would have problems distinguishing between the entities that they conventionally denote – such words as *bulldog* and *mastiff, pewter* and *britannia metal, paraffin* and *methylated spirits, rook* and *crow, judo* and *karate* would be examples. Nonetheless, on a particular occasion of use I expect to be able to understand an utterance containing one of these expressions, particularly if there is only one relevant type of object present in the context.

In such cases, a qualified expert, whose education and experience have been specialised in the relevant area, could tell us how to distinguish the members of the pair reliably. But we also know a great many words which are not always reliably deployed to make consistent distinctions in the world, and perhaps in principle cannot be reliably deployed. Labov, in a well-known experiment, asked subjects to label a set of shapes varying in the dimensions of height and width, using the terms *bowl, cup* or *vase*. No-one had any difficulty with naming the prototypical shapes, but the intermediate forms were judged variably, and judgments could be swayed in one direction or another by the uses to which the container was put (Labov 1973). This outcome seems to exemplify Quine's second kind of vagueness. Jackendoff (1983) remarks that we would hardly expect an expert to rule on whether or not something is correctly identified as a *puddle* or a *pebble*. Similarly Fillmore has discussed the domestic conditions under which today one might judge someone to be a *widow*. Is someone who is divorced, whose former husband has just died, now a *widow*? Suppose she has married again and has become the *wife* of the second husband, is she nonetheless to be considered to be the *widow* of the first? (Fillmore 1982, see also Lakoff 1987). We may claim to know the meaning of a word but it does not follow that we always deploy it in a consistent and reliable manner. This is an issue which we shall return to in later chapters.

We have noted that the genre which has traditionally been seen to be most threatened by the imperfections of language is factual discourse involving the exchange of information, particularly in the sciences. However, partial understanding is obviously an issue which is relevant not only to scientific discourse at some far-removed professional level, but to us all. In everyday life, each of us has a lively interest in the correct passage of information between air-traffic controllers and the pilots of the aircraft we are travelling in, between pharmaceutical companies and the doctors who are prescribing medicines for us, between our legal representatives and those who sit in judgment on us. In cases like these, we would be reassured if we could rely on a system of communication as ideal as that described by Locke.

1.2 Variable interpretation in different contexts

Once we admit the possibility that the same expression may be interpreted differently upon different occasions, there are two major issues to be confronted. The first is a familiar one: the same expression may be construed as having a different meaning in different situations of use. This variability is not regarded as fundamentally troublesome since it can be attributed to the effects of pragmatic interpretation in context, though quite how this relationship between utterance and context is to be articulated is an issue we shall return to.

The second issue, which we shall begin to consider in 1.3, is much more threatening to secure communication. It concerns different individuals arriving at different interpretations of the same expression in the same context of use.

1.2.1 The effect of context on interpretation

In this section we shall briefly discuss the first issue, which raises many interesting questions, only some of which will be addressed at this point. We shall begin by making the simplifying assumption, for the moment, that different listeners (and readers) will generally agree, within reason, on their interpretations of language under everyday conditions of use.

In 1.1 we considered the prevalence of polysemy in natural language as one source of variability of meaning. However, it is often the case that divergencies of meaning of the same expression derive not so much from polysemy as from the underspecification (vagueness) of word meaning which permits us to talk about a wide range of experience using the same words. Haugeland ([1979] 1990:664), in discussing the problem from the perspective of Artificial Intelligence, provides a neat example of the same sentence used in two different contexts which invite the reader to construct quite different scenarios, hence to interpret the two sentences differently.

Consider how you understand the second sentence in each of the following texts:

(a) When Daddy came home, the boys stopped their cowboy game. They put away their guns and ran out back to the car.

(b) When the police drove up, the boys called off their robbery attempt. They put away their guns and ran out back to the car.

The second sentence in each of these two texts is not strikingly ambiguous. Nor are we dealing here with obvious instances of lexical polysemy. Nonetheless most readers will suppose that 'the same sentence' means different things in these two different contexts, as you quickly find if you try to translate either token of the sentence into another language, or even try to paraphrase them in English. The referring expressions in the two different contexts cause the reader to construct somewhat different imaginary referents. In (a) the expression *they* will be understood as referring to 'boys' who are still young children, *guns* as referring to 'toy guns' and *the car* as referring to 'a car owned by Daddy' which, we infer, is the same car that 'Daddy' has just driven up to the back of the house to park. The expression *the car* in the second sentence in (a) will be interpreted as anaphoric to 'a car' inferable from the first sentence. However, in (b), the same expressions will be used to construct a scenario which involves older 'boys' (who may actually be young men, thus colloquially characterised), real firearms and a get-away car which has been waiting outside the back of the house and will now drive away from it. This car is distinct from the car which, again we infer, 'the police drove up' in the first sentence of this text so, this time, the expression *the car* will not be interpreted anaphorically. And whereas *put away* in (a) must be taken to mean something like 'put away in a toy cupboard', in (b) it must mean something like 'put away in their pockets or holsters'. The second instance of *ran out back* might be paraphrased as *ran away* or *fled*, but such an interpretation would be quite inappropriate in the first example, where the boys are understood to be running out towards their father's car.

Such examples make it easy to see why computers have problems in interpreting texts. And if human beings were similarly deprived of experience and imagination which could be brought to bear in constructing an interpretation, these problems would be shared by human interpreters. In fact, we typically arrive at different interpretations for the second sentence in each of the two texts perfectly smoothly, with no apparent difficulty.

There is, however, a problem for us lurking here, and that is the relationship between the interpretation which we construct for a sentence presented in isolation and the interpretation of another token of the same sentence constructed within a context. If you do not know the context set up by the previous sentence, in the case of our example, you can only develop an interpretation by constructing a context based on your own prototypical experience. You have to provide a context to arrive at any sort of interpretation since the 'thin' semantic meaning of a sentence, derived just from a series of vocabulary items in a syntactic structure, yields only such a sketchy and partial content that it cannot alone provide the material for an interpretation. It is not until the 'thin' meaning is enriched by the provision of extra material, which you infer from the immediate context and from your previous knowledge, that you know what the utterance means.

There is a real sense in which you could not confidently undertake a translation into a foreign language which would generalise to any situation of *They put away their guns and ran out back to the car* if the sentence is presented to you out of any context. Since you have to enrich the content of the sentence in order to understand it, you need to provide some prototypical context for its interpretation. If you choose the wrong prototypical context, for instance one that is appropriate to text (a) rather than one appropriate to text (b), and it later turns out that a text (b) context is the one required, you will have to do some radical rethinking, and, indeed, you are likely to have to begin again to construct a different interpretation. (And, if you have translated the sentence into a foreign language, a different translation as well.) There is a crucial relationship in real-life communication between the utterance and the context in which it occurs and what the participants are prepared to imagine, or to infer from their previous experience. In later chapters we shall return to considering how to characterise the notion of context and its function in interpretation. We should just note at this point that the type of relationship holding between the first and second sentences in these two texts, whereby the interpretation of the first sentence provides severe constraints on the possible interpretations of the second, will generally hold between the first and second (and subsequent) sentences of any text.

1.2.2 Speaker meaning and sentence meaning

A distinction is often drawn between so-called 'sentence meaning' and 'speaker meaning'. Those who draw such a distinction hold that it is possible to attribute a specific interpretation to a sentence taken out of any context, an interpretation which yields 'the real meaning' of the sentence (see Lyons 1977:643 who writes: 'the meaning of a sentence like "John is a brave man" is not affected by its being uttered ironically'). If a speaker utters a token of such a sentence, in a context of use, where the speaker's utterance is interpreted as meaning something radically different from the constructed decontextualised interpretation, then a distinction is drawn between 'the real meaning' of the sentence and the meaning apparently intended by the speaker.

But note that, to arrive at this result, it is necessary to compare two very different sorts of object, which it is not at all clear are strictly comparable. On the one hand we have what I have called (in 1.2.1 above) the 'thin semantic meaning of a sentence . . . (which) yields only such a sketchy and partial content that it cannot alone provide the material for an interpretation' and on the other hand, we have posited a fully interpreted utterance, interpreted in a context which will constrain the potential range of meaning of the sentence. We are only able to compare the two meanings if the listener/reader provides some (prototypical) mental context within which the interpretation of the 'thin semantic meaning' of the uncontextualised proposition becomes accessible to contemplation. As Fodor remarks: 'it is only *qua* anchored that sentences *have* content' (1988:50), where he uses 'anchored' to mean 'anchored within a context'.

Once we begin to look at language used for genuinely communicative purposes, rather than at language idling, it becomes apparent that we often (perhaps characteristically) mean far more than we explicitly express in propositionally representable terms. If I say *John is a brave man* in circumstances where John has just demonstrated that he is timid and fearful, it seems perverse for an analyst to claim that what I really mean is that 'John is not a brave man', since if that were all that I wanted to express, I could have expressed that content quite straightforwardly. Obviously, I want you to interpret the utterance as richly as I intend it to be interpreted in the context, and, if I choose to preserve a positive evaluation in these unpropitious circumstances, it may be so that you may think I am generous, or witty, or sophisticated – certainly something other than straightforward. There are many subtle possible interpretations which you could reasonably suppose that I might mean you to infer from such a bald utterance in such a context – that 'John is usually a brave man', or 'John is fundamentally a brave man', or 'John is a brave man when he's in the public eye', or 'John is not brave when he knows that nobody will be impressed'. Of course, if a scholar is committed to a belief in specific monosemy and a direct relation between the word and the world, he is surely correct in claiming that the propositional meaning of the utterance remains the same. It must be clear though, if we accept that (at least some) utterance types do not have a single correct interpretation which will hold in all contexts, which is the position that I have been arguing for, every one of them is going to involve the 'sentence meaning / speaker meaning' conundrum for those who believe that language is only used to express what it explicitly states, and that it is properly used in a fixed and conventional manner. (This issue is further discussed in 3.6.1 and 7.3.)

If you adopt a view that, in saying something, you really mean to assert one proposition (and perhaps also to imply one, and only one, other proposition), this suggests that you believe that there is a single, conventionally agreed interpretation which can be assigned to each word in isolation from any context, and that the 'real meaning' of a sentence is constructed compositionally, by putting together the set of conventionally agreed single senses which are assigned to each word. It also implies that you believe that there is a correct procedure for using language to talk about the world – that there is a proper way of constructing expressions which refer to individuals and that there is a proper way of constructing descriptions of their activities, indeed that there is a proper prototypical context which can appropriately be constructed in order to arrive at the correct interpretation of a sentence in isolation. I have tried to show, in the discussion of the examples in 1.2.1, and throughout the discussion of vagueness in language in 1.1, that it may not be possible to assign such prototypical contexts to develop the interpretation of all sentences in isolation. The following sections will offer further support to such a view.

1.3 Variable interpretation among listeners

It is now widely held that the underdetermination of most word-meanings when they are considered in isolation, as in a dictionary entry, contributes a necessary flexibility to human language. Such a flexibility enables the communication of new thoughts (or at least of thoughts in new relationships to other thoughts). This assumption is commonly associated with the view that communication does not consist of a fail-safe exchange of the same thought, but is, rather, a system which requires effort on the part of the speaker in constructing a helpful message and also on the part of the hearer in working out what the speaker might have meant. This implies the possibility that one individual may arrive at a different interpretation from that intended by the speaker, or a different interpretation from that constructed by another listener. One obvious reason for current sensitivity to these issues has been a shift of interest from the almost exclusive study of discursive written genres to include consideration of spoken language, particularly the spontaneous, relatively unreflective speech of co-operative conversation.

The shift of interest from formal written language to informal spoken language is found in disciplines as diverse as philosophy, social anthropology and linguistics. An important influence in the last forty years has been the later work of Wittgenstein who insisted on the importance of looking at examples of particular instances of use in attempting to determine the meaning of a particular utterance (for instance Wittgenstein [1953] 1978). A further seminal influence has been the work of Grice, in giving an account of (non-conventional) meaning which rests on the hearer's recognition of the speaker's intention to communicate a given proposition, thus frankly pulling into the study of meaning the cognitive dimension of the speaker's intentions in uttering (Grice 1956). The second crucial contribution of Grice ([1967] 1975) was in showing a way to give a principled account of how much more can be understood from the interpretation of an utterance in a co-operative conversation than is directly encoded in words. From his initial outline of the Conversational Maxims, there has flowed a rich literature, which provides insights not only into how we arrive at interpretations of expressions which relatively transparently encode the speaker's intention, but also how we interpret expressions which indicate only subtly and indirectly what the speaker wishes to convey.

From a quite different perspective, Goffman (1967) has illuminated the reasons why co-operative parties in a conversation adopt indirect modes of expression, seeking on the one hand to protect their own 'face' and, on the other, to preserve that of their interlocutors. Why might the person writing a reference, in Grice's ([1967] 1975) example, choose to mention the applicant's punctuality and handwriting rather than his unsuitability for the position that he seeks? Goffman's approach (particularly as developed by Brown and Levinson 1978, and Brown and Levinson 1988) would provide an account (or range of accounts) of the writer's social behaviour.

In yet another field, Reddy (1979) brought into focus the effects of pervasive metaphors in English on our conceptualisation of the nature of communication. His paper explores widespread metaphors which, he suggests, have contributed to the belief that communication is an easy no-risk affair, whereas, as he correctly insists, it always involves effort on the part of both speaker and hearer, and necessarily carries with it the risk of misunderstanding. It is only recently that such views have become widely accepted, but they are by no means new. To take just one earlier example of an approach which requires an active, participatory role on the part of the receiver of information, Bartlett wrote of the 'fundamental effort after meaning' which characterises all our cognitive experience (1932:227).

It is not, of course, only linguists and their traditional allies in philosophy of language and social anthropology who have become sensitive to the possibility that a listener's understanding of an utterance may not yield a thought that is identical to that intended by the speaker. A major movement in literary theory, drawing on the work of figures like Foucault, Barthes and, more recently, Derrida, has insisted on the many possible readings of a literary text. Such a view is still the subject of animated debate. David Lodge points to uncontroversial evidence of differences in interpretation: 'If Jane Austen's *Emma*, for instance, is a communication, what is its message? Hundreds of articles and chapters of books have been published, purporting to explain what the novel "means", what it is "about" . . . They all differ to a greater or lesser extent from each other in their conclusions and emphases' (Lodge 1990:103).

It can hardly be denied that there are multiple possible ways of understanding any extended text, depending on factors as simple as how much time is spent on reading it. Most readers would agree that their interpretation of a poem on first reading is rarely identical to their interpretations on subsequent readings. The range of differing interpretations of literary texts has given rise to a critical literature which is itself constantly reinterpreted.

Similar issues arise in the translation of literature. Translations of classic works, including sacred texts such as the Bible, carry meanings which are subtly or sometimes strikingly different from those expressed in previous translations, which must indicate that the original text has been differently understood by these different translators. Such evidence of differing interpretations by different individuals seems to be incontrovertible.

The acceptance of the notion of differing interpretations of the same text is, however, seen as a threat by those who believe that scholars and scientists must strive towards correct interpretations, who are concerned that it would become impossible to set bounds on the range of possible interpretations and to distinguish the true meanings of texts from false ones. In 1992, in the University of Cambridge, a flysheet was issued in the course of an extended public and private debate on the work of Derrida. This flysheet deplored what was described as his 'assertion of the impossibility of distinguishing correct from incorrect interpretations', and pointed out what its authors saw as the sorely damaging effects of such a doctrine for disciplines as diverse as literature, history, law, science, technology and medicine. The passions raised by this issue reflect its significance.

The issue is not simply a theoretical one without consequences in the world. At a practical level, it is easy to appreciate the difficulties arising from an extremely relativistic approach to multiple meanings for academics marking students' paraphrases of extracts from Chaucer, Shakespeare or Milton, or for teachers of modern languages correcting translation exercises, or for any of us who use computer manuals which have been translated from, say, Japanese into English.

1.4 Correct interpretation

The possibility of multiple interpretations of a sentence uttered in a context of use raises fundamental questions for those linguists and philosophers of language who are concerned with the implications of such a view for semantic theories based on the notion of 'truth'. Over thirty years ago, Quine (1960) raised the spectre of the indeterminacy of translation in a book which is still constantly quoted today, since many of the issues which it raises (notably those concerned with the (im)possibility of knowing exactly what someone intends you to understand by the use of a particular word) are still not laid to rest, and are perhaps incapable of being settled. Lycan (1990:342) suggests, perhaps implausibly, that he may be only restating Quine's position in an extreme form when he writes: 'any interpretation that suits anyone's convenience is good enough, and if two interpreters' interpretations conflict, neither is correct to the exclusion of the other' (the very position attributed to Derrida in the flysheet cited above).

Some philosophers have countered Quine's arguments by drawing attention to aspects of the nature of interpretation other than those solely concerned with understanding individual words or sentences in isolation. Putnam has suggested that a necessary constraint in interpretation is provided by the listener's own interests in the issue, as well as those which the listener attributes to the speaker (1978:44f). Davidson (1974) has argued that we are only capable of understanding language which is expressing fundamentally similar conceptual schemes to those that we ourselves share. But these proposed additional constraints on interpretation still do not solve the central problem posed by Quine, and are certainly not sufficient to guarantee that we understand a particular utterance 'correctly'. There will always be a doubt, even when I believe that my own interpretation of an utterance is identical to yours, in being sure that this is adequately the case. Fodor states the technical problem for those who wish to insist that correct interpretation is possible, and that it involves speaker and hearer having identical thoughts: 'how much (and what kinds of) similarity between thinkers does the intentional identity of their thoughts require? This is, notice, a question one had better be able to answer if there is going to be a scientifically interesting propositional attitude psychology' ([1986] 1990:426). He goes on to point out that thinkers 'would not be anything like neurophysically identical' since we have no reason to suppose that any two human beings are neurophysically identical.

Put differently, once you have abandoned the belief that a correct interpretation simply means recovering the original idea of the speaker, you have to take a view on what it would mean for my interpretation to be similar enough to a correct interpretation of what the speaker intended to convey by producing that particular utterance.

Hofstadter suggests that, whatever is required for one mind to understand an utterance in the same way as another mind understands it, it cannot be neural equivalence. Rather, he proposes, we might want to suggest that corresponding symbols in the two minds are linked, to some degree at least, in corresponding ways. However, like Fodor, he sees the problem of what might count as a partial functional isomorphism as 'a most difficult question to answer' (Hofstadter 1980:371). Even if it were, in principle, possible to demonstrate that two minds contained the same thought, it is by no means clear that the same isolable thought would receive the same interpretation or be thought about in the same way in the two minds.

A simple instance of this issue is provided by the interpretation of proper names and the troublesome fact that individuals bearing proper names play multiple roles which participants in a conversation may have different views on and different feelings about. Suppose you say of a mutual acquaintance *In some ways he's very like Margaret Thatcher*. Have I interpreted the utterance correctly if I simply identify the individual referred to by the expression *Margaret Thatcher* as 'the former prime minister'? In Fregean terms, presumably the answer must be *yes*, since I will have correctly associated the expression with a particular individual. But in terms of normal human communication this is surely insufficient. I must also infer what might be her relevant attributes and match them with those of the mutual acquaintance, in order to determine whether or not I think the assertion is true. These attributes may be physical, intellectual or moral. In addition, I will suppose that you have some view, either negative or positive, about the attributes which I need to assess. If I infer, correctly, that you are referring to Margaret Thatcher's tendency to fight for her beliefs in a particularly aggressive manner, since that is what our mutual acquaintance does, I seem to be on the way to a correct interpretation. But if the matrix of beliefs into which my interpretation is to fit (and from which it is derived) includes a belief that such a tendency is admirable whereas you, unknown to me, deplore that tendency, can I still be said to have understood your utterance correctly? Remember that Frege (cited in 1.1, discussed in Evans 1982) insisted that the listener must think of the object mentioned by the speaker in the particular way that the speaker thinks of the object. If this view is strictly limited to the relationship between the sense of the expression and the identification of the referent, then presumably I have understood correctly. But if affect is taken into account as well, and it seems highly relevant in this type of utterance, then surely you have to suppose that I have failed to understand completely and correctly the speaker's intention in uttering. This is an issue which will frequently re-emerge in later chapters.

Those working in the field of psycholinguistics often appear to support the view that there is a single correct interpretation for a given utterance. Johnson-Laird suggests that evidence for the existence of a correct interpretation is provided by the fact that failures of communication occur, and are known to occur, whereas if no discourse had a true interpretation, such failures could neither occur nor be rectified. He goes on to suggest that the position of Derrida and other deconstructionist literary critics is that they confuse 'the admitted difficulty of recovering the communicator's intentions with a wholly independent question: do communications ever have a correct interpretation?' (1990:9). However, Johnson-Laird's brisk commonsense approach does less than justice to the complexity of the issues under discussion here, because it pays attention to only one aspect of the apparent paradox which we are confronting. It is true that, in daily life, most of our communicative attempts appear to be successful (except perhaps in the context of stressful relationships where one or both participants compulsively arrive at paranoid interpretations of what the other meant). But it is also true that some forms of language, particularly extended texts, appear to be open to a variety of interpretations, and this is true not only of literary texts, which might otherwise be seen as exceptional in this regard, but also of non-literary texts, as is attested daily, for instance, in courts of law and local tribunals where experts trained to understand legal language fail to agree what it means.

What sort of account can we give of these apparently contradictory experiences?

1.5 Adequate interpretation

I shall propose, to begin with, that we may need to modify the notion that correct interpretation is the norm, and substitute for it a weaker notion of **adequate interpretation**, a position which will be argued for throughout this book. It will be necessary then to give an account of our common everyday experience, which is that we do, on most everyday occasions, apparently correctly understand what the speaker intended to communicate. We shall need an account of what it means to understand an utterance adequately for a particular purpose on a particular occasion, and how it is that it is possible to be reasonably sure that we have done so, stated from the point of view of the listener rather than that of the speaker. It will also be necessary to reconcile this daily experience of successful communication with the further common experience of justifiably different interpretations of the same text.

To get some sort of handle on understanding, we are going to have to distinguish carefully how we appeal to this term in different contexts of use. Much everyday language, particularly that which relates to familiar procedures in the real world – checking that someone has put the cat out, buying a bar of chocolate, co-operating in a surgical operation or in organising an academic conference – is intended by the speaker to have a specific correct interpretation in that familiar context which will generally be recognised correctly by listeners and, if it is not, the speaker will see that something has gone wrong. In such cases, as Johnson-Laird suggests, there may be a possibility of identifying and of rectifying the erroneous interpretation. It is, I believe, primarily from such areas of common experience that we derive the belief that utterances have a single correct interpretation. Successful co-operative procedures lie at the core of everyday life, and it is on them that the continued successful existence of social groups crucially depends. Hence, it seems reasonable to suppose that these successful procedures are based on correct assumptions. (Dennett (1990:194) claims that natural selection must guarantee that *most* of an organism's beliefs will be true.) Even in such highly delimited areas there is room for misinterpretation, but it will occur relatively rarely.

However, it is not at all clear that it is appropriate simply to extrapolate from the experience of understanding utterances in such familiar, repetitive, contexts, where a majority of judges might well agree upon a correct interpretation, to other contexts where language is being used in very different ways. As language use moves away from short exchanges which relate to the here-and-now, towards more abstract and complex genres, the opportunities for misunderstanding multiply, and there is room for a wider range of justifiable interpretations, any one of which may be adequate for the listener's current purposes. It is not the case that we require the same level of certainty in all cases of communication in our assessment of whether or not our understanding is adequate, let alone correct. It is always necessary to consider this issue in the context of the listener's intentions in listening, and to formulate the question as 'adequate for what?'. Popper, in discussing the certainty of our beliefs, points out that we operate with a commonsense notion of certainty which is taken to mean 'certain enough for practical purposes', but that we interpret this relative to the significance of a particular belief in a given situation: 'subjective certainty . . . depends not merely upon degrees of belief and upon evidence but also upon the situation – upon the importance of what is at stake. Moreover the evidence in favour even of a proposition which is, I know, trivially true might be radically revised if what is at stake is sufficiently important'(Popper 1972:78–9).

We must remember that understanding an utterance is rarely an end in itself, in the way that it might appear to be in a test of ability in a foreign language. In real life it is typically the basis for some further activity. The nature of that activity will often determine for the listener what can be accepted as an adequate interpretation. Similarly, we should be careful not to assume that an interpretation, once constructed, is immutably fixed, and stored in this correct state in a permanent mental representation. Rather, we must suppose, the interpretation is assimilated into the matrix of existing beliefs which gave rise to its construction in the first place, to support, in its turn, further interpretations of discourse yet to be encountered which may, in their turn, cause the original interpretation to be modified.

The process of the continual renewal of interpretation is nicely exemplified, on a small scale, in a story constructed by Sanford and Garrod which begins:

John was on his way to school last Friday. He was really worried about the maths lesson. Last week he had been unable to control the class. It was unfair of the maths master to leave him in charge.

(Sanford and Garrod 1981:10)

Most readers, using conventional prototypes, understand the 'John' of the first two sentences to be a schoolboy, but are then forced by the third sentence to revise this and to suppose that John is the maths master, a revision which the final sentence overturns.

1.6 The gap between speaker and listener

1.6.1 The speaker's role

I have argued that we cannot suppose that communication is achieved by a speaker having a thought and then putting it into the only possible set of words, ordered in the only possible way, before targeting the words at a hearer to whom only a single determinate interpretation will be possible. Rather, the speaker has to decide how to package the message in such a way that it is likely to be understood by the hearer in the context of utterance, while couching the message in a socially appropriate manner. This means taking into account what the hearer can reasonably be expected to know, as well as the nature of the social roles that the speaker and hearer are playing.

Thus, if my daughter and I see one of our neighbours passing the house, I might say *She came over to borrow the power-drill* with a reasonable expectation that the expression *she* will enable my daughter to identify the intended referent. If there had been no sighting, or immediately previous mention of the neighbour, I would probably use her first name and say *Mary came over to borrow the power-drill* and assume that, whereas we may know a number of people called *Mary*, the fact that the one I speak of came to our house to borrow a particular tool will enable my listener to pick out the right referent. In these cases I should be doing no more than referring to my neighbour. In a different social context, if I were explaining to a visiting overseas colleague why I had left the room to answer the doorbell, I should be quite likely to say something like *Mrs Butcher, a neighbour, came over to borrow the power-drill*, where I not only refer in a manner appropriate to people who do not know each other, but I also invite my hearer to construct a new mental address under which the information about the name (*Mrs Butcher*), the role ('a neighbour') and the errand ('to borrow the power-drill') will be entered. If, later in the day, I use the term *Mrs Butcher* again to the visitor, that expression may be adequate for him to identify the correct address in memory, or it may be necessary to choose a fuller characterisation as in *You remember the neighbour who came over to borrow the power-drill? Well, she* . . . . In all cases the speaker has to make a judgment about social appropriacy: whether to choose the expression *Mrs Butcher* or *Mary*, and whether to describe her as *a neighbour* or *The old ding-bat who lives next door*. Simultaneously the speaker must judge the amount of specification necessary to secure adequate uptake; whether to choose the expression *she* rather than *Mary* or whether it is necessary to elaborate even more and use *the neighbour who came over to borrow the power-drill*. There is nothing predetermined about such choices, no single laid-down way of referring. They always depend on moment-by-moment judgments by the speaker which may or may not be successful in stimulating the intended response by the listener.

The listener's side of the interaction is no more straightforward, since the listener always has to make an initial judgment about how much it is worth paying attention to what the speaker says, and then determine how much of what the speaker says is actually listened to. The keen, highly motivated, overseas visitor may choose to listen carefully and remember the details of what I say about the neighbour, even including the name, which few people retain after a single hearing. The mention of *Mrs Butcher* several hours later may be sufficient to permit this listener to access the relevant address in memory and identify the neighbour who borrowed the power-drill. On the other hand, if the visitor is laid-back, jet-lagged and not particularly interested in why I left the room to answer the doorbell, it is quite likely that a later mention of the name will mean nothing at all, and even the addition of the information about the power-drill may not be sufficiently salient to recall this entirely trivial incident to mind.

Speakers must, in general, suppose that the judgments they have made about how to express their thoughts are reasonably accurate and should be adequate for their listeners' purposes. If they get this wrong in some genres, casual conversation for instance, it may not matter if the listener has a rather confused impression of what it is that the speaker is trying to convey, since relaxed chatty gossip often has no specific outcome in the world. In other genres, where it matters that the listener correctly understands the speaker, such an outcome can have serious consequences. We shall see, in later chapters, examples of speakers failing to refer sufficiently specifically, of them giving inadequate and misleading information, and of them providing far too much information at a time for the listener to be able to process.

The choices available to speakers about how much detail is required to achieve satisfactory reference always carry some element of risk. If the speaker chooses a strategy of maximal specification, adding a great deal of identificatory information, there is a danger that listeners may find the level of detail so boring that they stop paying attention, or if they do try to process all the detail, their processing capacity may be over-loaded. If, on the other hand, the speaker chooses a strategy of minimal specification, which is particularly common among young children, there is a danger that the listener may fail to achieve a correct identification. It is often the case that the minimal strategy works well sufficiently frequently, and is sufficiently readily recouped if it fails, to make it the most effective choice for a speaker. A difficult task for a young speaker is to learn to judge when such a strategy is likely to be unsuccessful.

1.6.2 The listener's role

One of the sources of risk in communication is that whereas speakers may think that what they have to say is sufficiently important to be paid attention to, listeners may have other priorities and may not listen in detail but only partially, or perhaps not at all. Sperber and Wilson (1986:158) assert that every utterance comes with a presumption of its own optimal relevance **for the listener**. Despite the various caveats they offer, including the possibility of the speaker simply being a bore, this seems to be too strong a claim. If a stranger approaches a passer-by in the street and asks for *the price of a cup of tea* or asks to be told the time, both the speaker and the listener are aware that the utterance is intrusive into the listener's attention, and is in the sole interests of the speaker. We may agree that, in the speaker's judgment, the utterance must always be relevant to the speaker's own interests. However, from the listener's point of view the picture is different. We could agree that the listener will share the speaker's assumption that the utterance is relevant to the speaker's interests, but it must always be the case that the listener is conscious that what the speaker says may or may not turn out to be relevant to the listener's own interests. People who are shopping in a crowded market may be assailed by the noise of traders shouting to advertise their wares but the busy shoppers are able to 'detune' and ignore the detail of the spoken messages, having determined, even without having heard the content, that they are not relevant to their interests.

It is not necessary to postulate a universal guarantee of relevance to the hearer as the motivation for a hearer paying attention to what a speaker says. Such a guarantee would suggest that listeners will pay attention to every remark that anybody addresses to them. All that is necessary to motivate a listener paying attention to a particular speaker is to invoke Goffman's social model which will motivate the listener, when appropriate, to preserve the speaker's face by demonstrably paying attention to what the speaker says (Goffman 1967, cited in 1.3). Indeed, the same point may be derived from Grice's principle of co-operation, which suggests that it will ultimately be in the selfish interests of one speaker to humour the other, so that one will be humoured in turn.

Listeners choose whether or not they will pay attention to a message and, if they do pay attention, they may select which part of the message they will focus on. The listener always risks missing what the speaker takes to be the main point of what is said and is, in any case, bound to assimilate the interpretation of what was said into a different matrix of beliefs. Most accounts of communication assume a co-operative listener who is prepared to adopt the point of view of the speaker (see for instance Sperber and Wilson 1986). Careful analysis of conversations held while carrying out co-operative tasks suggests that the goals even of fully co-operative listeners are by no means always identical to the goals of speakers at a given point in an interaction. The listener must be credited with a distinct personality and point of view in any model of communication which hopes to give an account of how speakers and hearers actually talk to each other and understand each other.

The standard assumption in the literature on aspects of communication such as reference is that the speaker is the active participant in the interaction, while the listener plays a merely passive role (consider, for example, Clark's remark: 'All that counts in the end is the speaker's meaning' and the recovery of 'the speaker's intentions in uttering the sentence' (1983:328)). The speaker is normally assumed to be the initiator of the interaction, playing the dominant role, selecting the information which would be appropriate for the current listener for some reason determined by the speaker. This stereotype ignores those frequent occasions in everyday life when the listener, the receiver of information, was originally the prime mover in the interaction, and was responsible for requesting the current speaker to provide required information. When the customer in the travel agency who has requested information about package holidays in Venice hears the laid-back person behind the desk begin to provide information on holidays in Vienna, it is the customer, the current listener, who is likely to take the initiative in redirecting the speaker's attention. The police officer who is trying to extract details of how a traffic accident occurred from an impartial passer-by, may be impatient at the lengthy account of how the passer-by happened to be on the spot at the time, but ask searching questions about the accident, looking for specific responses. The patient who is trying to determine whether or not to have an operation on her foot, will quiz the specialist about the effects of the operation and try to extract a comprehensible answer to the question of how long after the operation it would be before she could walk comfortably again. Whenever we seek goods and services from others, we, as the agents who initiate the interaction, are likely to need to be provided with information by the speaker who possesses the relevant information. In such interactions, the co-operative speaker will of course attempt to select information relevant to the listener's stated interests but, in the end, it is the listener who determines what, of this selected material, is or is not relevant.

An account of communication which assumes that only the speaker's intentions need to be taken into account is as inadequate as one which assumes that speaker and listener will share common goals and a common context. Johnson-Laird points out the fallacy of assuming a simple shared context which is common to both speaker and listener: 'the notion of the context overlooks the fact that an utterance generally has at least two contexts: one for the speaker and one for the listener. The differences between them are not merely contingent, but . . . a crucial datum for communication' (1983:187). When a third person, an observer or an analyst, reflects upon the communication achieved by the speaker and listener, yet another context must be added.

It is time for the independently motivated role of listener to be taken more seriously in models of collaborative communication.

1.7 Minimising risk in communication

It seems obvious that some contexts and patterns of behaviour between speakers and hearers minimise the risk of misunderstanding between participants in a conversation. We must suppose that the situation in which small children learn to talk provides the most supportive environment for communication, with least risk of failure. For the 1–3 year-old, the typical experience of language is conversation with one or two familiar interlocutors. The conversation is likely to be about some aspect of the immediate spatial context, which means that no complex temporal relationships have to be understood. It is usually organised so that each speaker takes only a short turn, so there is no great burden on memory. It often involves physical procedures which make it quite clear when a successful outcome has been obtained. The language used will mostly be simple and repetitive.

I have a video of two children playing together in the garden. We see an 18 month-old girl standing at the edge of a paddling pool in which her 3 year-old brother is playing. He has filled a red plastic watering-can which he hands to her with the words, *Go and water the flowers.* She looks first at him, and then at the garden, and then she trots to the nearest flower bed and tips the water out over the flowers. He repeats the instruction on three further occasions, and she repeats the same set of responses. Then he gives her the full watering-can saying, *Now go and water the trees.* She is clearly less confident, looking first at him, then at the garden, and then at him again. He repeats the order, this time waving his hand towards the trees, and she trots over and tips the water out at the foot of the nearest tree. This interaction satisfies all the criteria for supporting successful communication which were listed in the previous paragraph. Note that we do not know whether or not the small girl understood the language addressed to her, but an adequate level of communication was apparently achieved to satisfy both of the participants.

In many everyday dealings, speakers choose to refer to what they are talking about with an expression which is, for them, the best current fit. In the least-risk context, the speaker knows that this expression is the one which the listener is familiar with in this context. Where the speaker wants to talk about something different and introduces a new referent into the conversation, a judgment has to be made on whether the expression used is sufficiently comprehensible in the context to secure the intended meaning for the listener, or whether it is necessary to check that the listener has understood correctly. Checking is a crucial resource for the speaker in face-to-face conversation. Similarly, the co-operative listener will often nod or produce one of a battery of 'fillers' whose function is to reassure the speaker that the hearer understands the message adequately. As anyone who has worked on interactive speech knows, one of the most striking differences between transcripts of speech and written texts is the density of signals from speaker to hearer about how to 'take' the message, and from hearer to speaker indicating whether or not the message has been adequately received and understood. It is this constant checking and reassurance which minimises the risk of misunderstanding in face-to-face spoken language. It does not of course remove it. Listeners must often suppose that they have understood what was said and only later realise that they had not. Or they may suppose that they have understood correctly and later accuse the speaker, who is simply reiterating the original point, of inconsistency. Or they may never come to realise that they did in fact fail to understand what the speaker said. (This issue is discussed in 7.1.)

1.8 Conclusion

To insist on the riskiness of communication, and to suggest a general criterion of **adequate understanding** rather than **correct understanding** is not to claim that we can never interpret what someone else says correctly. Many short familiar everyday utterances, particularly the enormous number which are constantly used almost formulaically (like *Can you tell me the time? – Five past four*) offer instances of language which do indeed appear to be fully and correctly understood, sufficiently well understood for society to function with a tolerable level of efficiency. Similarly a great deal of technical information must be exchanged satisfactorily, since mankind has succeeded in splitting the atom, transplanting hearts and livers, cracking the genetic code and exploring the far reaches of space. It seems reasonable to suggest that in the case of everyday language, it is the dense frequency of occurrence of familiar, or nearly familiar, utterances occurring in repetitively similar everyday contexts which leads to such automatic-seeming correct understanding. In the case of technical terminology, I have already suggested that the extended processes of education must play a part in ensuring that people working together in the same subject area will largely use terms in a similar way. The same is likely to be true of a group of people who work together on a day-to-day basis. This is part of what 'talking shop' means. On a more mundane level, we succeed in communicating names, addresses, telephone numbers and much of the paraphernalia of daily life correctly. As Johnson-Laird claims: 'People can and do communicate successfully' (1990:9).

However, as we have seen, even brief utterances of a familiar type are sometimes misconstrued and, it appears, the longer the discourse, the more likely it is that it will be capable of multiple and developing interpretations. Understanding is not an all-or-nothing affair which, if successful, yields a finite representation of the speaker's thought in the listener's brain. Rather, any interpretation, particularly the construal of a complex utterance, is capable of adaptation and modification as it is inserted into the matrix of beliefs which are themselves, in part, responsible for the formation of the interpretation in the first place. The understanding of some utterances (mostly brief formulaic or technical messages) may be said to be 'complete and correct', but the understanding of others may be partial but adequate (as in the case of the child asked to *water the trees*), adequate but partially incorrect (as in the case of the child checking whether it is possible to identify an acanthus by the expression *an enormous turnip*), quite incorrect, or not achieved at all. In chapter 2 we shall turn to consider some of these possibilities in greater detail.

2 · The Map task method

In this chapter, I shall introduce the Map task method, and begin to explore some of its benefits and limitations as a window on the processes of interpretation. First, I shall set the approach in context by rapidly reviewing existing well-established research paradigms.

2.1 Methods and problems with methods

There are two perennial issues which confront anyone who is engaged in a theoretical enquiry into the nature of interpretation, or even in an empirical enquiry which is simply trying to determine whether or not a listener has understood an utterance. The first lies in defining what will count as adequate interpretation. The second is the problem of method. I am going to put aside the first question for the moment, simply assuming a common-sense view of adequate understanding which I shall attempt to refine in later chapters. In this chapter I shall concentrate on the second issue. How do you decide whether or not an utterance has been understood? Since we have no access to what is going on inside people's heads as they work out what an utterance means, we can only observe their behaviour after having interpreted all or some part of an utterance as they put the utterance to use. Alternatively, or additionally, we may have resort to imaginative reconstruction of what we think that the listener has understood, based on an empathetic assessment of how, if at all, we would have understood the utterance ourselves, had we been the intended listeners. On a day-to-day basis, we all constantly make judgments about whether people around us have adequately understood what was said.

The essential prerequisite for understanding an utterance is to have heard it. If you speak to someone who gives no indication of even having heard you speak, you will want to check whether or not this most basic essential for communication was, or was not, achieved. I shall not review here the details of the various competing models of how a listener identifies an utterance as an utterance of English, recognises the words spoken, and the way the words are structured into utterances having phrasal and sentential form (Garnham 1985 offers a clear introduction to these issues). Nor shall I develop any detailed discussion of how listeners use rhythmic, intonational and paralinguistic features as cues to how the utterance is to be taken (but see Brown *et al.* 1980, Brown 1990). In the discussions of data which occur in the following chapters, such levels of interpretation will simply be taken for granted, except where there are cases of failure, or apparent failure, of these processes to operate normally.

If an utterance is greeted by the listener with a reaction which indicates that it was certainly heard, the speaker may still be cautious in assuming that it was necessarily understood. It is well known that nodding and smiling can be used as social masks to conceal lack of attention and also lack of understanding. One might, as a speaker, find a smiling reaction to be charming, but one would want to have some further indication that the import of what was said was actually understood. Typically this is judged by the listener's future behaviour. If you have been giving instructions or advice, you may watch to see whether the listener appears to be following your directions. If you have been chatting about the astonishing strength of interest in educational issues to be found among the French public, you will listen to what the listener says, when her turn comes to speak, to see if the utterance makes sense in the context of what you have already said.

As I have just remarked, discourse analysts must, in analysing data, make use of the same range of indicators that they use themselves in everyday interaction. Such a procedure has been objected to by Stich (1983), on the grounds that the ascription of content to an utterance will necessarily depend on the observer's judgment. A particular observer may have a belief-set so radically different from that of one (or more) of the discourse-participants that it is impossible for the observer to empathise with that participant. There is a danger that the analyses made by academic observers will represent the psychology of 'me and my friends'. (Recall Davidson's suggestion (1974, discussed in 1.4) that we are only capable of understanding language which expresses the content of conceptual schemes similar to our own.) The problem is acute where the observer is analysing overheard spontaneous conversation with randomly shifting topics between conversationalists who know each other well. In the data I shall discuss in this book, the objection holds somewhat less weight, since the external context of utterance and the information content of the conversation are circumscribed to a considerable degree by the analyst, but even here it is an issue which the discourse analyst cannot ignore, and sometimes it is only possible to make the most tentative stab at guessing what a current speaker might have understood in interpreting the previous speaker's utterance.

Where the listener takes a turn as current speaker, and responds appropriately to what the previous speaker said, the analyst may be satisfied that the response makes sense in the context, hence that the listener did, to some degree at least, understand the preceding remark. The situation is far more difficult if the current speaker fails to respond appropriately to what the previous speaker said. In such cases, the analyst is often quite unable to determine why this should be, since there are a number of possible reasons for such a lapse:

– the listener was not listening to what was said (or did not hear what was said)
– the listener heard what was said, but was so engrossed in interpreting a previous utterance that no immediate further processing of the current utterance was possible
– the listener heard what was said but did not understand what the utterance (or some part of the utterance) meant, for instance did not know the meaning of one of the words
– the listener understood the words of the utterance and parsed it correctly but could not interpret 'the thin meaning' in the current context and was waiting for more information before trying to respond
– the listener understood the utterance in the current context of information but was unable or unwilling to produce an appropriate response.

To distinguish between such possibilities, a method is needed which will probe into the difficulty which a listener is experiencing, and identify the reason for the failure to make an appropriate response. We might expect to find an instrument for such disambiguation in the armoury of experimental methods used in psycholinguistics.

The typical psycholinguistic approach to investigating verbal comprehension involves constructing a model of some aspects of comprehension and then performing a series of carefully controlled experiments which will yield information about each step in the postulated process. By such means, we have learnt a great deal about how listeners may identify sounds and words in the stream of speech (Marslen-Wilson and Tyler 1980; Morton 1969) and how they use syntactic and semantic information to arrive at one interpretation rather than another. We have also learnt about some aspects of text processing, particularly with respect to anaphora (Garnham 1985; Stevenson 1993) and the effects of various aspects of context (Clark 1992; Swinney 1979). More controversially, claims are made with respect to the ways in which subjects construct mental representations of discourse (Gernsbacher 1990; Graesser 1981; Johnson-Laird 1983; van Dijk and Kintsch 1983) and render some parts of such representations salient (Sanford & Garrod 1981). Similarly we are now much better informed about some of the conditions under which subjects perform less well, particularly the disabling effect of some syntactic structures (at least when they are presented in unhelpful contexts) (Frazier 1987; Markman 1981). Such studies typically raise more questions than they answer, which is presumably why there has been an explosion of interest in this field. Whereas the studies I have mentioned have illuminated our understanding of many of the detailed processes of comprehension, they do not, on the whole, address the types of issue which I listed in the preceding paragraph.

The listener, in the type of experiment typically reported in the studies cited above, is taken to have a single goal – that of correctly comprehending a short text in order to perform a specified task of recognition, reaction or inference. With respect to each such very specific goal, the subject is regarded as either wholly succeeding or wholly failing. The subject's behaviour in the experimental condition becomes one statistic among others which, together, constitute the basis for the report of the behaviour of the set of subjects. In such experiments, the relationship holding between the speaker of the text which is to be understood, and the individual who is undertaking an interpretation, is necessarily ignored. Moreover, the relationship between the sample of language which is to be comprehended and the individual listener, or between the language and the social context in which the utterance is understood, is also ignored, since it is, again necessarily, regarded as standardly controlled. The aim of the investigation is to isolate the focussed behaviour as far as possible from the exigencies of real life and social variability, and to find out how a set of listeners responds to controlled linguistic input in sanitised laboratory conditions, where the subject's response can be objectively characterised. The reasons for such control are obvious. Only by holding stable all, or at least as many as possible, of the relevant parameters, can one be sure that variation in experimental results is due to the one parameter which is being systematically varied.

There is, however, an evident difficulty in extrapolating from results obtained in strictly controlled psycholinguistic conditions, where the listener has no independent role, to language use in a normal human environment. An analogy may be sought in the field of visual processing. There was a long tradition in this field of strictly controlled, rigorously scientific experimentation, where points of light or single lines were presented as stimuli, preferably with the eye itself immobilised. But, in 1966, Gibson, in an influential work, argued that visual systems have not evolved to cope with fixed points of light or isolated lines, but with the changing forms which are created as animals move around in their natural habitat. Following this lead Neisser, in a series of publications (for instance, 1976, 1987), has stressed the important contribution to be made by what he calls 'ecological' methods of enquiry, which study the behaviour to be investigated in environments as near to normal as possible. In language, he proposes, it is not sufficient to study how subjects cope with lists of syllables, words, and sentences or short constructed texts in contexts where all-or-nothing judgments are made. It is important to see how human beings actually use language when they are telling or listening to stories, or describing places which they have seen (Neisser 1987:1–6). It is relevant also to know whether there are aspects of the communicative setting which give rise to problems of interpretation other than those which are manipulated in typical psycholinguistic experiments.

The cognitively focussed psycholinguistic approach typically ignores other aspects of communication in the experimental situation, for example the social predispositions which cause a listener to take a message in one way or another depending on who said it, and how and when it was said. However, a considerable literature has developed in sociolinguistics and in ethnographic anthropology about such social aspects of interaction. An area which has been particularly intensively studied is the way social roles indicating power, gender and solidarity are manipulated by people talking to each other (Brown and Gilman 1960; Goffman 1967; Brown and Levinson 1988; Schiffrin 1987; Tannen 1991). The focus of sociolinguistic as opposed to psycholinguistic investigations is usually on how speakers interact, rather than on the linguistic forms, the meanings they express, or the inferences which might be drawn from these meanings. In primarily ethnographic or sociolinguistic investigations of language use, the data investigated is typically spontaneous conversation between peers, or unscripted interactions in courtrooms, hospitals or classrooms, where some individuals are playing powerful roles and others are playing weak, even supplicant, roles. The focus of attention in such analyses is not usually directed to the cognitive content of the language used in such contexts. This appears to be seen as secondary to the expression of social goals in what Levinson has called 'the architecture of conversation' (1980). It is typically in the social structure of the interaction that the analyst perceives the interest of the data to lie.

In those cases where the analyst does pay attention to the interpretation of the content of utterances, the interpretation is usually offered in an authoritative and clear-cut manner as if the analyst had privileged access to the speaker's mind at the moment of speaking (see, for example, discussions of the interpretation of transcripts in Schiffrin 1987; Tannen 1991). The following example is quite characteristic:

> Sally: You said your teachers were old-fashioned.
>   Did they ever hit kids, or:
> Irene: a. Yeh. I had one teacher, her name was Frank,
>   b. we used t'call her Frankenstein.
>   c. So, yeh, she would hit kids with a ruler.
> Irene first answers Sally's yes-no question (a) and then diverts for a
> moment to mention the teacher's nickname. (Schiffrin 1987:199)

It is plausible that this account offers a correct analysis of Irene's *yeh* in (a), but there are other possibilities: for instance that Irene is acknowledging that she has heard Sally's question, or that she is agreeing with the correctness of the immediately preceding remark – that she did indeed say that her teachers were old-fashioned. However it would be distracting to consider such a range of possibilities when the author wishes to focus on a different point in the dialogue. Whereas in a spoken discussion it is possible to point out uncertainties and alternative interpretations as you go along, in a written presentation it is easy to become bogged down in the welter of possible construals. The outcome of such largely rhetorical considerations is that the content of discourse, particularly that which is not the focus of the author's attention, is frequently presented as though it is quite clear what the speaker meant, whereas what is actually being made clear is what the present writer takes the speaker to have meant. Stich's (1983) objection to the 'me and my friends' analysis of content has real force here. The problem is acute for anyone trying to present an analysis of an extensive body of discourse, particularly where the presentation is in the written mode (as it is, for instance, in this and the following chapters).

Each method of enquiry has its own focus of attention, its own domain of interest and its own limitations. Psycholinguists may have a firm grasp of the trunk of the elephant, in trying to infer the basic processes involved in the comprehension of short constructed inputs. Sociolinguists may have a good grasp of the elephant's tail as they examine the processes of construction of social meaning. It would obviously be foolhardy to ignore the gains that have already been made in these areas, but it is clear that a good deal of the construct of comprehension remains to be explored. Other modes of exploration will naturally also have their own limitations. The hope must be that the various modes of approach will be seen as complementary rather than in competition with each other.

In considering approaches to interpretation, we should not ignore the significance of empathetic imagination in arriving at an interpretation of what some other person says, when the utterance presupposes a range of experience which has hitherto been denied to the listener. No doubt each of us builds upon the structures of our own experience in attempting to understand what another speaker says, and no doubt we are, each of us, limited to some degree by the constraints of that experience, of the state of our personal perceptual mechanisms, and of our individual imaginative capacity. But we should not underestimate the power of imagination. Henry James puts this well: 'The power to guess the unseen from the seen, to trace the implication of things, to judge the whole piece by the pattern, the condition of feeling life in general so completely that you are well on your way to knowing any particular corner of it – this cluster of gifts may almost be said to constitute experience' ([1884] 1963:86).

There is an important limitation on the ability of the analyst who is concerned to present spoken data in the written mode. In the spoken record of an utterance the listener can hear the voice quality of the speaker, whether or not the speaker sounds interested, amused or bored, the ebbs and flows of amplitude, the rises and falls of pitch, the patterns of speeding up and slowing down, the length of pauses, hesitations, stutters, as well as characteristic features of elision, assimilation, segment reduction and syllable lengthening. The analyst has to decide how much of these characteristic features of speech to attempt to indicate. The more detail supplied in the transcription, the less the reader is denied access to cues which the analyst may have used in interpreting what was said in a given manner. If, however, a mass of detail is made available to the reader, the process of absorbing it slows up the reading of the text in a wholly artificial manner.

There is a further significant loss of information when a conversation is transcribed and represented orthographically. The transcription represents only what the participants say, the noises that they make. Participants in the conversation can observe fleeting expressions on the listeners' faces – raised eyebrows, slight smiles or puckered lips, nods and head shakes. That is, they can observe some of the listeners' reactions to what they are in the process of understanding. They can observe, as well, those moments when a listener leans forward, mouth beginning to open, apparently ready to take a turn as speaker. The very nature of transcription conventions concentrates on the speaker and what the speaker is doing while uttering, leading us readily to a view of the active speaker and a listener who is quite passive during the speaker's turn. But collaborative conversation does not consist of a series of discrete stages, as the physical nature of the transcription suggests, with a participant either being actively on-stage or passively off-stage. From each participant's point of view, that participant is constantly on-stage but playing different roles, which overlap and merge into each other. While listening to another speaker, the listener may be taking on information which will form part of the listener's own next contribution as speaker. Comprehending what the current speaker is saying and planning the listener's own next turn as speaker are not necessarily distinct activities, sequentially and separately organised in time.

Where two or more speakers are interacting, the form of the written record of the conversation has a profound influence on the way a conversation is read. The most common form of presentation is to allocate each speaker a new line and to represent each speaker as carrying on from where the last speaker left off, as in the data just quoted from Schiffrin (1987). This format constitutes an invitation to view the conversation as a thoroughly co-operative enterprise, with each speaker fully participating throughout the conversation, taking turns in a co-operative fashion and contributing to the harmony of the whole. The layout presents the conversation very much as the text of a play is presented, as an achieved work.

A very different impression is often given, particularly in multi-party conversations, if each participant is allocated a column within which that participant's speech is transcribed, as we see below in a three-party conversation between A1, B1 and B2:

A1	B1	B2
we saw the girl going into the office and answering a phone		
		the woman was on the phone when we saw it – just standing there
	++ well we think it was the girl – did any of the – others know about it?	
dunno + don't think so		
		+ no

This format facilitates the study of a single individual's contribution to a conversation, and highlights the way in which individuals often repeat their previous utterances in different turns and may often pursue their own interests in a conversation. In the extract above, A1 and B2 are speaking of the same woman, the woman on the phone, but B1 hijacks the topic of the conversation, speaking of a different girl who was mentioned several turns earlier in the conversation, whose role in the series of events B1 has been consistently concerned with.

One has much less the feeling of a harmoniously structured conversation when it is presented in such a format. However, the drawback with this mode of presentation is not only that it is massively wasteful of space, particularly when long extracts of conversation are transcribed, but also that the shortness of the line within each column necessarily reads in a misleadingly jerky and disjointed manner. We have to conclude that there is no thoroughly satisfactory solution to the problem of the presentation of oral data in written form.

2.2. Background to the Map task

This book presents analyses of data produced by subjects talking to each other in a range of constructed tasks. The set of tasks which we shall discuss in this chapter and which will be exemplified in chapters 3, 4 and 7, involves a speaker describing to a listener a route drawn on a map. The listener looks at a map of the same (imaginary) locality and draws on it the route described by the speaker. Apart from the route, the information on the maps is manipulated so that each participant's map contains some information which is not present on the other map.

The format permits a different perspective on the nature of understanding from those discussed in the previous section. It is, as far as possible, 'ecological' in the ethnographic tradition, but the focus of interest is nonetheless on the cognitive content of what is being expressed and how this is understood by individual listeners. The ecological aspect of the method is that subjects co-operate to undertake tasks which mimic familiar board-games and other similar activities. They typically work in self-selected pairs, talking to each other when they like and as much as they need to. In the tasks, one individual is provided with more, and more authoritative, information than the other. This builds into the interaction some reason for communication, as A, who has the authoritative information, tells B what B needs to know in order to complete the task. The structure of the task provides the two individuals with different roles and different intentions.

The analyst has access to records of the details of what each participant says and does at each point in the task, which permits some understanding of how an individual is tackling the task at a particular moment, and where the difficulties for that individual lie.

The input stimuli are controlled. The controlled aspect of the data derives from the construction of the tasks, and the types of mismatches of information which are provided to the participants. It is not only the case that A has more information than B, it is also the case that some aspects of B's information may differ from that of A, sometimes quite radically. Such mismatches of information typically provoke discussion, as the participants attempt to resolve the discrepancy. Control of the patterns of information allows direct comparison between the behaviour of many pairs of subjects as they confront the same relationships of presented information.

Observing where problems arise in communication, particularly when the analyst has constructed the cause of the difficulty, permits the exploitation of a method of enquiry which has been fruitful in other spheres of linguistic study. Clark and Clark (1977:260) remark that 'virtually all information about speech execution comes from speech errors'. The study of the breakdown of different aspects of lexical and syntactic control of language when patients are afflicted with different forms of aphasia has yielded an impressive range of insights into the relationships holding between concepts and linguistic categories (McCarthy and Warrington 1990). Similarly, in his search for a window on linguistic competence, Kiparsky (1968:174) suggests that linguistic change may offer such a window, since one can more clearly distinguish the shape of the tiger from the surrounding grassland once he begins to move. We can learn rather little about the processes of comprehension when they flow comfortably in a normal conversational setting. We have an opportunity of learning rather more where understanding is difficult to come by, where interpretation is only partially achieved, or where an attempt to communicate results in misunderstanding.

In free spontaneous conversation of the sort which is typically studied by ethnologists and sociolinguists (for instance Schiffrin 1987) each participant brings to the interaction a set of social knowledge and cognitive beliefs which is quite unknowable to the analyst (Stich's point (1983), mentioned in 2.1). As a result, an eavesdropper who is external to the conversation can have only a very general sense of how far the participants have actually understood each other. Obviously, even when subjects are undertaking a prescribed co-operative task, as they are in the Map task, each participant again brings to the interaction unknowable matrices of beliefs. But, in this case, the familiar, even banal, nature of the task requires subjects to call on only a limited part of their past experience, as they identify schematic drawings of familiar objects and apply to them appropriate simple descriptions, and interpret what they hear in the light of the visual representation in front of them. The strength of the analyst's position here lies in being able to find other examples of similar behaviour by other pairs of subjects confronting the same, or a very similar, communicative problem.

In chapter 1, I wrote of the crucial role of context in the interpretation of utterances. Whereas in a free conversation the potential context for each speaker is unlimited, and speakers may appeal to knowledge which the analyst does not share, in a mundane task the potential available context is powerfully constrained. Each subject has two overt current sources of information: what the other speaker says and what is visually displayed on the map. Together these constitute a salient part of the constraining context within which each speaker brings to bear his or her own inferencing capacities, together with knowledge of the world and knowledge of the language used by the interlocutor. From the analyst's point of view, the great advantage is having access to many aspects of the relevant overt context: overhearing what each participant says, and having the visual information presented to each of them immediately available.

It is not, of course, the case that each of the participants and the analyst share 'the same context' (as Johnson-Laird warns, 1983:187). A-role speakers, having been told that all the information on their map is correct, see a map with a route marked on it. The route typically focusses their attention only on the parts of the map contiguous to it, specifically on the path to the goal of the next move. The A-role speaker has been asked to plan how to get

B from one point on the route to the next in the most transparent and helpful manner. The B-role speaker initially sees simply an unstructured map, with no predetermined focus of attention. Once each move has been completed, B typically stays at the completion point of the last move, the 'anchor point', not knowing where the route will next move, unable to embark on a further move without understanding whatever A goes on to say next. The analyst, unlike either of the participants, knows where there are mismatches of information between the maps, hence where difficulties of communication are likely to arise. In this respect, the analyst is better informed than either of the participants. However, in other respects the analyst is much less well placed. Whereas when one of the participants takes a turn, each of them knows at least what he or she assumes at that moment, the analyst can only infer such assumptions from what is said. Whereas A and B presumably each know, for their own part, whether or not they have been listening carefully to some or all of what the other speaker says at a particular point, the analyst can only infer this from what follows, and is likely to have no information at all about which aspect of a visual feature either of them is paying attention to (for instance whether they are contemplating different faces of a cube, in a Necker's cube effect) or whether they see a given drawing of a feature on the map as 'a lake' or as 'an island'.

The task format has advantages, but it also has obvious limitations. It offers, on the one hand, the opportunity for subjects to converse with each other in a plausibly natural manner and, given the opportunity of strictly controlling the distribution of information, it offers the possibility of comparing the spoken behaviour of different pairs of subjects as they encounter the same presented sequence of more-or-less difficult configurations of information. However, the limitations arise from the constrained nature of an interaction imposed by a third party. The subjects are required to play a role on a toy stage in a toy-town world. (It must be said that it appeared to be an occupation which they enjoyed. Many subjects volunteered to perform again on future occasions.) Participants in the tasks are, of course, also subject to more general limitations which arise from the very nature of communication, which is such that the analyst, like the addressee – and perhaps even the speaker, once the utterance is completed – can never know just what it was that the speaker had in mind in constructing any particular utterance.

As a window on comprehension, the task-based format of enquiry offers only an indirect view. It makes it possible to observe what speakers say and what they do, as a result of having formed an interpretation of a preceding utterance in a highly constrained context. It is an essentially behavioural approach, with the well-known drawbacks entailed by such an approach. A listener might respond appropriately without having understood what was said, or respond inappropriately having fully understood what was said. Comfort for the analyst, such as it is, can often be drawn from numbers. Since so many pairs of subjects have engaged in these tasks, it is possible to generalise across the behaviour of many individuals at the same point in the task.

In these map tasks, one participant gives instructions and the other executes the instructions. I characterise this as a procedural task. Ryle draws a distinction between learned habits and the intelligent capacities which are involved in knowing how to do something. He distinguishes further between procedural knowledge about how to do things in the world, 'knowing how', and propositional knowledge about the world, 'knowing that' (1949:27). He suggests that the most basic form of knowledge is not propositional but procedural, and that propositional knowledge rests on knowing how to perform certain activities: 'Intelligent practice is not a step-child of theory. On the contrary, theorizing is one practice among others and is itself intelligently or stupidly conducted' (1949:26). I shall use the term 'procedural' here in a narrow sense, to refer to tasks where a relevant part of the context is largely externally constructed and where a series of instructions is provided about how to react to the external context. There are many reasons for supposing that straightforward procedural tasks located in the here-and-now constitute the simplest context for the practice of communication, as we saw in discussing contexts of least risk in 1.7.

Certainly procedural tasks, like procedural uses of language in the real world, offer a format in which communicative risk can be minimised, since they occur in a social context rather like that of the child's early experience of language. The subjects in these tasks were, in the main, 14–16 year-old adolescent volunteers, working in single-sex, self-selected, pairs in a small room in their own school. (All the tasks were piloted on graduate and undergraduate university students as well.) For each participant, the physical environment, like the other participant in the conversation, was thoroughly familiar. The cognitive content of the task was, similarly, of a familiar type. The conversation, which was about the immediate spatial context on the map, was organised by the participants so that each of them took only short turns at speaking. This means that neither of them had to hold extensive linguistically specified content in memory.

Similarly, because each move in the task was independent of previous moves, participants did not have to hold in memory the whole sequence of previous moves which led to the current position. In this respect, procedural genres are less demanding than narrative or argument where, in order to understand the present utterance, it is necessary to remember the sequence of events or arguments which brought you to the current position, and to maintain a constantly updated memory of previous events which have no external physical counterpart. If, for instance, you are reading *Hamlet*, it is essential to an understanding of Hamlet's later actions to remember as you read, that he believes that his father has been murdered by his uncle, perhaps with the connivance of his mother, and that his friends are being subverted. Similarly, in reading a novel or a detective story, what the character is doing now will depend on what has happened in the past, and on what the character intends shall happen in the future. All such information must be carried along in a cumulative, integrated mental model which is constantly updated and transformed. In a Map task, however, it is the external physical representation which is itself updated. Later on, in chapters 5 and 6, we shall consider differences between the cognitive demands made by narrative genre, but for the moment I shall simply observe that, all things being equal, the least cognitively demanding type of task is a simple procedural task and that what is true of relatively constrained ecological tasks may frequently be true also of similar uses of language in everyday life.

2.3 A simple Map task

In this section we shall look at data from a simple Map task, and begin to consider some of the implications of working within such a format. Many of these aspects will be developed more fully in later chapters.

The data derives from transcripts of recordings made of the language used by two speakers as they co-operated in undertaking the task. Additional data is provided by the added details on the map which were produced by the partner who was instructed by the authoritative speaker. Each partner works with a map which the other cannot see. The authoritative speaker, A, has a map of an island, with a set of readily identifiable features drawn on it – features such as a fort, a lake, a waterfall, a mountain, woods and so on. A's map has a route drawn across it. The second speaker, B, has a similar map of the same island, with similar features marked on it, but without a route. A is asked to tell B how to draw a route across the island on B's map, so that B's route looks just like A's. A and B are both told that A's map is recently and correctly drawn, whereas B has an earlier map of the same island. They are warned that some of the features on B's map, or their locations, may be incorrect. Both subjects hear (or are at least present during) all of the instructions given to each of them.

The material which the subjects are asked to work with does raise ontological and epistemological questions since it involves subjects each working with a slightly different map of an imaginary landscape. I find here helpful a suggestion made by Evans: 'In general it seems to be preferable to take the notion of *being in an informational state with such-and-such a content* as a primitive notion for philosophy, rather than to attempt to characterise it in terms of belief . . . the subject's *being* in an informational state is independent of whether or not he believes that the state is veridical' (1982:123). He goes on to say in the same paragraph: 'Our being placed in the appropriate informational state by someone telling us a story does not depend on our believing the story to be true'. I assume that, as far as the Map task is concerned, what is relevant is that subjects have particular information made available to them, that is that they are placed in informational states, rather than whether or not they believe that the maps in front of them are in fact true representations of locations in the world.

The combination of initial information from the experimenter which creates the basis for the interaction between the participants, and the visual information which is made available to each of them, creates a configuration of partially shared, partially similar, partially correct and, no doubt, partially assimilated information which is privately available to each participant in the task. This configuration mimics quite well, I would claim, the initial information states of participants in many normal everyday communicative interactions before they begin to talk to each other about their own informational states.

Varying the differences between features and locations on the maps offers a vast range of subtle possibilities for manipulating the informational states between the two participants. In a simple version of the task, the START was marked on both maps, there were rather few features, several of them had names written beside them, they were in any case readily identifiable by everyday expressions, the majority were held in common, and most features were in the same location on both maps. The route on a simple map proceeds in a reasonably consistent direction, without looping back on itself or crossing its own track. The route passes close to features which are distributed in a fairly regular manner over the map.

As A gives more information, B responds. We can examine every response by each speaker as evidence of what he or she has understood from what the previous speaker said. I shall give here a brief example of the format and the type of data which it elicits. The two subjects sit at opposite ends of a table with a low screen between them which prevents each of them from seeing the other's map but allows them to look at each other. A and B both have START marked at the bottom right-hand side of their maps. To the left and slightly above is a clump of palm trees with the words *palm beach* written beside it. Then the route, which for A is always the salient feature and determines where A looks on the map, moves further to the left, where A has a swamp but, unknown to A, in that position on B's map there is no swamp but there is, instead, a half-submerged crocodile. Further to the left, still on A's route, both maps show a waterfall. Here is one example of a transcript covering these moves, together with an initial analysis which indicates the information available to each subject at the end of each turn. (In the text, as opposed to the matrix, ++ indicates a long pause of over a second, + a pause of about half a second, and – a very brief audible discontinuity;? indicates rising intonation.)

(R & H)

	A	(A/B)	B	(B/A)
A. do you have the start marked	+	?	+	+
B. yes	+	+	+	+
A. all right	+	+	+	+
+ do you have palm trees?	+	?	+	+
B. + yes	+	+	+	+
A. right	+	+	+	+
+ the swamp?	+	?	−	+
B. ++ what swamp	+	?	−	+
A. + to the − left of the palm trees	+	+	+	+
B. no	+	−	−	+
− I've got a crocodile	−	+	+	?
A. aargh	−	+	+	−
++ have you got a waterfall?	+	?	+	+

The columns show the information potentially available to each subject at the end of each turn. The left-hand column for each subject represents the state of information provided visually for each subject, which is directly, demonstratively, available to that subject. A plus in this column indicates that the information is present on the map, not that the speaker has necessarily seen it or would recognise it under the description offered by the other speaker. A minus indicates that the information is not available to the speaker. A question mark indicates that the speaker has, as yet, no indication of the other speaker's informational status with respect to this feature, which is present on the speaker's own map, and that it is a feature currently under discussion. The right-hand columns, (A/B,B/A), represent what each speaker might reasonably infer at this point about the other speaker's information state from what the other speaker has said, that is, from descriptively available information. Again, it does not follow that either subject has necessarily drawn the relevant inference. This preliminary analysis does not represent the informational states of the participants, merely the information available. It does not follow from the fact of information being made available that a subject necessarily perceives it, interprets it rationally or remembers it correctly.

In spite of the fact that there is no direct external evidence available to the analyst that a participant has noticed a particular feature or inferred from what the partner said that the partner has a given feature, there comes a moment when the analyst has fairly clear evidence that the two participants are communicating adequately. Knowing that A and B both have 'the start' available to them, it seems reasonable by the end of A's second turn, *alright*, to suppose that B must now infer not only that A has the start, but also that A must know that B has it, and that A must know that B knows that A has it. Each must henceforth suppose that this feature is shared, part of their common ground (see discussion in 7.2).

If we examine the language A uses, we observe that A does not directly instruct B at any point, nor does A indicate specifically that the route marked on his map passes through or near to the features whose presence he checks on B's map. We might reasonably suppose that A knows, and B knows, (and each of them knows that the other knows since they were both present when the task was introduced to them) that A has been asked to tell B how to draw a route across B's map. When A asks B if he has *the start marked*, B immediately picks up his pencil and places it on the map where START is marked. He is listening with a particular purpose in mind, understanding in order to utilise the information which he is given. Clark and Clark (1977:45) draw a distinction between 'constructing an interpretation' and 'utilising an interpretation'. Procedural tasks, as we shall see, necessarily throw more direct light on the second of these processes, though what happens at such a point in the interaction may give some grounds for inferring what may have happened during earlier stages while the interpretation was being constructed.

Consider first B, as listener. He hears A ask whether he has *the start*, checks his map and replies *yes*. Since we know, independently, that he has START marked on his map, we assume that he has correctly understood A's question. Similarly he replies *yes* appropriately to the question about palm trees. He shows that he has (apparently correctly) interpreted A's intention in uttering, by drawing a line on his map from the START to the palm trees. However, when he is asked about 'the swamp' (which we know that he does not have), he indicates that he has a problem, though at this point he does not deny having a swamp. He does not indicate a problem in understanding the utterance of the term *swamp*, which he repeats correctly, incorporating it into a question with rising intonation (*what swamp?*). Rather, he indicates a problem in knowing how to utilise the utterance in the current context. (This is an example of the distinction, drawn by Clark and Clark (1977), between constructing an interpretation and putting it to use: the speaker has apparently arrived at an initial interpretation, having at least identified the words of which it is composed and, it is reasonable to suppose, having parsed it as an NP, but does not see how it might relate to his map.) It is a relevant feature of the B-role that B does not know, at this point, which direction the route goes in, so potentially the whole of the map, except the area he has just come from, might need to be scanned before he could identify a swamp. B appears to indicate by saying *what swamp?* that he needs more information. When A says *to the left*, we must suppose that B looks to the left but only to a plausible distance from his current anchor-point, the palm trees, beyond the region he has just come from, rather than back towards the beginning of the route.

The notion of **plausible distance** for a move is one which has to be inferred by each B-role participant from the initial moves of each new task, and from taking account of the general distributional pattern of features on the map. Most, but not all, listeners appear to assume that the next move will be to an immediately proximate feature. The area circumscribed by an arc of plausible distance pointing away from the territory just traversed, typically constitutes the locational context for B's search for the next mentioned target. This constrained area will be referred to as **the search field**. In the plausible distance location to the left of the palm trees, B finds no swamp – which is what he may be indicating, non-specifically, by *no* – but he discovers that he has a crocodile where, it is reasonable to suppose, he infers, A's swamp might be.

A striking feature of the discourse of the subjects undertaking this task is how underspecified the language is. In the extract we are considering, at no point does B explicitly deny that he has a swamp, or make it clear that his crocodile is in a position to the left of the palm trees. Even without having been offered any practice before beginning the task, subjects bring to bear appropriate constraints from their individual previous experience, and construct inferences which enable them to bridge the gap between the context of utterance and what is explicitly stated.

The reaction of the first speaker, A, to each of B's first two positive responses is to move immediately to speak of the next feature on his route, but as soon as B gives notice that he has a problem finding the swamp, A shows that he understands that further specification is needed. Although B's utterance, *what swamp?* is minimal, A must reason that the relevant reply in the context of this task (where, so far at least, only one swamp is at issue) is not a detailed description of the swamp but, rather, some information about the location of the swamp. A supplies the information about the location with respect to an already agreed feature, B's current anchor-point, the palm trees. Similarly when B says *no – I've got a crocodile*, A indicates by a groan, *aargh*, that he now has some unspecified problem and apparently understands that B not only has no swamp on his map but has a crocodile in what may be the same place. At this point, A resourcefully moves on to check the next feature on the route, the waterfall, prior to fixing the location of the swamp with respect to the palm trees and the waterfall.

2.4 Context and interpretation

In 2.2 we observed that the context of utterance was not identical for speaker, listener and analyst. This is nicely illustrated in the transcript which we have just discussed, and in the problems posed for the analyst by attempting to interpret what each speaker intends to convey by what he says at each turn.

We have noted that A asks B a series of questions about whether or not B has a particular feature on his map. From the analyst's point of view, this is a surprising strategy, since A was asked to tell B how to draw a route across his map. The analyst's immediate reaction might be to identify each of these questions as an Indirect speech act (in the sense of Searle 1979), where B should first interpret each question as a direct question about having a feature and then, finding that inadequate in an instruction-giving context, reinterpret it as an indirect instruction to draw in a route from the last mentioned agreed feature (the anchor-point) to the currently mentioned feature. To some extent B's behaviour gives credibility to such an analysis since he does, in each case, first reply appropriately to the question posed by A and then, once the feature is agreed, draw in the route. There is, however, a problem for the indirect analysis from the listener's perspective, in that B does actually respond verbally to the direct questions. Despite this anomaly, for an analyst who reads the text as an achieved whole, rather than considering the informational condition of each participant after each new utterance, and who believes in mutual 'negotiation of meaning' and a mutually present context of utterance, this might seem an attractive analysis.

However, it is worth pondering why it is that A undertakes this particular strategy. Jarvella and Engelkamp (1983:225) give a timely warning: 'A too cooperative view of linguistic communication runs the risk of failing to recognise that many linguistic choices are probably dictated by states of the speaker's mind rather than the listener's, or out of consideration for the listener'. Why does A repetitively ask direct questions about whether or not B has the next feature and then fail to give explicit instructions about how to relate the feature, once agreed, to the route? One plausible answer is that, for A, B's answers to his questions about whether or not he shares a feature may constitute the most interesting aspect of the task. A, after all, knows where the route goes, and knows which features it passes, so for him the route is only that which he has an imposed duty to indicate, rather than a point of personal interest. He and B were told, before they began the task, that there might be mismatches of information between the maps. A's questions appear to be directly addressed to finding out where the mismatches are. Some support for such a conjecture may be drawn from A's failure to specify any information, at any point, about where the route in fact goes – for example, that it passes below, rather than through or above, the palm trees. If such an analysis is correct, A's questions are primarily intended as simple direct questions to satisfy his own interests in the potential mismatches of information (and only incidentally, if at all, intended as indirect instructions to B).

Some A-role speakers in other pairs adopt a similar strategy to A's and concentrate on the mismatches of information rather than on the route itself. Yet other A-role speakers first check the presence of the features relevant to the route and then, having secured the set of features, go back to the beginning, telling B exactly where the route goes with respect to each feature. It may be that A, in the extract we have been discussing, intended to do this originally, but then found that B had completed the drawing of the route, or – in his interest in the mismatched features – he may simply have forgotten to specify the route.

It is clear that in each of the utterances which he produces, A may have any one of a number of intentions in speaking (or a combination of several intentions) which the listener, like the analyst, can only guess at. Without doubt, it is this rich range of possibilities which gives rise to the most obvious possible divergences in interpretation even in so banal and trivial a task, where each speaker takes only a very short turn at speaking. A familiar experience for any discourse analyst who publishes an analysis of such a stretch of discourse must be the number of letters written by correspondents who have interpreted some part of it differently, and are convinced that *their* interpretation is the only fully correct one.

We should note that B, as listener, appears to be quite unconcerned by the possible range of A's intentions on any particular occasion of utterance. He must assume from what A says that A's *general* intention in uttering is, minimally, to address B, and to refer to the map. This general intention appears to hold throughout the interaction. However, B has no access to A's specific intentions in producing a particular utterance. He appears to take from what A says only that which he is interested in. At no point in the interaction does B comment on the fact that A is asking questions rather than giving instructions, and nor do the partners in any of the other pairs where the A-role speaker adopts a similar strategy. For B, the focus of interest in the task is quite different from A's, since B's aim is to draw the route correctly. We might suggest that B 'correctly' understands A's utterances as direct questions, and responds appropriately, but additionally, stimulated by his own focus of interest, B infers that A is likely to mention only those features which are relevant to the route and is likely to mention them in the order in which they occur, because that is what he would have done in A's place. So he puts the mentioned features to use in drawing his own route.

When listeners interpret what speakers say in the context of a task which interests the listener, it does not seem to be the case that 'all that counts in the end is the speaker's meaning' or the recovery of 'the speaker's intentions in uttering the sentence' (Clark 1983:328). Certainly it could only be with respect to the most general intentions governing the conversation that such a statement could be held to be true in the case under discussion, rather than to the specific intentions in producing any particular utterance. As Putnam 1978 (cited in 1.4) suggests, it is the focussing effect of what the listeners wish to pay attention to which leads them to be able to select a particular interpretation relevant to their own interests from among the plurality of meanings which might have been intended by the speaker. We shall return to these issues in later chapters.

2.5 Conclusion

This first brief introduction to the Map task raises a number of issues to which we shall return. We have seen that a listener may understand the form of an expression intended to refer (*the swamp*), and presumably the denotation of the expression (since he expresses no surprise at being asked about the presence of such a feature) without being able to locate a referent for it or to put it to use in the current context. This raises a question about the nature of reference and the part it plays in the processes of understanding which we shall return to in later chapters. We have seen how the constraining context of the task makes it possible for listeners to achieve an adequate understanding in spite of remarkably underspecified language – for instance, A at no point tells B where the route goes, and B never explicitly states that his crocodile is situated to the left of the palm trees, and yet both listeners demonstrate that they have adequately understood what they have not been explicitly told. And, in addition, we have seen that a listener may achieve an interpretation of a particular utterance which is adequate for the task in hand, without necessarily having recovered the speaker's specific intentions in speaking.

What the participants say while they are undertaking a Map task is necessarily constrained by the limits of the task. It would be absurd to claim that all human life is represented here. However, the claim is that these limitations do have advantages in allowing us to explore how speakers communicate information to each other, since the discourse analyst knows to a very large extent where the limits of relevant information lie. Although we should only cautiously extrapolate from speakers' behaviour in such a constrained environment, we should note that speakers do on the whole succeed in communicating remarkably efficiently in these imposed circumstances, presumably relying on already well established habits of communication in the wider world.

3 · Identifying features in a landscape

3.1 **The nature of reference**
The term **reference** is generally held to hold between a linguistic expression and a referent (for example a particular individual or entity in the world). However the term has been used in a variety of ways and in this short introductory discussion of the nature of reference I shall begin by making use of the three-way terminological distinction introduced by Lyons (1977: chapter 7) between **sense, denotation** and **reference**. His account relates to that of Frege, who called attention to the importance of the distinction between **sense** and **reference**, a distinction widely accepted in philosophical discussion. However, Lyons uses the term **sense** to describe meaning relations holding between linguistic units. His use of the term **denotation** is in some respects closer to Frege's use of **sense**. The distinction between these terms is not always easy to maintain (though see Lyons' discussion of the issues in Lyons 1977). Despite the difficulties of drawing a clear boundary between these categories on all occasions, we shall nevertheless find it useful to call upon the distinction in analysing certain types of misunderstanding.

3.1.1 Sense
The term **sense**, as used by Lyons, applies to words taken out of context, as they are when they appear in a dictionary. (Strictly speaking the term applies not to words, but to those meaningful elements which are common to a set of words related in meaning, to **lexemes**. Thus the words *rook, rooks* and *rookery*, each of which is a morphologically distinct form, will be said to

share the lexeme ROOK. For our purposes in this discussion it will be adequate to think of sense relations as holding between words.)

In 1.4, we began to discuss how language relates to the world. (I shall frequently talk in these simplified terms, rather than continually insisting that language can only relate to the world via human perceptions of the world.) I listed there a set of pairs of words whose meanings I in some sense know, but whose relationship to the world I am uncomfortably unsure about. I shall take the pair *rook* and *crow* as an example for each of the categories sense, denotation and reference. I shall not consider the range of possible meanings which can be attributed to these forms – for instance when they are categorised as verbs. I shall only be concerned with these words insofar as they are related in sense to the term *bird*: they are hyponyms of *bird*, which means that any dictionary entry will include the information that the word *rook* or *crow* means, at least in one of its senses, 'a type of bird'. From the information that *rook* (or *crow*) means 'a type of bird', other information flows – that a rook will be a member of the class of animate beings, but not a *mammal* or a *fish*. Additionally, and here I extend Lyons' formal approach, that it will typically have *feathers* and *wings* and a *beak*, that it will *fly*, and that females will *lay eggs*. All these word senses which relate to *bird* will be inherited by the terms *rook* and *crow*. A dictionary entry would probably also include the information that the words *rook* and *crow* mean a type of *bird* that is *black*, and that it is *big* (for a British bird). It will also be possible to infer a set of further sense relations – that *rook* does not have the same meaning as *crow* (or *blackbird* or *coot* or any other word denoting a 'big, black, bird' which has a separate dictionary entry). A dictionary entry will supply a range of terms related in sense. What it will not do is provide information which would enable you to distinguish between the types of birds referred to by these terms.

Since the sense of a word involves its relations with other words, it will be clear that this aspect of the meaning of a word has a good chance of being held in common between users of a language. All speakers of English, we must assume, have to understand the words *rook* and *crow* as meaning, minimally, 'a type of bird'. However, such absolute commonality of meaning cannot always be assumed, particularly in those areas of vocabulary where words refer to issues which people have very strong feelings about. For instance I may believe that the word *abortion* **means** 'a type of murder' and you may believe that it **means** 'a type of therapeutic operation'. For each of us the word would enter into an only partially overlapping set of sense relations. In such cases it is difficult to draw a principled sense/denotation distinction since our knowledge of the world is so intimately related to our understanding of the meaning of the word. Nonetheless, where the distinction can be clearly drawn, it will be helpful in our analysis.

For all of us, there will be many words which we only know in terms of sense-relations with other words, words which we have heard used or have read and can relate to other words in a relevant field, but have no cluster of beliefs concerning what whatever-it-is-that-they-denote looks like, sounds like or functions like. Terms such as *neutrino, differential* (when used of a car), *broil, phonematic unit, triforium, romneya, epistemology, pearl* (knitting), *echolalia* might offer one or two examples of words which you can identify as meaning 'a type of X' which will entail that whatever-it-is-that-they-denote will inherit the characteristics of X, but you may still not be quite sure what it is exactly that the particular word denotes. Thus you may know that *pearl* is 'a type of stitch used in knitting' but know no more than that about it. For instance you may not know how to make such a stitch or know anything about the function of such a stitch, nor how to identify the product of such a stitch if you were shown a piece of knitting. We might say of the small boy who asked whether an acanthus was *an enormous turnip* (discussed in 1.1), that he had understood part at least of the sense of *turnip* (that it was a *plant*, that it had *leaves*, that it would have *green leaves*, that it would grow *in soil*, for instance) but that he was unable to apply the term correctly with respect to the world.

3.1.2 Denotation

Whereas the sense of a word is expressed in terms of its relations to other words, the denotation of a word is expressed in terms of its relationship to the world outside the language system. In philosophical and formal linguistic discussion, the relationship is usually expressed rather briskly, as in 'the word *rook* denotes the class of rooks' (see Lyons 1977:206–217 for an extended discussion of some of the issues raised by the notion of denotation).

In discussing denotation, I shall adopt a cognitive view (see for instance

Jackendoff 1983; Bechtel and Abrahamsen 1991). From the point of view of an individual speaker of a language, the denotation of a word may be taken as the (changing) cluster of beliefs held by the individual about what is meant by the word. Among the beliefs may be sets of visual images, or auditory or olfactory impressions which may be iconically represented in the mind in a modality specific representation, as well as propositionally expressible beliefs which are widely believed to be represented in some other manner. I can conjure up some rather non-specific visual images for *crow* and for *rook*, which are unfortunately not distinguishable. Similarly, I can evoke the sound of wings flapping heavily and a harsh 'cawing' sound for both of them, sound impressions which are similarly non-distinguishable. But I have sets of beliefs about them which are quite different, many more for the crow who appears more frequently in folk-tales and in children's literature. My beliefs about crows include the beliefs that they are solitary birds, that they are sinister, that they raid dustbins and eat carrion, that they kill baby birds and are a threat to other small creatures. Rooks on the other hand, I believe to be quite cheerful gregarious birds which circle their communal nesting areas at the top of groups of tall trees on summer evenings, apparently conversing with each other.

I am assuming that the denotation of an expression is constituted by the cluster of beliefs held by each of us about what an expression means, not simply on the austere basis of its relationships with other words, but on the basis of the assorted experiences which each of us assembles from a variety of sources – the real-world, what we learnt at school, what we have read in newspapers, magazines or literary works, what we have seen on television, what we have been told, what we have inferred on the basis of apparently related experiences and what we have constructed from our own imaginative resources. It will be obvious that whereas the sense of a word has a reasonable chance of being largely held in common by many speakers of a language, there is a much greater likelihood of considerable variability in what each of them takes to be the word's denotation on a particular occasion. As Locke remarks, abstract words denoting complex thoughts seldom have the same signification for different individuals 'since one man's complex idea seldom agrees with another's, and often differs from his own, from that which he had yesterday, or will have tomorrow' ([1689] 1971:301).

Since the denotation of a word may include a large amount of assorted information, often derived from different modalities, it seems reasonable to suppose that such clusters of belief are structured so that some (perhaps more frequently used or more salient) are more central, while others are more peripheral. Prototype studies (see Rosch 1975; Bechtel and Abrahamson 1991:148) certainly suggest structured representations, though more recent experimental studies, reported in Barsalou 1989, show that such structures are remarkably unstable and appear, for the most part, to be recreated on each occasion of use. The context of a particular occasion of use may make salient one aspect of this bundle of beliefs rather than another. This issue was raised in 1.1 where we noted the experiment conducted by Labov (1973) which showed subjects' variable use of the terms *bowl* and *vase* when the exemplars shown were not obviously prototypical, though the terms were used quite consistently of prototypical examples. A similar point was made in the discussion in Fillmore (1981) which suggests that whereas people are quite clear about the **sense** of the word *widow* they are unsure about how to deploy it appropriately in a society whose customs have changed, where a woman can divorce her husband and remarry while one or more former husbands are still living, one of whom then dies. Is she 'the widow' of that man, while being 'the wife' of another man?

I have not tried to draw a distinction between **denotation** as a set of neutral beliefs and **connotation** as a set of subjectively coloured beliefs, since it seems to be a distinction which is even more difficult to maintain than the sense/denotation distinction. Each of us inhabits a world which we perceive by means of our own individual senses which may be in excellent working order or not. If you suffer from some form of colour-blindness and I do not, is there any neutral denotation of the terms *red* and *green* which we share (granted that we share the same sense relations)? Or if I suffer from tone-deafness and you have a fine musical ear, can we share the same neutral denotation of the expression *D-minor*? My assumption is that we cannot, and that such variability in the ability of each of us to perceive, in any of the senses, is commonplace. I adopt therefore an individualist stance, which accepts that my own abilities to perceive, to observe, to learn, and to generalise over experience are likely to be in some respects and to some degree rather different from yours, which will lead to us having somewhat different clusters of beliefs about the meanings of many words which we both use. This variation between us will in many cases also colour our attitudes and aesthetic responses, indeed what might be called our 'gut reactions', towards the denotation of a particular word. Thus, in the context of a visit to the dental surgery, the proposal that *an injection* should be given may not, for all patients, be given a neutral, rational, interpretation.

While I believe that we are forced into adopting an account of the denotation of words which relates to individual experience, I also assume that we are social animals inhabiting a Darwinian world, and that most of us will modify our beliefs, or adopt new beliefs, when it appears to be necessary, to some degree at least, to achieve a modus vivendi with those with whom we are trying to communicate and, indeed, to permit a necessary integration into society. Recall Dennett's remark, quoted in 1.5, that natural selection must guarantee that most of an organism's beliefs will be true (1990:194). Thus we must suppose that over the years of upbringing in the family and education in school, children learn to categorise the world in largely similar ways, and to use words in similar ways, demonstrating generally similar values to their parents, their teachers, their schoolfriends or whichever peer-group they aspire to join. Obviously, some of these influences may conflict with each other, but we might suppose that, during this extended period, children learn many of the conventions of discoursal interaction in a range of interlocking speech communities (for an authoritative technical discussion of convention see Lewis 1969, discussed in Bennett 1976 and Pateman 1987).

Perhaps the most striking evidence of the need for distinguishing between the categories of word sense and the cluster of beliefs and experiences which contribute to the mental representation of the denotation of a word is provided by neurolinguistic data. Damasio and Damasio (1992) report that the concepts of colour (which I presume must constitute part at least of their denotation) are located in a part of the brain which is quite distinct from that where the words which relate to colour are located. Patients who suffer a lesion in the area of the brain where memory and perception of colour (denotations) are stored (the occipital and subcalcarine portions of the left and right lingual gyri) develop a condition called 'achromatopsia' in which they lose not only their perception of colours, but also their memory of colours, so that they are unable even to imagine colour. However, their knowledge of words relating to colour is reported to be still fully intact, which presumably means that they will still retain the full range of colour words and the appropriate sense relations, in that they will know of the term *red* that it is a hyponym of the term *colour,* and that *red* is not a synonym of *blue, brown,* or *yellow.* They will also know, via relationships of sense, though no longer by denotation, that *red* can collocate with *tomato* and that *yellow* can collocate with *lemon.*

3.1.3 Reference

The terms **sense** and **denotation** can be used of isolated words, taken out of any particular context of use. You may be able to guess the sense of a word which you have never encountered before, if you meet it in a word list, simply on the basis of its partial similarity to other words whose senses you do know. Or you may recognise the word, say *red* or *patriot* or *university,* and be able to supply not only some of its sense-relations but also those aspects of the denotation of the word which rise most readily to consciousness in the absence of any relevant constraining context.

Whereas the terms sense and denotation may be applied to words taken out of context, this is not true of the term **reference**. The term reference is used to describe one of the actions of a speaker in using language to mean something particular on a particular occasion. The term is used of a relation which a speaker tries to establish for the hearer between an expression used to refer and a referent out there in the world (in the simplest case). The type of expression used to refer is best thought of, in this initial discussion, as a **noun phrase** (a syntactic structure which will include such types of definite expressions as the forms *Peter, the cathedral, it* or *that one*). Evans suggests that we may think of the act of reference as the speaker taking aim (by constructing a helpful referring expression) at a target (the referent in the world, which is to be identified by the hearer) (1982:325). If the act of reference is successful, the hearer homes in on the correct target. In 1.6 we discussed the sorts of cognitive and social considerations which might lead a speaker to choose one expression rather than another to refer to 'the neighbour who came over to borrow the power-drill'.

The act of referring by a speaker takes place in a context of utterance. The

context of utterance will often narrow down the potential range of the referring expression used by the speaker so that the listener arrives safely at the
intended referent. I have confessed to my problem in distinguishing
between rooks and crows. If we are standing in a garden in which one large
black bird of a generally appropriate look is standing in a visually salient
position and you say *look at that crow* (or indeed *look at that rook*), I have a
good chance of identifying your intended referent. If, however, there are a
number of large black birds of the appropriate type circling some trees, and
you say *look at that crow*, I am unlikely to be able to identify your intended
referent without further help. Your attempted reference, then, will be held
to have failed by any standard account of reference (for instance Evans
1982). However from features of the context such as the direction of your
gaze, and the fact that there are no other suitable birds in the vicinity, I may
be able to identify the **range** within which I believe your referent is to be
found. Having identified the range gives me a reasonable hope of being able
to identify the specific individual if you add some supplementary descriptive
detail. We shall return in later discussion to the notion of **range of reference**.

Lyons argues that the relationship of reference must be thought of as
holding between the intentions of the speaker in uttering the referring
expression and whatever the expression is used to refer to (1977:177). He
adopts, however, as terminologically convenient, the practice of speaking of
an **expression** as referring to a referent, an approach which is widely found
in philosophical writings. From the point of view of a discourse analyst such
a practice appears to be the only possible convention to adopt, since the
analyst (like ordinary human listeners) has no reliable independent access to
the speaker's intentions in speaking other than the resulting utterance. It is
true that in some contexts it is possible to use features of the context itself,
features like gaze-direction, or what is currently being paid attention to and
is salient in the context, as supplementary information from which to infer
what it is that the speaker intends to refer to. Such inferences are necessarily
risky but it is hard to see how it is possible that vague and underdetermined
expressions are so frequently understood by the listener, apparently adequately, if some such processes are not postulated (an issue we return to in
chapter 6).

In most linguistic and philosophical discussions of reference, the crucial relation is seen to be that which holds between the speaker's expression and the entity to which the expression is intended to refer. The listener plays a minimal but crucial role. Only if the listener correctly identifies the speaker's intended referent can the speaker be said to have achieved 'successful reference', to have hit the target aimed at (Evans 1982:317). In standard accounts, the listener is not credited with any intentions which are independent of the speaker. This study adopts the unusual stance of looking carefully at how listeners appear to understand linguistic expressions which are apparently used to refer in a world where the speaker and listener do not share identically specified minds, or identical views of the world, or even overwhelmingly co-operative intentions. It is also forced to observe that, in collaborative conversation, it appears to be the case that a speaker and listener can successfully converge upon the same object in the world even when the speaker uses an expression which would not standardly be taken to be a referring expression (see discussion in 3.4).

3.2 The priority of reference in understanding language

It seems reasonable to suppose that the most crucial feature of each utterance, the feature which a listener must minimally grasp in order to begin to understand the utterance, is the expression used to identify what the speaker is talking about. This identifying expression typically fills the role of the subject of the sentence and, again typically, is intended to be understood as a referring expression. Understanding an utterance may be thought of as necessitating at least two stages. First the referent must be identified, for without this the listener cannot ground the information contained in the utterance, judge its truth (or appropriacy) or act upon the utterance. Secondly, it is necessary to connect the referent with whatever is predicated of it. Put differently, the new information contained in the predicate must be filed under the correct 'address in memory'.

In early life, the pre-linguistic infant apparently learns to follow its parent's eye gaze, thus beginning to pay attention to what its interlocutor is paying attention to. A few months later, following a well-established behaviourist tradition which does not seem pernicious in this case (see Quine 1960, chapter 3 for a helpful discussion, but note that such an approach cannot account for the acquisition of syntax), the young child shows that it is learning to understand referring expressions, having heard an expression used in a context which renders the object referred to particularly salient, for instance when an adult says *Give me the doll* while pointing to the doll, or *Granny's coming* as the grandmother comes into the room. In the ideal low-risk context of communication (see 1.7), a demonstrative expression which appropriately characterises the referent is used to refer to an object saliently situated in the immediate local context. The mutuality of the physical context between speaker and hearer supports a reasonable expectation that they are both contemplating the referred-to object in the same way, seeing it in the same light (see Clark and Marshall 1981). Such circumstances are most likely to fulfil the weakened Fregean requirement (that is, that speaker and listener have 'the same thought') expressed by Evans in the words: 'Understanding the remarks we are concerned with requires not just that the hearer think of the referent, but that he think of it in the right way' (1982:315), suggesting that this will require 'thoughts that are pretty similar on the part of speaker and hearer'(ibid.:316).

I have suggested in the preceding chapters that I am going to distinguish between **correct interpretation** with its requirement that a listener must have 'the same thought' as the speakers or at least 'thoughts that are pretty similar' to those of the speaker, and **adequate interpretation**. Adequate interpretation takes account of the relationship between the utterance, the context and the listener's intentions in interpreting the utterance, rather than concentrating exclusively on the relationship between the intentions of the speaker in uttering (which may be far from transparent) and the utterance. The question then arises how far it is necessary that the listener should recover the referent intended by the speaker and think of it in the same (or a 'pretty similar') way in order to understand adequately what the speaker is saying. (We have already noted the risk involved for the analyst, and the listener, in trying to discern the speaker's intentions independently of the form of utterance which the speaker produces.) We shall begin to explore this question in the next section as it is illuminated in the context of the Map task where speakers attempt to refer to objects represented in a highly constrained spatial context.

3.3 **Sources of information**

Reference may be achieved in a number of ways, but we shall begin the discussion by considering how listeners understand referring expressions, where what is referred to is an entity which the speaker can currently see, located in a spatial representation, and where the speaker wishes the listener to pay attention to this same entity.

Each participant in the Map task has two current external sources of information, and one prior external source, in addition to the inferencing capacity and the knowledge of the world and of language which each brings to the task. The prior external source is the information given to the participants about the nature of the task, the conditions under which it is to be carried out (notably that neither may look at the other's map), A's role in instructing B, and the fact that whereas A's map is correct, some details on B's map may be incorrect.

Of the two current external sources, that which appears to be primary for the participants is the visually presented source, the map. It is primary in two respects. First, it is information which each participant has available prior to any passage of verbal information between them. Secondly, it appears that participants prefer to believe that their own maps represent the correct state of affairs, a state of affairs which will be shared by the other participant. In spite of having been warned that the B-map is unreliable, and in spite of remarks by the other participant which suggest that there must be a discrepancy between the maps, subjects frequently resist adopting the belief that a given discrepancy does exist. This is particularly true of B-role participants who sometimes resist making alterations to their maps, even when this means attributing quite irrational and unco-operative behaviour to their interlocutors. Extract (3a) illustrates both participants' reluctance to accept that differences exist:

(3a)   (J&L)
    A. you go over a bridge ++ got that? +
        have you got it yet
    B. I haven't got the bridge + where's the bridge
    A. on the big river
    B. what part of the big river

A. down from the wood ++
B. where's the bridge
   (*4 lines of transcript omitted*)
A. on the big river + you got it yet?
B. you got a bridge on yours?

In response to A's instruction to go over 'a bridge', B states explicitly that he has not got a bridge (which may mean either that no bridge is represented on his map or that he has not yet located it) and asks where the bridge is located. A apparently assumes that B is simply making an interim statement (as he may be) and gives the approximate location of the bridge. When B requests more specific information, A again responds appropriately, by specifying where the relevant part of the river is to be found. When B yet again asks where the bridge is located, A reverts to his first answer, and then asks whether B has succeeded in finding it, apparently still assuming, in spite of B's previous failure to find it, that the maps will contain the same information. More surprisingly, B, having initially apparently accepted that A does have a bridge, having used A's authoritative statements on its location during his search of the map, and having asked two questions, each of which presupposes the existence of a bridge, nonetheless appears in his last turn of speaking to challenge not only the grounding of A's information but also, in a quite fundamental way, the rationality and co-operativeness of A's behaviour.

This reluctance to abandon earlier established information in favour of contradictory information resembles the behaviour of Oxford undergraduates in an experiment reported by Wason (1960). The subjects in this experiment were presented with a set of numbers and asked to generate a hypothesis which would account for the structure of the series. Once they had evolved a hypothesis, they were invited to explain it to the experimenter who would tell them whether or not their hypothesis was correct. If it was incorrect, they were invited to try again. The curious and interesting tendency which Wason noted was that subjects who were engaged on second and third attempts typically did not produce a different hypothesis, which was what they had been asked to do, but presented their original hypothesis in a different manner. This tendency to conserve already established information/beliefs, even when they have already been shown to be faulty, is common to members of our school population and to Wason's Oxford undergraduates. Wason's conclusion was that: 'These experiments demonstrate, on a miniature scale, how dogmatic thinking and the refusal to entertain the possibility of alternatives can easily result in error' (1977:314).

We discussed in 2.2 the issue raised by presenting subjects with differing maps of the same imaginary island. Despite the difficulties introduced into the communicative situation by the doubtful status of B's visual information, participants appeared to behave as they might if they were in a comparable situation in the real world – for instance where A, who is driving the car and whose eyes are on the road, has a different memory of the desired route from that which is proposed by B, who is looking at the map. Subjects in the Map tasks regularly assume that those who constructed the maps adhered to conventions of trustworthiness in, for instance, representing features common to both maps in the same way.

Johnson-Laird (1983:165), in his discussion of the nature of mental models, characterises them as 'structural analogues of the world'. In a procedural task of the type that we are considering here, where the current state of the subjects' information is represented visually, 'the images which are the perceptual correlates of models from a particular point of view' may be considered as directly represented by the token of the map which the subject is looking at in the case of A. The same is largely true in the case of B, though here the model has to be updated as the route and other missing features are drawn in. The great advantage for the participants is that this external representation, which they have constant access to, minimises the burden on memory since the map constitutes a stable representation of their current state of information about this imaginary world.

The second current external source of information which the participants have access to is what the other participant is saying or has just said. We have already remarked in 2.4 that this source is of greater interest to B, who needs to know about A's information in order to draw in the route and the missing features, than it is to A, who already knows the correct information and where the route goes. We now turn to consider how the participants manage the transfer of verbally conveyed information.

3.4 Referring in a spatial domain

Given the structure of the task, the A-role speaker must constantly introduce into the interaction reference to features (entities) which have not been mentioned before, which are present on A's own map, hence fully informationally grounded for A, but whose informational status for B is in doubt. A has a range of possible moves here:

(a) to assume that B does share the feature and utter a direct instruction to move to the feature. This is typically expressed by an instruction or descriptive statement which incorporates a definite description as in:
   - *go up to the palm beach*
   - *you start below the palm beach – right*

(b) to assume that B probably shares a feature, using the same range of syntactic structures, but with an indefinite expression:
   - *go up to a palm beach*
   - *now – there's a palm beach*

(c) to check whether or not B shares a feature, using an interrogative structure (which may be uttered on a falling pitch or a rising pitch) with either a definite expression or an indefinite expression:
   - *have you got the palm beach*
   - *have you a palm beach?*

(d) to hope that B shares the feature and to use this hitherto unmentioned feature as a staging-post on the way to a more distant goal, using either a definite or an indefinite expression:
   - *go up and left – past the palm beach and the swamp – across to the waterfall*
   - *now you go left around a palm beach and past a swamp – just a bit above it*

From the point of view of the hearer, who has a palm beach marked on the map at a plausible distance from the point marked START, all of these formulations appear to be understood as instructions (or at least as a justification for B's decision) to draw a route from the START to the palm beach. That is to say, in this context, listeners appear to treat both definite and indefinite expressions, whether they appear in statements, questions or instructions, as if they were intended to be understood as referring expressions since, for the listener, they do indeed succeed in referring.

On a traditional account of reference, it is doubtful if A would be held to be referring when an indefinite expression is used. Indeed Quine asserts that 'indefinite singular terms do not designate objects' (1960:146). By choosing such a form of expression, A would not normally be held to indicate a presupposition of the existence of a palm beach on B's map (yet the informational link which A has with his or her own map, together with the knowledge that his or her map is correctly specified, might be held to justify a presupposition of existence for both A and B, if B assumes that A is behaving rationally, see Lyons 1977:184). A striking feature of the issues posed for analysis by data such as this is that it forces us to confront the question of how interlocutors cope with two distinct sets of information which are sometimes in accord and sometimes not. In many ways this configuration seems a better paradigm of everyday interaction than the conversational structures postulated by the philosopher or theoretical linguist where the imagined speaker's intentions are fully known and the imagined listener's sole raison d'être is to understand correctly what the speaker intended to say.

The use of indefinite expressions to refer is problematical in many accounts. Allan (1986:123) suggests that an indefinite expression is used when the speaker (S) intends the hearer (H) 'to recognise that S believes that H cannot identify the denotatum'. Hawkins (1978:184) puts a rather different case when he insists that if a speaker uses an indefinite expression together with a singular count noun he may refer, but 'a prerequisite for a + singular count noun to be able to refer to an object in some speaker-hearer shared set is . . . that there must exist at least one more such object in that set which the reference can exclude'. Neither of these positions gives a good account of the data under discussion. Allan's position seems to be too strong. The speaker, A, may wish to indicate that he or she is not sure whether or not the hearer can 'identify the denotatum' but the speaker is not in a position to entertain a belief that the hearer cannot identify it. And with respect to Hawkins' assertion, we have observed that both A-role and B-role speakers treat indefinite singular expressions as referring to the one unique example of a palm beach on their map, with their listeners moving unquestioningly to that feature. It might be argued in defence of Hawkins' position that since the Map task participants have individual maps which differ from each other in some respects, they cannot be said to 'share' the set of information that they hold in common. It should be noted, however, that the participants behave as if the information, which they confirm that each has, is indeed shared. When B-role speakers are asked if they have 'a palm beach', they typically reply *yes, got it*, or even *I've gone up to the palm beach*. There is only a single palm beach represented on each map and, once B has confirmed sharing the feature, both participants appear to assume that they share 'the same feature'.

It seems that indefinite expressions indicate no more than that the speaker, by using one, indicates that the epistemic status of the referent is not (or may not be) well-grounded for both participants. It is often true that the speaker does not know whether or not the listener has (knowledge of) an entity, as in the instances cited in (a–d) above. Or the lack of groundedness may be the speaker's own, as when the speaker indicates to the listener that some feature is not held in common (as in *I haven't got a bridge*), warning that the listener should not assume shared knowledge of this entity. Occasionally, as in (3f), an A-role speaker begins by checking whether or not B has a feature, using a definite expression, apparently with the expectation that B will share the feature, and only after learning that B does not share the feature does A switch to an indefinite expression:

(DC & LC)
A. you got + *the church*
B. +++ no
A. right – there's *a church* there

(See Brown 1987 for extended discussion of this issue. Wright (1990) describes an experiment working with the same data which demonstrates how the sensitivity of speakers to information about whether or not a feature is shared is revealed in their use of definite and indefinite expressions.)

Speakers in these tasks use a wide range of types of expression to mention entities on their maps. These expressions include, as we have seen, indefinite noun phrases occurring within interrogative sentence tokens (as in *have you got a bridge?*). Where the listener has such an entity in an appropriate position, the listener appears to take the expression as a referring expression. The pair, by linguistic means, succeed in converging their attention on to the same feature on the map.

3.5 Understanding referring expressions in a spatial domain

3.5.1 Shared features: the paradigm case of reference

We shall first consider the paradigm condition in which reference is normally considered – the case in which the speaker refers to an entity which is visually present to both speaker and hearer. In the case of the Map tasks the speaker and hearer are looking at different, type-identical, tokens of a given entity. They are looking at type-identical tokens located within the same set of spatial relationships on a map which is, in the relevant respects, identical to that which the interlocutor is looking at. This seems at least as close to the ideal of 'visual co-presence' as that described by Clark & Marshall (1981) where interlocutors are seated across a table from each other with a visually salient object – a candle, or a bowl of fruit – on the table between them. In such a case, obviously, speaker and hearer are not looking at identical visual presentations. They are looking at enantiomorphs, where the two faces of the object can be thought of as manifestations of a single token of a type, which is rotated through one hundred and eighty degrees for each viewer with respect to what the other is looking at. If the candle as seen by A is blowing slightly to her right, then the same candle as seen by B is blowing slightly to his left. If A can see the rosy side of the apple, slightly obscured by the orange but with the pear behind it, B can see the pale side of the apple, somewhat obscured by the pear, but with the orange behind it.

Even if this standard configuration is changed, and the interlocutors sit side by side, their angles of vision will necessarily be slightly different (and the image that each cognitively represents will of course depend on such variables as short-sightedness, colour-blindness, relative sensitivity to shape or colour and so on). In everyday life, we are prepared to adapt to such common mismatches in shared visual properties, assuming a loose interpretation of 'seeing the same thing', in just the same way that we are prepared to adapt to mismatches of absolute identity of meaning in our interpretation of utterances.

Where A and B have both started from the same anchor-point on the map and are both looking at the same object on the map, in these loose terms, B usually successfully interprets the referring expression if speaker A uses a familiar expression which reasonably describes the shared feature. As we saw in 3.4, under these conditions, B will assume that A intended to refer, no matter what form of expression A used – definite or indefinite expressions, in declarative, interrogative or imperative sentence-forms or even bare noun phrases – all will be taken by B to refer, if the conditions are seen as appropriate from B's point of view. We, as analysts, are in exactly the same position as B, in that we cannot know whether or not A intended to refer on any particular occasion. However, the default expectation of any listener must always be that, if A utters what appears to be a rational utterance, containing an expression which could be understood as a referring expression, A does intend to refer. Certainly no A-role speaker in this data ever denies having intended to refer, or denies having intended that B should take an utterance of whatever form as an instruction to make a move. We assume that successful reference has occurred when B understands A's utterance to refer to the feature on B's map which is appropriately characterised by A's choice of expression and which is located in the same set of spatial relations.

3.5.2 Different descriptions of the same feature

For simple drawings of familiar objects which the A-role speaker appropriately describes as *a crashed aeroplane* or *a church* or *a house*, the listener normally understands readily what it is that the speaker intends to refer to when the object is present on both maps in the same location. However, even in this standard ideal condition, occasionally a speaker uses an expression which does not immediately identify the referent for the listener, in spite of the fact that the referent appears on both maps in the same location, as in 3b and 3c:

(3b)   (FB & BM)
    A. go – erm – up very slightly diagonally + about two and a half
        inches + so you'll be level with the top of the mound

    B. ++ top + of the mound
    A. you know the little hill at the bottom
    B. got it

(3c)   (NE & ME)
    A. then you go north – north-west until you're almost off the page
    B. what – below that bump
    A. bump?
    B. hill
    A. yes + just below the hill

In each case here, the listener appears to be uncertain of what the speaker intends to refer to by means of the expression used: *the mound / that bump*. It seems likely that the listeners in both exchanges recognised the senses of the words used, and were aware of their rather vague range of denotation but, in this particular case, the intended referent did not obviously fall within that denotational range for them. It is not until the speaker uses the more type-specific term, *(the little) hill* that the listener in each case is able to identify the intended referent.

The disparity of denotational range between speakers is again, this time quite extensively, illustrated in 3d. Here, once again, the feature at issue is present on both maps in the same location. The forms of interest are italicised:

(3d)   (FB & BM)
    A. *a boat* in the lake?
    B. erm – yeah I've got *a two-sailed yacht*
    A. yeah
    B. about half way down
    A. yeah well – from the house – from the side of the lake where *the boat* is – put an ambulance
    B. what just –
    A. by the side of *the boat* – not in the lake
        (15 transcribed lines later)
    B. what just straight down in between *the yacht* and the + er + ambulance?

(2 lines later)
A. from *the boat*
(6 lines later)
A. towards *the boat*

If we take the language which they use as evidence of their thinking about the feature, it is clear that A and B do not share total similarity of thought with respect to the boat, which A seems to regard as a vague prototype-like boat falling within the denotational range of the superordinate term, whereas B describes it by the more specific term, *yacht*, which is a hyponym of *boat*. B is initially enabled by the denotational range of A's term to pick out the relevant feature on the map. Nonetheless she evidently feels that she needs to check the correctness of this identification by checking the location: *about half way down*. Once A has agreed to the correctness of the proposed location, B appears to accept that the referent is shared and is prepared to use it as a shared anchor-point for locating other features. In spite of the apparent difference in their views on the precise nature of the referent, as reflected consistently in the terms used by each of them, the participants nonetheless succeed in understanding what the other means on each further occasion of use. Such an instance would hardly satisfy the strict criteria of **correct interpretation**, which requires similarity of thought with respect to the referent, but it certainly appears to achieve 'adequate interpretation' for the purposes of the task in hand. B for instance not only interprets each utterance satisfactorily, but also knows how to proceed on the basis of having arrived at that interpretation.

Such an accommodation to other people's viewpoints is common in everyday interaction. It must often be the case that you refer to a mutual acquaintance, Jim Smith, as *Jim*, since you know the individual quite well, whereas I, who have only met him once, feel that to call him *Jim* would give an inaccurate impression of how well I know him so I speak of him as *Mr Smith*, yet reference is comfortably achieved between us. It is also of course a commonplace in any extended discourse that an individual introduced under one description may later be referred to by other descriptions. Thus you may successfully introduce a reference to a colleague into a conversation by using some neutral expression like *your neighbour on the corridor* but go on to refer to her in more subjective terms as *your friend*, and then later as *the source of the rumour*. In all cases, reference may be achieved, even though the listener may wish to dispute the presuppositions (which appear to be assumed by the speaker to be shared by the listener) which are denotationally encoded in the terms chosen to construct the later referring expressions.

Listeners are obviously able to cope with considerable variability of expression in referring to the same individual. On some occasions, we must assume, each participant in an interaction may accommodate the other speaker's point of view only to the extent of using the denotational range of the other's preferred expression, to secure reference, as in the case of A and B in extract (3d) above, while nonetheless preserving a different individual view of the referent. On other occasions, A and B may initially have different conceptions of the nature of a referent, which initially impedes understanding but where one of them eventually appears to surrender her original conception in favour of the denotational category identified by the other's referring expression:

(3e)   (NE & ME)
   A. and straight up towards the house + which is on the side of the lake
   B. I haven't got the lake – I've got a boat
      (*2 pages of transcript omitted*)
   A. see where the rocks are – on the right hand side of the lake
   B. no I haven't got – oh yes the rocks – that island's the lake – right

A surprising number of subjects initially failed to identify what was intended to be seen as a large lake with a boat on it, set in the middle of a landscape which has features such as a church, a house, a campsite and an electricity pylon dotted about in it. Rather, these subjects saw it simply as 'a big shape' or, as in the case of B in transcript (3e) as 'an island'. Another B-role subject shows such a difficulty, when he says *I've got a boat – on the island + what looks like a boat –* or *maybe the sea*. When his partner replies *is that a big – is that the big lake in the middle – have you got a big . . . ,* B unhesitatingly replies *yeah I've got a big lake and there's – there's a boat in there.* (This is an example of a belief, apparently entertained by some participants in the task, which the analyst is unable to account for coherently, because, to someone who is used to seeing the shape as a lake, it seems entirely implausible that the shape could be perceived as an island which has a boat on it, set in a surrounding area which has a campsite, a house and other terrestrial features depicted on it. Such a dissonance of views reminds us of Stich's concerns with 'me and my friends' psychology, discussed in chapters 1 and 2.)

In extract (3e), A's first use of the referring expression *the lake* is unsuccessful, in that the denotational range of the expression for B does not enable B to identify what it is that A is referring to, even though we have evidence that B is looking in the right location since she states that she has *a boat*. On the second occasion of reference, B initially begins to deny having (at least one of) the mentioned features. It appears to be only because she has been able to identify 'the rocks' that B is now (as in a Necker's cube effect) able to see 'the island' as 'the lake'. This time, the denotation of the expression *the lake* has enabled B to reinterpret her previous interpretation of the figure and to reconstitute it as a representation of a lake.

In this last example, we see an act of successful reference functioning not merely to draw the listener's attention to a shared feature in a static display, but constitutively. The identification of the rocks permits the listener to home in confidently on the feature 'the lake'. The act of interpreting the denoting expression *the lake* and trying to apply it to the model world before her, constructs the listener's interpretation of the model world, thus permitting her to achieve an interpretation of the referring expression. The reason, we must suppose, for her being prepared at this point to abandon her previous interpretation of the shape as an island is because the new interpretation makes better sense of the perceived world, which now has a boat on the lake and a campsite on dry land. We shall return to this issue in 3.6.

3.5.3 Similar features in different locations
The preparedness of participants to tolerate underspecification and to overlook what they must suppose to be minor variations in their informational states ('minor' at least for their current purposes) can be dangerous if participants do not undertake frequent checking of the correctness of their interpretations. Such checking is particularly important on the more complex maps, which presented to B as few as eight out of the twenty landscape

features which were represented on A's map. Thus, in one version of the task, there was a group of tents on A's map (below the lake to the left) and a caravan (below the lake to the right). As one pair worked on this task, A referred to the group of tents as *the campsite*. B, who had no tents featured on her map, apparently assumed that this expression referred to the area where the caravan was marked, which must have made reasonable sense from her point of view, since her experience of the world may well have informed her that caravans are often found on campsites. This mis-identification involved a long detour from her current anchor-point, which she failed to query, and she also failed to check the location. The problem for the participants here was that each was using the same term, *campsite,* to refer to a different entity which was situated in a different location, a position which led to rapidly compounded difficulties.

We have observed a range of configurations of information between A-role and B-role speakers which give rise to problems in the interpretation of referring expressions. One of the most problematic is when both participants have identical features on their maps but these features are represented on each map in different locations. In maps where the features were in radically different locations, where for instance for B to follow A's instructions would have involved leaping over a number of intervening features to reach a feature appropriately described by the referring expression, there was rarely a problem. Since a competent B-role listener typically scans only the search field bounded by the plausible distance for the next move, most B-role participants simply ignored such distant features, sometimes even denying, at that point in the task, that they had such a feature on their map. For a few, academically weaker, subjects, whose search fields were apparently not so constrained by a notion of 'plausible distance', such distant features did constitute a confusing and misleading piece of information when the expression used by A reasonably described them, since subjects would take off for these distant points and then, sure that they were in the appropriate position, find it impossible to interpret B's next instructions (discussed in Brown 1986).

The importance of the search field being constrained by a notion of plausible distance is well illustrated in the interaction of two Scottish undergraduates who worked on the pilot stage of the first Map task. Here the

A-role speaker repeatedly produces more information than B can scan within her immediate search field. Since this is a long extract, line numbers are provided to facilitate discussion. The expressions of particular interest are italicised.

(3f)   (ug K & S)

 1 A. go – up towards between the mountains and
 2   across *the bridge* on the big river
 3 B. what *bridge* on the big river?
 4 A. the river on the –
 5 B. och aye
 6 A. and you go + round towards *the wood* + but
 7   you cut off between + the top of the – river
 8   and *the woods* ++ and then up towards the
 9   castle
10 B. I go up to the top of the river + right
11 A. you go across *the bridge* right + up towards *the*
12   *wood* + then go between the two rivers right +
13   one at off the top of the right hand corner +
14   and the river with *the bridge* on it + between
15   that and then up towards the castle
16 B. say that again Karen
17 A. right you go across *the bridge* + and you go up
18   towards *a wood*
19 B. wait a minute where's *your bridge* + I've not
20   got *a bridge*
21 A. across the big river ++ you go across the big
22   river
23 B. aye
24 A. then you go up
25 B. across it?
26 A. uh-huh
27 B. right
28 A. then you go up towards *the wood* + but + then you
29   go between the two rivers + one that comes in at

30   the top end at the corner
31   B. aye
32   A. and the big river
33   B. wait a minute what did you say about *woods*?

The maps of both participants show two rivers, both marked in the same locations. However, whereas A's map has a bridge across the big river, B has no bridge on her map. A has woods marked above the end of big river. B has no woods marked in that location, but has a similar set of woods marked quite a way off to the west, beyond a lion's den.

In line 3, B shows that she has understood A's expression but that she cannot find a referent for it. A begins to offer a location for the river but B, at this point apparently locates the big river and assumes that that will be adequate as a goal for the next move. In lines 11–15, A gives a set of instructions which include references to *the bridge, the wood, the two rivers, the river, the bridge* and *the castle*. It is not possible for B to follow all of this immediately, presumably because the information in the search area which she is focussing on in her map is not immediately compatible with what A is saying. She asks for a repetition of the entire instruction (adding a placatory *Karen*). A apparently realises that she has provided too much information too quickly, because in her next turn (17–18) she mentions only two features, 'the bridge' and 'a wood'. Now B becomes aware of the relevance of the expression *the bridge* (which she did actually repeat as part of a larger expression in line 3, so she had clearly heard and identified the word even if she had not appreciated its significance). She asks for the location of A's 'bridge', explicitly stating that she does not have such a feature. A offers a brief reply, *across the big river,* perhaps meaning that the bridge spans the big river, which would be a helpful answer to B's question. But this may not be what she means, since her next, immediately following, utterance sounds like an expansion of the first, echoing the intonation pattern of the first, with the words *across, big,* and *river* stressed in exactly the same way: *you go across the big river.* If this second analysis is correct, her first utterance was not a direct answer to B's specific question about the location of her bridge, but rather a more general instruction about what B should do next.

B, meanwhile, has set to work to draw a bridge across the big river, and apparently has not heard, or not interpreted, or not remembered, A's second utterance in 21–22, because in line 25 she asks *across it?* A's next instruction (28–30) mentions 'the wood' and 'the two rivers' and describes where the second river is to be found. B's *aye* in line 31 presumably indicates that she has found the second river. A completes her description in 32, and then B, who has now been within hearing, though not apparently paying attention, while 'the woods' were mentioned on five different occasions asks (33) *wait a minute what did you say about woods?*

It is not possible to say whether or not B interpreted the expressions *the bridge* and *the wood(s)* on each occasion when A uttered them. What is clear is that, if she did hear them, and if she constructed an interpretation involving their denotation, she did not utilise the interpretation in looking for a referent on her map at that point, to appeal once again to Clark and Clark's distinction (1977, cited in 2.3). Her primary attention appears to be focussed on where she is on the route which she is drawing. Her strategy seems to be to take in information which relates to where she is at the moment, to examine her map only within her search field, and, in particular, to pay attention to only one feature which she can find within her search field, even when several features are mentioned by A. B's strategy is summarised in Table 3.1. The potentially troublesome expression *the wood(s)* has little chance of misleading a listener who chooses to constrain her search field in such a consistent manner.

In an interaction where the listener has a specified goal which is different from that of the speaker, it must be obvious that the listener is not simply listening sympathetically to everything that the speaker says, nor is she attempting at all times to discern the intentions of the speaker in uttering. The listener here is trying to use the speaker as a database which will provide the information that she needs at the particular moment when it will be useful to her, and when she has the processing capacity available to deal with it. She apparently ignores anything else that the speaker says, until she is ready to take on a new piece of information which relates to her search field. Indeed, we have evidence from what she says in this extract that she ignores some parts of what is said to her, even though she has heard it and processed it to the extent of being able to repeat an expression such as *the bridge*. At the

Table 3.1

showing how the listener selects for attention only part of what the speaker has said

mentioned by A	focussed on by B
the bridge / the big river (2)	'the river'
the wood / the top of the river /	
the woods / the castle (6–8)	'the top of the river'
the bridge / a wood (17–18)	'the bridge'
the wood / the two rivers (28–30)	'the two rivers'

point when she repeats the expression, it seems to be little more than an echo of the form of the expression. She appears not to have paid attention to the content of the expression and its implication for her next move in the task. Similarly, in line 33, she reveals that she has at least heard the expression *the woods,* and presumably made a judgment that whatever was said was not immediately relevant, but she retained the form of the expression in memory until she had sorted out her immediate problem and had time to return to pay attention to it.

In such an interaction, the listener cannot hope that everything that a speaker says comes with a guarantee of its own optimal relevance, as Sperber and Wilson propose (1986:158, discussed in 1.6). The context within which B is working is sufficiently different from that of A to make it impossible for A to judge how much information B needs and, in particular, to judge what would be the optimally relevant piece of information to provide for the listener, since 'optimal relevance' must surely be defined with respect to the time of speaking – and what might be relevant to B in a few moments' time is not necessarily relevant now.

A similar refusal to take on new information before the current anchor-point is thoroughly secured can be discerned in the responses of other B-role speakers, for instance in (3g) (which shows some Scottish dialectal features). (The forms of interest are italicised.)

(3g)   (R & S)

    A. go – across + towards the swamp ++ and draw a line round the
       swamp

    B. swamp – whereabout is the swamp

    A. on your left

    B. the crocodiles?

    A. aye + draw rou – draw a line round it – is there *a waterfall* there?

    B. (*muttering to himself while drawing*) just – right just – draw it –
       right round the + the + crocodile

    A. no + not right round it

    B. a line going up to it?

    A. just a curve going – across the back of it

    B. right

    A. have you got *a waterfall*

Here B appears quite to ignore A's first question about 'a waterfall' while he is concentrating on drawing the route around the crocodiles. His muttering at this point appears not to be addressed to A, rather it seems like an expanded rehearsal of A's earlier instruction which he addresses to himself. It could be of course that the reason that he utters this instruction to himself *sotto voce*, rather than silently, is to make it obvious to A that his attention is engaged on his drawing rather than in listening to what A is saying. If this is his intention, he is treating A at this point as an overhearer rather than as an addressee (see 7.1 for a discussion of this distinction). A evidently recognises that B is not responding appropriately to his question, and helpfully returns to the point where B is working, correcting B's view of how 'the line' should be drawn, and waits to repeat the question about the waterfall until B indicates a readiness to take on more information by saying *right*.

This extract also raises a further issue, which concerns not the behaviour of B as listener, which is what we have so far paid attention to, but the behaviour of A as a listener with respect to what B says. It must be the case, to say the least, that A takes a considerable risk in simply assuming that B's offered referents, 'crocodiles', which A does not share, are in the same location as A's swamp. Such risks are frequently taken by some A-role participants, as we shall see in the following section.

3.5.4 A-role interpretations of B-role utterances

Among the most interesting insights provided by this data are those which derive from the problems arising for A-role speakers when they are required to respond to utterances by B-role speakers who are objecting that they have problems with following A's instructions. It is sometimes the case, particularly with less academically successful A-role speakers, that they find it difficult to combine the role of the person-giving-the-instructions-to-B with the role of conversational-interactant-with-B as (3h) below illustrates:

(3h)   (K & S)
    A. you go up + between a swamp and the palm beach
    B. eh?
    A. between a swamp and the palm beach + and you go round the swamp
    B. what swamp?
    A. to the waterfall
    B. (*loudly*) what swamp?
    A. +++++ have you got a waterfall?
    B. er yes
    A. right
    B. do you go past the crocodiles?
    A. +++++ go round the waterfall + near the cliffs – go round it though – round the waterfall + and up towards the mountains

B, in her first response, indicates some unspecified problem. A responds to this by co-operatively repeating the first instruction. However when B asks *what swamp?* apparently indicating that she has understood the denotation of the expression but has not located an appropriate referent, A simply ignores B's question and continues with the next instruction. It is not until B reiterates the question, this time a good deal more loudly, that A appears to demonstrate an awareness, by leaving an extended pause, that B has a problem, but she still does not directly address B's question. She simply checks that B has the next feature on the route, which is presumably the goal of A's planned move for B, and leaves B to shift for herself in drawing the route between the palm beach and the waterfall. When B raises the question of 'the crocodiles', A again appears to ignore B's question, though she does pause for a moment before continuing with her plan for B's next move, which suggests that she has at least heard the question even though she makes no attempt to respond to it.

A similar example of an A-role speaker behaving as if, in his role of hearer, he had not paid attention to B's question, arises in (3i):

(3i)   (H & D)
    A. up the hill ++ and over the bridge
    B. I've not got a bridge
    A. and keep going + until you reach the fort

In each of these excerpts it is clear that A hears that B is saying something, since A does not continue talking while B speaks, and waits until B's turn is completed before speaking again. It is at least plausible that each of them does process what B says, but finds it impossible to cope with B's incompatible information, to 'put it to use'. We may speculate that, particularly for academically weaker subjects, the processing load involved in working out the instructions which will be necessary for B to draw the route is so great that they cannot also simultaneously construct a model of a hearer's state of knowledge which is incompatible with their own. Far from acting as though the B-role speakers' contributions come with a guarantee of their relevance, these A-role listeners systematically appear to treat inconsistent information offered by B as quite irrelevant to their own purposes.

In several interactions between academically weaker students, A explicitly abandons the attempt to formulate a route for B, when B indicates a mismatch of information:

(3j)   (C & D)
    A. right + you're going to have to cross the river
        now
    B. how
    A. dunno – any way you want

(3k)   (J & L)
    B. where's the wood
    A. ++ doesn't matter about the wood
    B. yes it does

In each of these extracts we have evidence in A's reply that A has understood B's question (or at least has understood that B has asked a question) but is not prepared, or does not feel able, to construct a co-operative reply. Such examples of an apparent refusal by the A-role speaker to attempt to process the problem raised by B are relatively rare. However, they draw our attention again to the difference in motivation for A, who already knows where the route goes, as opposed to B, who does not have this information but needs to know it to complete the task. (This difference in motivation was discussed in 2.4.) They also remind us once more of Jarvella & Engelkamp's warning against taking 'a too co-operative view of linguistic communication' (1983:225).

In a very small number of cases in this data, the A-role speaker seemed quite incapable of producing a coherent set of instructions for B, even with a simple map. However, it was always the case that the B-role speaker would endeavour to extract sufficient information from A to complete the task. An extreme example of this can be seen in extract (3l):

(3l)   (S & S)
    B. I'll start drawing a line up the way + how far
       do I go
    A. erm ++++++
    B. do I go near a lake
    A. ++++++ no
    B. right + which way do I go
    A. left
    B. left ++ do I head towards the waterfall?
    A. ++++++ what?
    B. do I go near a waterfall
    A. aye + round it

The A-role speaker in this extract, and throughout the whole interaction, rarely takes the initiative and produces only minimal responses to B's questions. B is, however, highly motivated to extract the information which he needs from A. He recasts his questions when he fails to elicit a helpful response from A, making them more specific by indicating a particular feature and by choosing simpler lexis, as in *head towards* / *go near*. It is unclear whether A fails to respond to the first question because he has not understood it or because he does not know how to formulate a reply. It seems more likely to be for the second reason, since it seems that when he has not understood (some aspect of) a question he tends to say *what?* He takes some time while he is apparently searching the map, looking for 'a lake', but he correctly replies *no* and correctly indicates that the route goes to the *left* and, after apparently failing to understand the first question about 'the waterfall' (though perhaps merely failing to identify the feature at that point) he responds appropriately to the second formulation. This is an extreme, almost pathological, instance of A failing, or perhaps being unable, to adopt a helpful stance in the interaction, and of the more highly motivated B being forced into using A simply as a source of hard-to-come-by data.

3.6 Understanding constitutive expressions

We have considered a range of conditions under which various types of expression are interpreted by a listener as referring expressions, and we have enquired whether or not it is necessary for a listener to have the same, or at least a very similar, thought about the object of reference in order to be said to have understood the speaker adequately. We now turn to consider how a listener is able to interpret an expression which introduces into the discourse a particular individual or entity which the listener has no previous knowledge of. As Levy (1979) remarks: 'a speaker by making reference may not simply identify but may construct a referent by selecting from a field of relationships those properties that are relevant at the moment of utterance'.

From the point of view of a speaker, who does not know whether or not information on an individual or entity is shared by the listener, each attempt at mentioning a new referent involves a stab in the dark. The speaker, hoping to achieve reference, has to select a form of expression whose sense and denotation will permit the listener to identify the individual or entity which the speaker wishes to talk about, or, failing that, will at least enable the listener to identify the type of individual or entity at issue. Where the listener is unable to identify a referent, it is necessary to use the denotational information carried by the linguistic expression and relate that information to the currently relevant context to establish a sufficient identity for a new entity or individual to which further information can be added.

As we saw in 3.4, new referents may be introduced into the discourse either by an indefinite expression, in the traditionally approved manner, or by a definite expression. Either of these types can occur presupposed in an instruction (as in *go up past a lion's den to the woods*), or the existence of the referent can be directly asserted (as in *there's a palm beach just above the Start*) or mentioned in a question which checks whether or not the B-role speaker has the referent (as in *have you got the waterfall*). We remarked earlier that, if the listener does share the mentioned feature, any of these formulations appears to be taken by the B-role speaker, in the highly constrained context of the Map task, as an instruction to draw in the next section of the route on the map.

From the point of view of the B-role speaker who is trying to interpret what A has just said, the initial problem of trying to identify the relevant feature within the search field circumscribed by the plausible distance is exactly like that of trying to identify a feature which is present but which has not yet been located (or has not yet been appropriately identified). B, having achieved an interpretation for the expression, immediately attempts to put it to use, working with the denotation of the expression produced by A to try to locate a feature on the map, which could reasonably be described in such a way, within the appropriate search field.

In many cases, even where a feature was missing on B's map, this provided few problems for the participants, if A and B were both moving from the same location at the beginning of a move, if there was no other token of the same feature in a different location on B's map, if B's map was quite highly structured so there was a plausible 'move-sized gap' where a feature was missing, and if what was missing was a feature which has a common conventional depiction, for instance 'a house', 'a church' or 'a fort'. In such circumstances B, having failed to find a feature within the search field which corresponded to the denotation of the expression used by A, would typically ask for details of the location and proceed to draw in a stereotypical token of the type of object which might appropriately be described by the term used by A. The denotation of the term, in such cases, typically permits B to create an entity which is then available for mutual reference – the denotation functions constitutively, to permit B to construct a picture which is then available to be referred to. Occasionally, B would require specific pictorial detail. All of these processes are illustrated in (3m):

3m   (DC & LC)

    A. you got the + church

    B. +++ no

    A. right + there's a church there with a big spire just touching + well a little way down – from the top of the page

    B. yeah – about well is it sort of ++ northeast of the erm – end tree

    A. yeah

    B. right + church with a spire + how how's it drawn

    A. it's got well it's like a + big tower – 'n then you know – it's got the body of it

    B. has it got a pointed thing on top?

    A. yeah

    B. right + 'n then it's got a cross? yeah? well – just a spire

    A. yeah – cross – cross on top of the tower

B first of all searches his map to see whether or not he can find a church in a move-sized area from his current anchor point. Failing to find an entity which could reasonably be described by the term *church*, he replies that he does not have one. A then offers a very brief description – *church . . . with a big spire* – and locates the top of the spire with respect to the top of the page. B checks where the church is located on the east-west dimension and, having ascertained that, and repeated the description *church with a spire*, asks how the church is drawn.

The underspecified nature of the information provided by A, with repetitive non-specific anaphoric reference, seems bound to be misleading if the text is simply read as a text taken out of context. However for B, who is drawing the church as he listens to what A says, the pieces of the church have to fit together in a logical manner and B draws a church which is remarkably like that on the original map. He first draws a tower, a simple vertical rectangle, and then to the right of that a horizontal rectangle with the outlines of two gothic windows and a gothic door, and then asks whether the tower has *a pointed thing on top*. Why does he ask this question when he himself has, but a moment earlier, repeated A's expression *church with a spire?* We may speculate that it may be because A first used the expression *a big spire,* and then, later, the expression *a big tower.* B might reasonably wonder whether A is confusing the terms *tower/spire,* or using them loosely, so rather than repeat the term *spire,* B constructs a synonymous expression, *a pointed thing on top,* to check that A really meant to denote 'a spire'. Once A has reaffirmed that he did mean a spire, B now draws in a tall acute angled triangle on top of the tower and then asks whether *it's got a cross.* Finally, he draws a cross on top of the spire. From a position with no church marked anywhere on his map, B now has a representation of a church which is quite similar to A's, though more crudely drawn, and which is in a quite similar location. A, in speaking, has described his own church and enabled B to constitute a new, reasonably similar, representation of that church on his map.

That B is able to achieve this degree of similarity demonstrates well the amount of previous knowledge which participants bring to bear in constructing an interpretation of what they hear, and the imaginative manner in which they put this previous knowledge to use. It is B who, presumably on the basis of previous experience, proposes the addition of 'a cross' – note that B does not specify where the cross should be placed. It is A who now checks the map and confirms that there is indeed a cross which, he states, is *on top of the tower,* which B correctly understands as relating to the top of the spire which is located on top of the tower. If A's utterance is considered simply in a textual context where both a spire and a tower are at issue, there appears to be a startling difference here between speaker meaning and sentence meaning which might well have been expected to mislead B. A speaks of the cross being on top of the tower, when in fact it is on top of the spire. However, in a discourse context where B has already suggested that the spire might have a cross on top of it, and where B has drawn the base of the spire so that it takes up the available space directly on top of the tower, B has no problems at all in interpreting what A apparently meant. Whether this could be said to be a correct interpretation of what A *said* could only be claimed, I suspect, if one were to assume some part-whole relationship between spire and tower, which hardly seems warranted in this case where they have each been treated by both speakers as separate entities.

Data such as this, involving features which are not shared by the two participants, poses interesting general questions about the nature of communication. Recall that the position adopted in this work is that each participant develops a necessarily individual view of the world, which is constantly modified and formed into a socially more-or-less normal shape, by interaction with other members of society. The maps which each of the participants can see nicely model some aspects of these individual states. When A initially says *you got the church*, A speaks of 'the church' which he can see on his map and which he assumes that B can see depicted on his. A, in speaking, attempts to refer. When B hears what A says, he recognises that A is attempting to refer to what A presupposes to be a shared referent and uses the denotation of the expression *the church* to search his map in the relevant area, but he fails to find the church. A's attempt to refer fails, in that B cannot identify a referent. B's map represents a different state of information. However B now knows of A, that A can see a church on his map, and B also knows the type of entity that the expression *the church* is likely to denote in the context of the Map task (a stereotypical outline shape of the elevation of a building, rather than, say, a three-dimensional church, or an elaborate ground-plan of a church). B also now knows that he must understand A's utterance constitutively, rather than referentially, and that he must update the information on his map, to bring it more closely into line with the information on A's map.

Once A has understood that B does not share his information on the church, he begins to use indefinite expressions, *a church*, *a big spire*, to describe the drawing before him, rather than continuing to use expressions which apparently presuppose that B knows about the church. And yet at this moment A is speaking of a single specific church, and A knows that B must have inferred from their previous exchange that A has a single church on his map which he is currently paying attention to. At this point he is speaking of a church which B must already know exists. Why then does A use indefinite expressions? It is not until he offers some meagre information about the location of the church that he feels able to revert to using definite expressions. As soon as the information about location has been offered, both A and B feel able to use the expressions *it* and *the church* to refer to 'the church' as a feature which the other shares. In this task, which requires a certain degree of specificity for success, a co-operative A-role speaker will frequently continue to use indefinite expressions, as DC does here, until information about location has been specified. Once that is established, however sparsely, the entity appears to be treated as constituted for the B-role speaker, and available for mutual reference, even before any details of the entity itself are specified.

But note the difference in their knowledge of it as the dialogue proceeds, and remember Evans' requirement that for reference to succeed the speaker and hearer must in thinking of the referent 'have pretty similar thoughts' (1982:316). A, throughout this piece of dialogue, can see the full drawing of the church in its correct location on the map as it relates to other features and to the route. B, at this point, has only heard the church spoken of, has no external visual picture of it and is still unsure about its precise location. Yet he can now refer to it as *it*, confident that A will be able to secure the reference. B next begins to narrow down the location of the church, working presumably on the basis of his search field which depends on perceiving a rational pattern in the distribution of the features on the map, together with A's description *just touching + well a little way down – from the top of the page*. He then sets to work to draw the feature in. As he does so, with details increasing as he adds 'a tower' and 'a spire' and 'a cross', it must be clear that the details are unlikely to be precisely like those which are depicted on A's map in terms of precise size, shape and location and yet, when A later goes on to describe how the route relates to the church, B feels able to ask *through the middle of the church*? as though this were a thoroughly shared feature, quite on a par with those which were originally provided as shared features on the two maps.

The drawing of the church by B and its location on his map are surprisingly similar to those on A's map, given the paucity of information which passed between the two participants. (I have suggested that this similarity arises in part because both participants are working within the context of past relevant general experience and also their current experience of working within the context of the Map task where all the features are represented in simplified stereotypical elevations as line drawings.) Yet, on the other hand, since B has only received minimal specific information from A, there are, not surprisingly, some differences in the size, in the proportions, shapes and locations of the feature on the two maps. As I have suggested, the situation here provides us with a good model of normal conversational interaction where both speakers share a certain amount of culturally similar information about a referent, and the denotations of the words used to describe it, and yet the specific knowledge that each has about it has been acquired by different means and may in some respects be strikingly different. Nonetheless, even over such considerable informational gaps, reference and adequate communication can be achieved, as we have seen.

Whereas, in earlier sections of this chapter, we were sometimes able to speak of B achieving a correct interpretation, in using the denotational range of A's expression to locate a shared feature, here – where the description of unshared features is at issue, features which may, in principle, never be mutually shared in specific detail – it is demonstrably necessary to speak of adequate interpretation rather than of correct interpretation. Here, B has no independent knowledge of the particular church to bring to bear, but simply a shared available location and a general knowledge of churches and of this Map task, as well as of previously encountered similar tasks. When he speaks of 'the church' he speaks of the church which he has constructed and located on the basis of what A has said, and of what he has used from these other sources of knowledge and his own imaginative resources. This seems very like the sort of knowledge that the overseas visitor might have, when I have explained that *Mrs Butcher, a neighbour, came over to borrow the power-drill* (discussed in 1.6.). The visitor can only have a minimal mental representation of someone who might appropriately be called *Mrs Butcher* (an adult female, probably British with a name like that), *a neighbour* (the sort of person who would live in this type of neighbourhood) – and possibly a few inferences about the sort of person who might 'borrow a power-drill'. Yet on the basis of this minimal constructed representation I, who know a great deal more than that about my neighbour, would confidently go on to make reference to her and expect my visitor to achieve an adequate interpretation of my referring expression.

3.6.1 Unshared features: problematic constitutive expressions

A particularly striking example of the success of underspecified language in communicating constitutive information arose on the same map which we discussed in 3.6, with respect to an electricity pylon situated on the A-map in the top left-hand corner. This feature did not occur on the B-map, where the relevant location was blank. The majority of A-role speakers referred to this as *the (electricity/electric) pylon,* or used expressions such as *a big sort of pylon thing.* Their B-role counterparts were able to use the denotation of these expressions constitutively, drawing on stereotypic knowledge, just as the B-role participant in (3m) did. However, many other much less specific terms were used by other A-role speakers and, characteristically, the B-role partners then requested further information to enable them to identify just what sort of object A was trying to describe. In most cases, it seemed that it was the combination of several pieces of information which enabled the listener to identify the intended type of object and to draw it in. This is illustrated in (3n)–(3q).

(3n) (FB & BM)
  A. have you got an electric power cable there
  B. er ++ no
  A. oh well + now draw an electric power cable
  B. what sort
  A. the one like four-pronged + you know they've got really big high tension power cable leads on them
  B. right ++ hang on then

(3o) (SC & EA)
  A. you come to this ++ is er erm ++ a + power ++ sort of thing
  B. ++ what?
  A. one of those triangular things
  B. what triangular things
  A. those metal frames with the like + pole sort of things
  B. oh yeah – got it – hang on

(3p) (JA & TP)
  A. have you got a tower?
  B. what sort of a tower
  A. one of those skeleton towers – that (?) got electric cables on
  B. OK – I'll put one in

(3q) (DB & NK)

    A. and just there you should have a colon

    B. a what?

    A. a colon – one of them posts with electricity wires coming off them

    B. oh right – hang on – I'll do the colon

(3r) (TR & MP)

    A. you should come to a ++ big ++ set of wires

    B. what?

    A. I don't know what else to call it

    B. leave that one then

In all these cases the A-role speaker fails to use a conventionally established expression to denote the pylon, and uses instead an expression which the B-role speaker recognises to be inadequate. The denotational range of the expression is either not sufficiently constrained to permit B to identify what A is speaking of; or perhaps the expression does not seem to make sense in the context. In (3n), A's initial expression, *an electric power cable,* seems positively unlikely as a feature in a landscape but B, presumably using the denotation of the expression co-operatively, nonetheless searches her map. She fails to find anything corresponding to this denotation and, when A uses the same expression again in her instruction to draw the cable, B merely asks *what sort.* A now elaborates, but minimally helpfully with her *like four-pronged . . . really big high tension power cable leads on them.* In spite of the apparently unhelpful nature of A's remark, there is sufficient additional information for B to discern that what is at issue is a pylon to which electric power cables are attached.

In all cases except the last, (3r), where the pair abandon the effort to communicate on this issue, the B-role participant is eventually successful in drawing what is recognisably an electricity pylon in a roughly appropriate location. Despite some initial expressions whose denotations seem positively misleading, notably *electric power cable* and *colon,* sufficient extra information is added to enable B to infer the sort of feature that might be found in a landscape represented in such a way.

Curiously enough, in the case of (3q), B appears to understand the term *colon and* concurs in its use. However we should note that B's initial response to its use is to say *a what?* It is not until A fleshes out the description with *one of them posts with electricity wires coming off them* that B recognises what is being described. We might speculate that both of the terms *pylon* and *colon* are relatively unfamiliar to these subjects, certainly rarely used by them. The phonological (and the related orthographic) similarity of the words might have led to A selecting the wrong member of the pair and to B understanding the word in the sense intended by A rather than in its conventional sense. If B had had ready control of the term *pylon,* confusion, or at least further discussion, might have resulted. But confusion does not, in the event, arise since both participants proceed as though the term *colon* was the term *pylon.* We shall see what appears to be a rather similar instance of a wrongly chosen word, which is phonologically quite similar to the word presumably intended, in the selection of *alcove* for *cove* in chapter 4, in extract (4c). The effect is familiar in the 'Colemanballs' column of the magazine *Private Eye*, where readers of the magazine contribute examples of transcribed speech heard on radio or television where speakers apparently frequently produce lexical slips which, in the main, no doubt pass unnoticed by listeners and, since they are not corrected, are presumably not consciously noted by those who utter them.

3.6.2 Expression meaning and speaker meaning

Since the participants in the Map tasks are undertaking a controlled task, we can be reasonably confident that we know what it is that the A-role speaker is attempting to identify in each of extracts (3n)–(3r), and we also know that, at the beginning of each of these extracts, the B-role speaker does not know what is being referred to.

In 1.2.2, the issue of how a distinction might be drawn between sentence meaning and speaker meaning was raised. In extracts (3n)–(3r), the question arises of the distinction between speaker meaning and expression meaning. Unlike standard examples in the literature, it is not the case that these speakers are exploiting one well-articulated expression from which their listeners are supposed to infer an indirect and well-articulated further interpretation (as proposed, for instance, in Searle 1979). These speakers are struggling to express the description of an entity whose name they probably do know well, which they would almost certainly recognise, but which does not come readily to mind when needed. Like speakers of a foreign language whose command of vocabulary in the foreign language is imperfect, they are forced into trying to construct a synonymous expression. Their initial attempts suggest inexpert proddings with an ill-designed tool:

(3n) an electric power cable
(3o) a + power ++ sort of thing
(3p) a tower
(3q) a colon
(3r) a ++ big ++ set of wires

What are we to understand by **speaker meaning** here? We have good reasons to believe that these speakers intend to refer to whatever the term *pylon* describes. That meaning, we must suppose, is what they would like to be able to convey. But given that they are apparently unable to call to mind the correct term, do we have to accept that what they actually intend to express by what they say is something other than what is conveyed by the term *pylon*? William James expresses one view of the relationship between thought and utterance: 'And has the reader never asked himself what kind of a mental fact is his intention of saying a thing before he has said it? It is an entirely definite intention . . . as the words that replace it arrive, it welcomes them successively and calls them right if they agree with it, it rejects them and calls them wrong if they do not' ([1890] 1981:167).

What is not clear of course, in the instances we are discussing, is whether or not the intention in each case did indeed 'welcome' the utterances which were eventually produced, or whether they were simply accepted as the best that could be managed.

In the case of (3q), we may feel reasonably justified in suggesting that speaker A has made a tongue-slip (though it is rather more difficult to make the same claim for speaker B). It is harder to separate what the other speakers might have intended to express from what they actually said, if what they actually said is extremely vague, simply selecting what is for them a single salient attribute of the landscape feature, rather than arriving at characterising the whole feature as an entity. In such cases, perhaps it is necessary to accept that the speakers in these extracts have indeed expressed what they are trying to express. In the case of (3n) and (3r), the speakers may be trying to convey a sense that the main feature of a pylon is the cable or the wires attached to it, whereas in (3p) the speaker may be more impressed by the tower-like structure of the pylon. The most vague and abstract description is provided by the speaker in extract (3o). In all these cases, it seems reasonable to suggest that the words used by the speaker may reflect the meanings which the speaker is trying to express reasonably well.

In the case of (3q), however, we seem to be forced to distinguish between expression meaning and speaker meaning, and to assume that, as the result of an error in selecting a particular word, the speaker has said something other than that which was intended. The fact that the speaker's expression, together with additional description, is successful in denoting the correct type of entity to the listener, so that the listener adequately understands what the speaker intended to convey, is, we might suggest, merely a fortunate spin-off from the phonological similarity of *colon* and *pylon*.

A stronger claim is expressed by Davidson, in his paper *A Nice Derangement of Epitaphs* ([1977] 1986). Davidson says of malapropisms generally: 'What is interesting is the fact that in all these cases the hearer has no trouble understanding the speaker in the way the speaker intends' (1986:434). With malapropisms he is prepared to include the interpretation of garbled or incomplete utterances, tongue slips, new idiolects and words which we have never encountered before (1986:437). Davidson's account involves the listener recognising that the speaker has, either by error or design, selected the wrong word, though he goes on to say that it makes no difference whether both speaker and hearer are mistaken, since things would still go as smoothly. The listener may have an initial theory (what Davidson calls 'a prior theory') about what this speaker in this context is likely to say. If the speaker then says something which cannot be accommodated within the listener's theory, the listener will produce a change in his or her prior theory, and construct a fresh one-off theory, a 'passing theory' which will permit the interpretation of what the speaker intended, indeed will converge on the speaker's own passing theory. The interest for Davidson lies not so much in the fact that the speaker has apparently made an erroneous choice of words, but in producing an account which will 'distinguish between what a speaker, on a given occasion, means, and what his words mean' (1986:434).

The conclusion which Davidson is driven to is to suggest that 'there is no such thing as a language, not if a language is anything like what many philosophers and linguists have supposed'(1986:446), and to suggest that an attempt to account for communication by an appeal to conventions should be abandoned. Dummett (1986), in commenting on Davidson's paper, suggests that there are two 'natural' extreme accounts of meaning, one of which depicts words as carrying meanings independently of speakers, and the other of which depicts speakers as attaching meanings to words. Davidson, he suggests, is, in this paper, committing himself to the second view. Against this view, Dummett urges that there must be some meanings conventionally associated with words independently of any speaker. If this were not the case, it is difficult to see how we would be able to recognise a malapropism when we encounter one (or, indeed, how anyone could ever have contemplated constructing a dictionary).

Chomsky (1988) draws a now-familiar distinction which may be helpful in pondering these difficult questions. He recognises what he calls an **I-language** (internal language), which is the language known to an individual, which constantly changes as the individual develops and hears and produces words used in different ways. The I-language, we might suggest, constitutes the sum of the relevant linguistic (and associated contextual) experience of that individual. Hence the I-language of one individual must differ quite strikingly in some respects from that of another individual, since their linguistic experience and the contexts of the occurrence of this experience have been necessarily different. The notion of I-language is to be sharply distinguished from that of **E-language** (external language), which is available in some 'ontologically mysterious' manner to members of a speech community. Chomsky, like Davidson, proposes that, for the purposes of his own area of study, the notion of E-language should be dispensed with. He is interested in I-languages: 'As for Jones, who uses "disinterested" to mean "uninterested", he might be in error if his own I-language happens to yield a different consequence; many factors interact in behaviour . . . so our behaviour might not correspond to our knowledge' (Chomsky 1988:67). This seems as good an account as we are likely to be able to propose of the use of expressions like that in 3q. These issues will be taken up again in 7.3.

3.7 Achieving adequate interpretation of referring expressions

We have noted that listeners, in achieving an interpretation of expressions used by speakers in these spatially structured tasks, put to use a range of information, which includes not only their knowledge of the world and of the language, together with expectations of truth and co-operativeness in communication, but from the nature of the task in hand:

— the denotation of the expression used by the speaker
— the current point of departure and the search field bounded by a plausible distance from it
— the established direction of the route
— their expectations of the types of entity likely to be found on the map — derived from observing the map

It will be obvious that much depends, in a task which is focussed on locations and the spatial relationships holding between them, on the directional and locational expressions used by the A-role speaker, expressions such as *above, across from, just touching, straight up, past, a little way down from, northeast, down from the top of the page* and so on. The issue of the specification of spatial relationships and the identification of locations, particularly where these involve the use of deictic expressions, will be discussed in chapter 4.

Verbs play a minimal role in such discourse having apparently only five significant functions:

— used by A to establish whether or not B has a feature, relevant forms are: *got, have, see, find*
— used by A to instruct B to draw a new feature: *put, draw, should have, be*
— used by A to move B's focus of attention about the map: *go/come (up/down/around/across etc.), start, leave*
— used by B to announce success in interpretation or discovery of an entity: *got you/it, see, know, do*
— used by B to ask A to go more slowly: *wait, slow down, hang on, hold on*

The range of verbs used in these interactions is remarkably restricted, unsurprisingly since the range of associated actions is so limited. Many of the instructions consist simply of prepositional phrases without any overt verb. These prepositional phrases, when they are sufficiently specific, have the effect of pointing the listener in the right direction within the search field. The interpretation of noun phrases which describe the relevant feature is constrained, for most listeners, by the denotation of the expression and the area within which they expect to find the entity.

We can summarise the configurations of information which give rise to relative ease or difficulty of successful interpretation for the listener in the Map task:

(1) Immediate success is likely if the feature is shared by A and B, if A and B are both at the same point of departure for the new move, if the feature lies within a plausible distance of the point of departure, following the established direction of the route, and if A uses an expression whose denotation is understood by B to include, specifically and conventionally, entities like the relevant entity. Such a configuration typically gives rise, we might claim, to B **correctly** interpreting an expression used to refer (if we make the charitable assumption that B is thinking of the relevant entity in a manner sufficiently similar to A). Note that it may not follow that B has correctly understood A's intentions in producing the utterance, as we saw in the passage we discussed in 2.3 where B apparently correctly identified the referents of A's expressions and appeared to arrive at an interpretation which was adequate for her purposes in listening, but which may not have been that intended by speaker A.

(2) Delay in a confident interpretation by B is likely when all the conditions stated in (1) are satisfied except that A uses an expression whose range of denotation does not enable B to home in on the relevant feature. We saw examples of this in extract (3b) where A used the expression *mound* which B failed to see referred to what A then successfully described as *the little hill*. A difference of perception in extract (3c) left A and B using the distinct terms *boat/yacht* to refer to the same entity. In extract (3e) we saw B eventually able to interpret her *island* as A's *lake*. In the first and third of these examples we might suppose that B eventually **correctly** interprets A's expression. In the

second example this is less clearly the case, as each one of the pair continues to entertain somewhat different views from the other, albeit of the same entity. In that B does light on the intended referent, the reference may be held to be successful. In Evans' terms, the arrow does indeed appear to hit the target but it is not clear that B thinks of the target in the same way as A. B certainly **adequately** identifies what A is speaking of, but apparently continues to view it in a slightly different manner (a difficulty raised in 1.4 in interpreting the utterance *he's very like Margaret Thatcher*).

(3) There are some cases in the data of B-role listeners neglecting the constraints of the search field bounded by a plausible distance, and taking an expression of A's, whose denotation reasonably picked out an entity in a distant location, to refer to that entity. They assumed that they had correctly understood the language used. Clearly, they had indeed correctly understood the language, in the sense of having correctly identified the appropriate type of denotatum. What they had failed to do was understand the language in a sufficiently constrained context of use. Such cases must exemplify failure of reference.

(4) In the case of unshared features, A informs B of the presence of an entity which B does not have on the map, so here there is no question of B achieving uptake of an expression which A may have intended should function as a **referring expression**. B has to understand such an expression, rather, as a **constitutive** expression which will permit the construction of a representation of a new entity on B's map.

3.8 Conclusion

In this chapter we have explored the success, partial success, and apparent failure of a wide range of expressions used to refer in a variety of contexts, while considering the question of what it means for a listener to think of a referent in a way which is 'pretty similar' to the way in which the speaker is thinking of the referent. We have observed that dissonance between how the speaker thinks of an object and how the listener thinks of an object (revealed by the way they each construct referring expressions in their turn as speaker) does not necessarily block communication. We have, as well, observed that, in spite of the participants having considerable variation in what they know of a feature, communication is not necessarily blocked.

In many examples, we have seen that expressions which would not standardly be held to be referring expressions, are used by the speaker and are successful in focussing the listener's attention on the feature which the speaker is speaking of (as in *have you got a bridge?*). Such examples present a problem for theories of reference which restrict the form of referring expressions to definite descriptions used in declarative sentences, and see the relationship of reference as holding between the speaker's intention in uttering (or the speaker's utterance) and the world, while assigning only a marginal role to the listener.

We have also taken note of the fact that there are occasions when a speaker cannot know what is the relevant information to offer a listener, where the listener treats the speaker as providing a database from which the listener selects that information which is apposite at the moment of listening, and where the listener apparently ignores information provided by the speaker which is not currently relevant to the listener's own interests.

4 · Guiding the listener through the landscape

4.1 Locations and landscape features

In chapter 3, we observed a range of instances where the initial referring expression used by the speaker was insufficient to enable the listener to locate the landscape feature referred to, at least initially. In such cases, since all of the entities were represented in a spatially structured context, the standard response by B was to request information on the location of the entity, either in order to constrain the search field, or to insert a new feature on to the map. In the first section of this chapter, we shall note some of the issues raised by expressions of location in English, before going on in later sections to consider how some expressions of location can be used to create and structure the context if they are interpreted as terms of spatial deixis.

Lyons (1991:142) draws a distinction between entity-referring and place-referring expressions, and between entities and places, suggesting that 'it is . . . arguable that places (as distinct from spaces) are ontologically secondary, being identifiable as such by virtue of the entities that are located in or near them'. Such a characterisation seems appropriate to entities mentioned in prepositional phrases of a type such as *behind the barn, on the shelf, over the sea*, when such phrases are used to locate an object. Such an analysis is also consistent with the classic psychological distinction drawn between **figure** and **ground** (see the discussions in Clark 1976, Hanks 1987). It seems, however, less obviously true of *London, France* or the *Gobi desert* in expressions such as *x is located in the northern hemisphere* where, one might argue, these locations appear to have attained the status of entities, which they hold simultaneously with their function of identifying locations. Indeed, in English, it is frequently unclear whether the speaker wishes to refer to an entity or to a location. It appears that any entity can sometimes be seen as a location (as in *Sit in the chair beside John*) and, on the other hand, as we have seen, it appears to be possible for any location to be conceptualised as an entity (as in *Can you see a lake?*). It might be possible to clarify the ontological status of entities and locations, for instance by expressing a set of necessary and sufficient conditions for primary membership of one category rather than another. But it seems more likely that these categories are the temporary products of different modes of conceptualisation on the occasion of a particular utterance, which in English are revealed by the speaker using either entity-referring or place-referring expressions. The mode of conceptualisation appears to depend on whether the entity referred to is the topic of an utterance (as in *France is much bigger than you think it is*) or whether it is used to locate some other topic (as in *Avignon is in the south of France*).

Certainly in the Map task data, there is a notable diversification of strategies between those A-role speakers (a majority among the school population, but rare among undergraduates) who characteristically introduce new features by speaking directly in terms of entity referring expressions – *have you got a church? / you should have a pylon* – and those who typically first specify the location in terms of a place referring expression and only then state what is located in this place, as in: *and straight up towards the house / go – erm up very slightly diagonally + about two and a half inches + so you'll be level with the top of the mound*. For the first set of speakers, very little appeal is made to location, surprisingly in the context of a spatial task. Rather they simply refer to a list of target entities along the route. For them, if any reference is ever made to location, what prompts the use of a spatial expression appears to be when they learn that B does not have the relevant entity on his or her map.

It seems clear that the expression denoting a particular type of entity, the referring expression, has a clear informational priority over a simple expression of location, in that a referring expression can appear alone, whereas a locational expression simply denotes the location within which the referent is to be found. We have sporadic evidence from the Map task that, when a listener sees an appropriately denoted entity on the map, which is in a different location from that which is specified by the speaker, the listener may ignore the locational discrepancy and proceed to that entity. In a further task, the Ogre's castle task, this relation was systematically explored and, again, it was found that where there was a conflict between the information about the type of entity denoted by the referring expression and the specification of location, listeners would quite often prefer to believe that the information in the referring expression was correct and that the divergent locational information could be ignored (see discussion in Brown and Markman 1991). In both tasks, when such divergent information appeared, those subjects most prone to ignore the divergent information carried by the locational expressions were those judged by their schools to be among the less academically able.

It is obvious that the special nature of the task which these subjects are engaged in will predispose them to use place-referring expressions, just as one frequently finds dense use of such expressions in conversing with very small children, as in: *give me the ball + the ball + no it's over there – there – on the floor – no Tom look – on the FLOOR + behind you.* In such contexts, it seems appropriate to suggest that the location is actually not, from the point of view of information, secondary to the entity, rather the intersection of the space described by the entity-referring expression and the place-referring expression will get you into the appropriate area, the range, where you can expect to locate the entity. It is not simply that it is on the floor – behind you – that you will find the ball. It is also the case that the particular ball that you are to give me is that ball which is in that place on the floor. More generally, it is not simply that you will find x in y, but also that it is the x which is in y which is the one of interest.

Some versions of the Map task were specifically constructed to explore the ability of participants to construct and to interpret expressions referring to locations (which might be viewed as features of the landscape) for which no simple conventional label exists. It was hoped that, under these circumstances, listeners would not be able to rely on conventional denotations of expressions in their search for the feature but would have to work imaginatively, beyond the bounds of conventional lexical relationships, to interpret what their interlocutors were referring to. For instance in one version of the

Map task, an unshared windmill was situated in a prominent location on the edge of the (shared) lake. The location received a wide range of descriptions, most of which were successfully interpreted. The relevant expressions are italicised in the following extracts:

(4a)   (FB & BM)
   A. OK have you got a – a windmill
   B. no
   A. well y'you go down where the – you know – where the lake is
   B. yeah
   A. the big lake with – there's *a little + indentation like – little bit of rock – few rocks* in't there
   B. yeah

(4b)   (WL & RA)
   A. well and go round that ++ as far as the windmill
   B. I ain't got no windmill
   A. (*laughs*) alright + that's *below the boat + where there's no water – it's just in that little alcove bit – where it's got little squiggly lines near it*
   B. oh I see it

(4c)   (DC & LC)
   A. er ++ there's a windmill *directly below the boat – the rocks –*
   B. the boat + oh got you + there's *this little cove thing* isn't there
   A. yeah + and that windmill's just sitting in there

The speakers in (4a) and (4b) appear to have conceptualised the relevant landscape features rather differently. In 4a speaker A ignores the boat and speaks of *a little + indentation* and then mentions 'the rocks', which are the feature described by the speaker in (4b) as *little squiggly lines*. Whereas the speaker of (4a) mentions the outcome of the intended representation, the speaker of (4b) mentions the means of representation. The use by the 4b speaker of the term *alcove* is odd, though it appears to be successfully interpreted by B, since the conventional denotation of *alcove* hardly seems appropriate to the particular feature. It may be that the speaker was searching for the term *cove*, used by B in (4c), whose denotation more appropriately fits the feature and whose sense seems more appropriately related to *lake* (an issue discussed in 3.6.1). There is a striking variety of ways of conceptualising this particular feature of this map which is revealed in further verbalisations such as:

– *where the lake's got a big bit that suddenly comes out*
– *you see where the shape sort of breaks up and it goes into little sort of bumps*
   – there's a windmill just there
– *as you go up the – er – coastline – when you get to that little bulgy bit –*
   not the bulgy bit on the left hand side – the bulgy right hand side

We see that speakers in this spatially oriented task appear to construct place-referring expressions in a manner which suggests that the various locations on the map are characteristically treated just as though they were entities – *a big bit, little sort of bumps, that little bulgy bit*. English appears to be particularly prone to express locations as entities, an issue which will arise again in the next section.

In this part of the task, A-role speakers were driven to invent descriptions for a unique landscape configuration, thus to stretch the denotation of existing words to fit a new situation, very much in the mode characterised by Ziff in 1.1. In spite of the fact that the listeners were confronting the task of interpreting an utterance which was using language in a novel and inventive manner, in what Clark (1983) calls interpreting a 'nonce sense' which can only be understood in the context for which it was created, they had no difficulty in interpreting these utterances. Using the search field as a guide, they tracked up (or down, depending on how the A-role speaker had elected to describe the route) the side of the lake, until they reached a point where the configuration changed, sometimes using the boat, or the representation of the rocks, as a check that they were in the appropriate area.

So far I have written in rather general terms of the notion of the search field. It seems, however, that in this task at least, we can characterise it even more narrowly. To attempt this, we need to examine the use of deictic expressions.

4.2 Deixis
The function of deixis in language is usually held to be to anchor the utterance to the speaker at the moment of speaking (Fillmore 1977, 1980, 1982;

Lyons 1977, 1991; Levinson 1983, 1992). As Bühler writes: 'what "here" and "there" is, changes with the position of the speaker just as the "I" and "thou" jumps from one interlocutor to the other with the exchange of the roles of sender and receiver' ([1934] 1982:94). Deixis encodes features of the context of utterance, hence its interpretation requires the listener to be able to appreciate, and if necessary to construct, the relevant context. In cases where the entities, events and locations are not previously known to the listener, the listener can use the deictic features of the utterances to create an appropriate prototypical context, as we saw when we attempted to interpret sentences cited out of any context in 1.2.1.

The three major deictic categories are taken to be the categories of person, place and time. I shall have little to say in this chapter about the category of temporal deixis, though this will be discussed further in chapter 6. I shall briefly mention person deixis in this chapter, and this topic will arise again in chapter 6. To begin with, we shall concentrate on spatial deixis.

4.2.1 Spatial deixis

The primary ontology of spatial deixis is considered to derive from an individual, the speaker, pointing at some object or location in the immediately surrounding space. Given the nature of the Map task, the focus of interest here will be on how subjects use language (since they are inhibited from using gesture) to direct their interlocutor's attention in a spatial domain, to relate entities to each other in space and, in particular, to consider how listeners use deixis to create restricted contexts which enable them to locate themselves in a pictured landscape.

Within spatial deixis, a distinction is often drawn in terms of three planes which, it is suggested, are in many languages understood as directly relatable to the body parts of the speaker:

(1) the first plane is symmetrical, cutting through the vertical centre of the body between the eyes, which yields the distinction:

LEFT/RIGHT

(2) the second plane is asymmetrical, cutting through the horizontal plane of the body at some point, which yields the distinctions:

UP/DOWN, ABOVE/BELOW

(3) the third plane is also asymmetrical, cutting through the vertical centre of the body and slicing through both the ears, which yields the distinction:

BEFORE(IN FRONT OF)/BEHIND

Within the physical space around the speaker, thus characterised, a proximal/non-proximal distinction is drawn in English, between a place relatively near to the speaker, and a place which is relatively more distant, yielding the distinction HERE/THERE. Of these, *here* is taken to be the marked member of the pair, since its use regularly implies a contrast with *there*, whereas *there*, used on its own, implies no such contrast. The relatively neutral denotation of *there* has permitted the range of functions of this form to develop more widely than those of *here* (Allan 1971, 1972; Lyons 1977, 1991) and, indeed, it has assimilated the distal function of the now largely defunct term *yonder*, sometimes expressed in modern English as *over there* (in contradistinction to *there*).

A further distinction is often associated with these static spatial distinctions, and it involves movement in space towards or away from the speaker, exemplified in the verbs:

COME/GO and BRING/TAKE

Still utilising the proximal/non-proximal parameter, a further type of space-indicating Deixis is often identified, this time relating to the person or object referred to in the utterance. The proximal/non-proximal demonstrative forms, THIS/THAT, are generally recognised as deictic. These expressions appear to be able to encode both the proximal/non-proximal distinction and person or entity reference as in *this*, 'the one near me' versus *that*, 'the one not near me'. Again, the proximal *this* is taken to be the marked member of the pair, since its use typically implies a contrast with *that*, whereas non-proximal *that* is taken to be unmarked and has acquired a wider range of functions than *this* (see Allan 1971, 1972; Lyons 1977, 1991).

We shall also, in this context, need to take some account of categories of person or entity deixis. Lyons (1977, 1991) has suggested that we should identify the definite determiner, THE, together with the personal third-person pronouns HE/SHE/IT etc., as constituting a further deictic category, an issue which we shall address in a later section (4.4). For the moment we shall focus on spatial deixis.

It is assumed that space, time and person deixis was, in its distant origins, developed to permit the expression of relationships in what Lyons (1977) has called the 'canonical situation of utterance', where a speaker addresses a hearer who is physically present in the here-and-now, and speaks of some object which is within view of both of them – the typical situation of utterance for the very young child. Some linguists and anthropologists suggest that original pure spatial deictic systems can be substituted for, or accompanied by, pointing, but that once they begin to be used to refer to objects out of sight of the speaker, no longer in the here-and-now of utterance, these linguistic expressions increasingly lose their deictic characteristics (Heeschen 1982, quoted in Senft 1992).

There are two major sources of problems in the analysis of spatial deictic expressions in discourse. The first is raised by the issue of whether terms deriving from the so-called deictic categories are being used in a deictic or a non-deictic way. Consider the following sentences:

(1) The ball is in front of the tree.
(2) The ball is in front of the man.

Here, it is suggested, the first usage is likely to be deictic, and to indicate the relationship between the ball, the tree and the speaker (or possibly the listener), where the ball lies between the tree and the speaker. The second usage may be similarly deictic, but it may, in contrast, be non-deictic, because a man, unlike a tree, has an intrinsic front, so even if the man is facing away from the speaker and the ball lies at his feet, it would still be necessary to use sentence 2, in spite of the fact that the ball may now be on the side of the man away from the speaker. Potentially ambiguous uses, it is suggested, will arise with all spatial deictic expressions, whenever the entities to which they relate have intrinsic tops, bottoms, sides, fronts or backs. This distinction is sometimes seen as contrasting a **positional** system of reference, which relates to the speaker or to the speaker's position, as opposed to a **dimensional** system of reference which directly relates one object to another independently of any speaker.

A second potential problem appears when the speaker employs what has sometimes been called **empathetic deixis**. This arises when the speaker appears to transfer the deictic centre, at least for some period of time, to the listener, and it appears to be a product of the movement out of the canonical situation of utterance, when the speaker speaks of some entity or event not in the here and now, and not mutually visible. If a speaker in London addresses a friend in New York saying *I'll COME to see you on Tuesday*, the deictic centre appears to be transferred to the listener in the choice of the term *come*. This transference of the deictic centre to the listener is held to indicate that the speaker is projecting him or her self into the point of view, and perhaps into the emotional state, of the listener. If a speaker employs empathetic deixis without making it clear to the listener that deictic expressions are now to relate to the listener's deictic centre rather than to that of the speaker, misunderstanding can readily occur.

4.3 Deixis and the search field

Thus briefly armed with some terminology, I shall turn to examine how speakers in the Map task exploit spatial deictic expressions to guide their listeners through the maps.

As we have seen, the most economical way for a speaker to move a listener from one position on the map to another, seems to be simply to use a nominal expression which could identify the type of landscape feature which constitutes the goal of the next move, and which will also, incidentally, identify the location of the goal of the next move. Such instructions simply ignore the configuration of the route, and give no information about how it relates to each landscape feature. In responding to expressions which simply describe features, rather than the route, listeners appear to search their maps for a feature which satisfies the denotation of the expression and draw a route directly up to it.

We shall briefly elaborate here the characteristics of the restricted search field which appears to be created by most listeners (discussed in 3.7), and then go on to ask the question: what justifies its creation? In general, listeners appear to assume a co-operative, Gricean, A-role speaker, one who will mention only features which appear on A's map, and, of those, only features which relate to the route, and one who will, moreover, mention them in a helpful order, so that the next move will always be to a proximate point, hence the route can be achieved in an orderly manner, step by step.

Listeners also make a number of assumptions about the nature of the task. Firstly, they assume that they should begin their search for each newly-mentioned entity from their current anchor-point, that is the point which they have most recently arrived at and agreed with the speaker. Secondly, if the features on the map are distributed at fairly regular intervals about the map, listeners appear to expect a new move to be of the sort of size which they have already experienced, to an immediately proximate feature, with no intervening features. Thirdly, if the speaker gives no counter-indication, they appear to expect the route to continue in the direction which has already been established. Fourthly, listeners import real-world knowledge and assume that features represented on the map which would, in the real world, offer obstacles to someone walking through it, should be skirted around: thus landscape features such as rivers, lakes, ponds, mountains and coastlines, all have the effect of constraining the direction in which it is possible to move from the current anchor-point. The combination of these four constraints means that most listeners search in a move-sized arc, on land, pointing away from their current anchor-point in the established direction of the route.

Extract (4d) illustrates this process working, though with some local difficulties, at the beginning of a simple map. In this extract, we begin to see some attempt at a description of the nature of the route. (These are Scottish subjects.)

(4d)   (B&P)
1   A. you've got the start
2   B. hm
3   A. have you got palm trees – palm beach on your map
4   B. aye
5   A. well go – about an inch down from them and go left
6   ++ have you got the swamp on your map?
7   B. crocodiles
8   A. yeah well ++ you avoid that + you go round it –
9   round in nearly a circle – round it ++ so that

10   have you got the waterfall
11 B. mhm
12 A. you go round the waterfall
13 B. left or right or what
14 A. eh + left round the waterfall + and up

The A-role speaker first locates B at 'the start'. Then, in line 3, she asks whether B has 'palm trees' and B, searching from the position of 'the start', in the bottom right-hand corner of the map, with only a ninety degree arc of search available, finds the palm trees which are the nearest feature to the start, situated above it. She draws a line from the start to the palm trees, which is what most B-role subjects do, having heard what they take to be an expression indicating the goal of the next move. However, the route on A's map does not, in fact, go all the way up to the palm trees. It goes half an inch up in the direction of the palm trees, and then turns towards the west. It seems reasonable to suppose that A simply intended to use the palm trees to indicate the direction of B's first excursion away from the start.

When in line 5, A says *go – about an inch down from them and go left*, this must be a problematic instruction for B, since if she obeyed it, it would bring her back to the start. She apparently assumes that A's use of the expression *about an inch down* is intended only vaguely, and draws a line of about half an inch down from the palm trees towards the start which then turns towards the left-hand side of the page. B arrives at A's intended anchor-point but having made, unknown to A, an excursion up to and half-way down from, the palm trees.

Having indicated the direction of the next move with the instruction to *go left*, A then enquires whether B has 'the swamp'. The direction *go left* is apparently interpreted by B as meaning by default 'go horizontally left', and this enables B to identify the relevant area of location, since her 'crocodiles' are located where A's swamp is to be found on A's map.

B's elliptical reply, *crocodiles*, to A's enquiry does not appear to impinge on A's consciousness, since she proceeds just as though B had agreed to having a swamp. It seems likely that A heard B's response, in that her own next contribution does not overlap B's utterance and leaves a normal gap between turns, but it is at least possible that she did not interpret what B said, since her use of the singular form *that*, together with the singular anaphoric forms *it* in lines 8 and 9, seem to relate more readily to the singular 'swamp' than to the plural 'crocodiles'.

How much of this language is to be interpreted deictically? We shall begin by considering only the obviously spatial expressions. In line 5, A's expressions *go* and *go left* must surely be interpreted as empathetically deictic, as meaning 'go from where you are' in each case, rather than 'go from anywhere', or 'go from the start', and so indeed B appears to interpret these expressions. The expression *left* is ambiguous as between a deictic reading 'change your direction of travel and go to your left' and a non-deictic reading 'go to the left of the page' (which has a clear top and bottom because features such as mountains, waterfalls and forts each have a clear top and bottom as they are represented in stereotypical profile on the map). Again, the expressions *go round*, in lines 8 and 12, must be interpreted as 'go round from where you are'. The expression *left round the waterfall* is ambiguous as between a deictic and a non-deictic construal, since the waterfall has a clearly drawn top, bottom and sides, hence an inherent left hand side.

Even in this extract (4d), where A gives very little locational information, we can identify some forms which must be interpreted deictically, in particular expressions containing the word *go*. In many other interchanges in the data drawn from the series of Map tasks, the speaker's intention that the spatial descriptions should be interpreted deictically is made quite explicit, as the speaker addresses the hearer as though the hearer were travelling through a landscape, rather than drawing a route on a piece of paper. In the more complex maps from which the next set of examples is drawn, the route does not simply move across to the left and then up the page as in the simple maps, where it might be argued that terms like *right* and *left* could simply relate to the sides of the map. In these later maps, the route goes up, down and across the maps, sometimes doubling back on itself. In such cases, listeners have to keep the orientation towards landscape features implied by what the speaker says steadfastly in mind, if they are to see the next move in the right way, and limit the search field in an appropriate manner.

Extracts (4e)–(4h) illustrate collaboration between speakers and hearers on more complex maps:

(4e)   (A & P)
   A. and head on a line + that would be sort of in line with your first oil well
   B. ++ go back up there?
   A. no d' + not ++ go up + go up to the sort of um + have you turned – sort of turned round in front of the logs
   B. yeah
   A. well you've come down from that + from the oil well
   B. + yeah
   A. gone round the back of the stones
   B. yeah
   A. and turned back up again

In extract (4e), note B's explicitly deictic question: *go back up there?* (GO from where I am, BACK to where I was, UP from where I am, THERE away from here) and A's expressions:

– *you've come down from that* (YOU – my listener, HAVE COME DOWN – from where you were to where you are now, FROM THAT – the further-away place from where you are now)
– *gone round the back of the stones* (GONE – away from where you are and/or were, ROUND THE BACK OF THE STONES – behind them as seen from your viewpoint in front of them)
– *turned back up again* (TURNED BACK UP – from where you were then, AGAIN – with relation to what you have done before)

Note the consistent use by the speaker of referring expressions as part of locative expressions marked by prepositions. All these expressions imply a viewpoint which relates to the speaker's view of how the listener is moving in the landscape, a view which the listener needs to shadow closely in order to interpret them adequately and which, in the case we are looking at, appears to pose no problems for the listener who re-traces the already agreed route while listening to, and agreeing to, A's summary of the most recent stages of the route.

In extract (4f), the expression *the far side of the little pond* assumes a being in a landscape from whose viewpoint one side of the pond is further away, in a manner very similar to the way in which the expression *round the back of the stones* was used in extract (4e). These expressions must be being used deictically, since these entities have no intrinsic 'backs' and 'fronts', 'nears' and 'fars':

(4f)   (B & D)

   A. then you turn and go towards the far side of the little pond

Extracts (4g) and (4h) further illustrate the LEFT/RIGHT dimension when it has to be interpreted deictically, rather than with respect to the fixed sides of the map or page:

(4g)   (A & N)

   A. from the fuel tanks go ++ turn ++ turn right and go straight on ++ and erm – walk down – through the twin crater and then turn back to face the crater

In extract (4g), the expression *right* relates to the right of the speaker or listener facing down the page in imagination, when the intrinsic right hand side of the map as it lies on the table before each of the participants, would be on the left of each of them. Note the instruction *walk down* where 'walk' suggests that the speaker is indeed imagining a perambulation through a landscape, and the overt suggestion of the orientation of the speaker's view of the listener as B is instructed to turn within the landscape to *face the crater*, thus reversing not only the direction of walking but also the LEFT/RIGHT dimension.

Again in extract (4h), the LEFT/RIGHT dimension is explicitly relativised to B's deictic centre by each speaker in turn, rather than to the page or to the map:

(4h)   (D & D)

   A. then go to your left round the fuel tanks
   B. yeah
   A. then – down in + on your right hand side you've got twin craters – in – in the middle +
   B. do we pass – do we pass it on the right hand side or on the left

Whereas LEFT/RIGHT expressions may occasionally refer to the left and right hand sides of the map (or of the page), and are often ambiguous between deictic and non-deictic readings in simple maps, in these more complex maps they are standardly used to refer deictically from the point of view of B as perceived by A or B, and listeners generally understand them in this sense. Only two pairs throughout these tasks used standard orientational terms (*south* and *west*) rather than terms which are capable of being relativised to the speaker or listener.

The depth dimension, IN FRONT OF/BEHIND (NEAR/FAR), is exclusively used deictically, relating to the point of view of the speaker or listener.

Similarly GO (from where you are) and COME (to where you ought to be / where I, the speaker, am looking) appear only to be used deictically.

On the other hand, the vertical dimension UP/DOWN, is used non-deictically, to refer to the stable intrinsic form of the map (or page), which must necessarily be interpreted as having a top and bottom since so many features on the maps (mountains, churches, boats, windmills, etc.) have intrinsic tops and bottoms.

4.3.1 The tour approach and the map approach

The majority of A-role speakers (more than 80%, in most of their turns) apparently adopt the view that it is their responsibility to lead the B-role speaker through the landscape in the manner exemplified in the previous section. Linde and Labov (1975), in a sociolinguistic study, reported that 97% of their subjects gave descriptions of their houses and apartments in terms of what they call 'the tour approach', rather than in terms of a description of the ground-plan as seen from above, which they call 'the map approach'. This is perhaps hardly surprising, since an imaginary tour, moving through the apartment, would be consonant with everyday experience. It seems more surprising that we should find this high incidence of tours in the Map task, which is presented as a two-dimensional map. Nonetheless, even in the descriptions of those who adopt an explicitly diagrammatic, bird's-eye view approach, describing the route in terms of vectors relating features, it is still the case that many instructions require a deictic interpretation. Thus instructions such as *draw, continue, move up,* etc. must in all cases be interpreted as 'do whatever-it-is starting from where (I think) you are'.

In interpreting expressions referring to landscape features in these tasks, it is necessary, as we have seen, for each B-role participant to interpret most locative expressions and instructions as deictic. Such a procedure permits the possibility, indeed creates the probability, of B approaching a new feature from the same viewpoint as A. The careful interpretation of deictic spatial expressions allows B both to secure such a viewpoint and to delimit the search field for the next move.

We now turn to discuss the interpretation of referring expressions which are not apparently being used as locative expressions.

4.4 Person/entity deixis in referring expressions

I mentioned earlier, in 4.2, Lyons' suggestion that definite articles and third-person pronouns should be seen as having a deictic function, parallel to that of the demonstrative pronouns *this* and *that* (or *these* and *those*). Earlier writers, both in linguistics and in philosophy, have considered the viability of this approach, but Lyons adopts an unusually strong commitment to it.

One reason for making such a suggestion is that, historically, these forms all derive from two proximal/non-proximal deictic sets, each of which had three forms distinguished by gender and could be used either pronominally or adjectivally. At that point in the development of early English, there were no distinct articles, definite or indefinite, and there were no separate third person pronouns (Quirk and Wrenn 1955:69–73). As Lyons (1977:647) points out, uncontentiously, the definite article evolved from one of the non-proximal demonstrative pronoun/adjectives (from the neuter non-proximal *that*), which has now lost its gender and number content and is today used only adjectivally, whereas the third-person pronouns (*he, she, it,* etc.) which derive from the same set of pronoun/adjectives, retain their number and gender content but, nowadays, these can only be used pro-nominally. In Modern English, just like the definite article, the personal pronouns no longer indicate a proximal/non-proximal contrast.

The second reason for suggesting that these forms should be seen as part of the deictic anchoring mechanisms of the language is synchronic. It concerns the way in which these forms contribute to how reference is made. Just as, with a demonstrative, the addressee is invited to look into the context and identify the referent, so, it is suggested, a definite description invites the addressee to look into the context and identify the referent. There are, as I pointed out earlier, two ways in which we can identify an object in the here-and-now context. First, we can characterise the object, by informing the listener of its properties or of the class of entity to which it belongs. As we have seen, on simple maps, this was the strategy preferred by many of the Map task subjects. Secondly, we can indicate the location of the entity and suppose that by looking in that place, the listener will find the entity. Again, we have seen conditions, where there are mismatches of information and in the more complex maps, in which Map task subjects have preferred to use explicitly locative expressions first, before moving on to specify the type of entity which should be located there.

Lyons (1977:648) suggests that the demonstrative pronouns *this* and *that*, when used as referring expressions, indicate the general location of the entity referred to, so that *this* can be understood as 'the one near me'. The personal pronouns, he suggests, indicate not location but type, so *he*, for instance, indicates 'the male one'. In this respect, demonstrative pronouns and personal pronouns each encode part of the information expressed by a definite noun-phrase. Thus the phrase *go to the waterfall*, where the expression *the waterfall* both identifies a type of entity and indicates a location, might be paraphrased as *go to the next one* or *go over there*.

If we accept Lyons' position, then every definite expression and personal pronoun is potentially deictic. The Map task offers data where the effects of this suggestion can be explored, since this task is particularly prone to throwing up deictic referential usage, as we have seen, because speakers undertaking these tasks must refer to specific spatially located entities. Our subjects stick to the mundane task in hand. They do not discuss creatures of their imagination, or abstract theoretical constructs, nor do they speculate about the nature of the world using generic or attributive expressions while they are doing the task. They speak only of each other ('you' and 'I') and the features on the map. Can all the definite expressions which they use be described as deictic?

4.4.1 Deixis and anaphoric definite expressions
If we consider part of extract (4e) again (now renumbered as 4i), we can see examples of referring expressions which are plausibly analysed as deictic:

(4i)   (A & P)

A. and head on a line + that would be sort of in line with *your first oil well*

B. ++ go back up there?

A. no d'+ not ++ go up + go up to the sort of um + have you turned – sort of turned round in front of *the logs*

B. yeah

A. well you've come down from *that* + from *the oil well*

B. + yeah

A. gone round the back of *the stones*

When A speaks of *your first oil well* to B, and then of *the oil well,* he speaks of an entity in a location which he, as speaker, is in relation with and which he knows that B, as hearer, is already in relation with. He speaks of 'the first oil well that you and I mutually know about and have just recently on this very map agreed on'. If A and B were each standing on a large version of his own map, which the other could see, A would be able to point to the oil well on B's map appropriately using the expression *that one*. On the second mention, in this extract, he says *you've come down from that,* using a clearly deictic demonstrative, before adding the full prepositional phrase *from the oil well,* presumably to ensure that his meaning is quite clear. Similarly, when A refers to *the logs* and *the stones,* he refers to entities and locations which have just recently been mutually agreed between the two participants as present on both maps, as part of their common ground in Clark's terms (1992). These seem to be clear examples of anaphoric use which is deictic, in that the verbal expressions plausibly substitute for pointing, and in that they anchor the content which they express in the shared past of speaker and hearer, as seen from the speaker's deictic centre at the moment of speaking, and from the speaker's view of the hearer's point of view. As Lyons (1977:670) remarks, recency of mention and salience within the discourse are deictically based notions, since both depend upon the speaker's judgment at the moment of utterance, hence it is reasonable to assert that anaphora rests on deixis.

4.4.2 Deixis and introductory definite expressions

Is it the case that the definite article is to be considered deictic in all contexts (like *this)*, or is it only used deictically in some contexts (like *that)*? We must already be predisposed to expect that it will only occasionally be deictic, because of the existence of apparently non-referential use of definite expressions in generic expressions of the type *the lion is a noble beast* and in the type exemplified by *the man who can solve this is a better man than I am,* which are held to be simply attributive and not to refer to any individual (Donellan, 1966).

If we turn back to another extract which we have already considered, and look again at part of extract 4d (now renumbered as 4j), where entities are introduced into the discourse for the first time by definite expressions, we might be able to determine whether or not these expressions are used deictically:

(4j)   (B & P)
1   A. you've got *the start*
2   B. hm
3   A. have you got palm trees . . .
6   A. have you got the *swamp* on your map?
7   B. crocodiles . . .
10 A. have you got *the waterfall*

In line 1, A, seeing 'the start' marked on her map, suggests that B has it on hers. She uses a definite expression. In what sense could this be said to be deictic usage? At this point, A has no specific information about what B has depicted on her map. She, apparently, simply makes the (reasonable) assumption that B too will have 'the start' to which A is informationally visually related, so the expression could be glossed as meaning 'the start that I know about'. It is, I think, hard to suggest that this is an occasion when a referring expression is, in some sense, standing in for pointing to a particular entity, since it could be that B does not have such an entity marked on her map. It is of course true that the expression *the start* is ambiguous as between 'a type of entity called *the start*' and 'the location where the start is'. A must know that B must necessarily have the location of 'the start' on her map, and A could, if permitted, point to this location, even if the start were not marked there. The potential pointing argument seems weaker here though, in that A knows only that she could identify the location on B's map, she does not know that she could identify the entity itself. If, on interpreting the denotation of A's referring expression, B still cannot identify the entity 'the start', B will also be unable to identify the location.

The pointing argument becomes even less plausible if we consider the definite expressions in the interrogatives in lines 6 and 10, where A does not presuppose that B shares the information on a specific landscape feature but rather asks whether or not B has such a feature. By speaking of an entity in this context, A indicates that she herself is in relation with the relevant referent. Thus the expression *the waterfall*, in *have you got the waterfall*, might be understood as 'the waterfall that I know about and that, seen from where I stand, I intend to be the goal for your next move'. Is the fact that the *speaker* can identify the thing spoken of all that is necessary to permit an expression to qualify as deictic? Lyons suggests that 'the deictically neutral pronominal component of the English definite article can be thought of as having just this function: it informs the addressee that some specific entity is being referred to without giving him any locative (or qualitative) information about it' (1977:654). On Lyons' view then, it appears that we could claim, in such cases, that the definite article is used deictically.

If such an interpretation is accepted for *have you got the waterfall* in extract (4j), it is hard to see that the same type of claim should not equally be made with respect to the indefinite expression *have you got a – a windmill* in extract (4a). In such cases, whether definite or indefinite expressions are used to introduce a new entity, the speaker is informationally related to the features of which he or she speaks in exactly the same manner. In these cases the features are *located* in the landscape, which means that A could potentially point to the relevant location on B's map. But in none of these cases does A know at the moment of utterance whether or not B is capable of identifying the feature itself, hence whether or not B would be capable of identifying the location. Unlike the anaphoric usage case, there is no shared past information which A can invoke here. If, in such circumstances, definite expressions are allowed into the deictic club, it is not clear to me by what principle one would exclude indefinite expressions from it, at least when they are used, as in the data under discussion, to instruct the listener to search the relevant domain and to attempt to identify the entity described in the expression.

Rather than opening the door to such an extended application of the term **deictic** which may, under further importunities, eventually imperil the utility of the term, it seems to me prudent to restrict its use to the traditional categories, including anaphoric expressions, and to analyse *the* as like *that*, in that it is sometimes used deictically and sometimes not.

4.5 **Conclusion**

It seems that the primary effect of deixis in the interpretation of speakers' instructions and questions in the Map tasks derives from the traditional deictic categories which, typically, sufficiently constrain the context to enable the listener to home in on the target entity when it is present, and to identify, at least in general terms, the *location* of the entity as it must be on A's map when it is not present on B's own map. Similarly, anaphoric expressions have a clearly deictic effect, since they must be understood as pointing the listener back into a context which, seen from the vantage point of the speaker's here-and-now moment of utterance, has already been established in the discourse as common ground and is available to the listener from the same temporally established vantage point.

Insofar as listeners are able to complete these spatial tasks successfully, this is largely due, I have suggested, to the fact that they apparently construct a highly constrained search field, within the wider context of discourse, within which they interpret locative expressions and anaphoric definite expressions deictically, thereby ensuring that they are not only, in general, thinking of the same feature as the speaker, but also approaching it from a similar perspective.

5 · The Stolen letter task : understanding reference to individuals in a narrative

5.1 Narrative tasks

In chapter 3, we considered how listeners made sense of expressions used to refer to features in a static visual display where the only salient relations were spatial relations. To understand adequately the instructions given by the A-role speaker, a B-role listener had to locate a feature which was appropriately characterised by A's description and ensure that it was in a location situated within a plausible search field. As we saw again in chapter 4, it was frequently the case that B could make sense of an underspecified message from A by locating a feature plausibly characterised by the denotation of the referring expression within a constrained search field, where the location is viewed by the listener from a particular perspective which is (largely) shared with the speaker.

We turn now to a different type of task, one which looks initially simple, but which turns out to be far more demanding for participants than the Map task. In the temporally structured task which I shall describe here, there are no enduring external aids to memory, no external model world whose stable features can be consulted, as in the Map task. Participants watch short episodes from a silent narrative which they see only once, enacted before them on a video screen. They then learn details of a further episode of the narrative which they were not shown, but which help them to interpret their own experience as they hear fellow participants talk about them. Their only access to this further information, which is crucial to the completion of the task, is through understanding and remembering what

125

others say and through making coherent sense of that in the light of details that they remember having watched themselves. In this task, subjects had no access to an external representation with a stable current anchor-point and, leading from it, a move-sized arc of search field of the type which was exploited so impressively by most subjects in the Map task. Now, subjects had to rely on their memories of the episodes that they had seen and interpreted as they watched, and they then had to combine these memories with their interpretation of what their partners in the group were saying. What is of particular interest here is how, if at all, a listener can construct a constrained search field, an adequately localised context of interpretation, in interpreting language heard in a much less constrained context.

Since any temporally structured task makes demands on memory and, in our experience, academically weaker students frequently fail to recall crucial features of narratives (or, at least, have problems in recalling them at appropriate points), this task was undertaken by quartets of subjects. Each quartet consisted of a pair of 14–16 year old adolescents taking the A-role, working with a further pair of pupils taking the B-role. Where each member of a pair could remind the other of what he or she had witnessed, the burden on memory was shared, and even those quartets composed of academically weaker subjects could make a useful contribution to the completion of the task.

5.2 The Stolen letter task

This task was created to reflect, as far as possible in a temporally structured task, the salient features of the Map task:

- Once again this task is, in Neisser's sense, ecological, in that subjects spoke to each other spontaneously, organising their own turns of speaking and talking for as long as they wished (Neisser 1987).
- Again, there is a shared basis of information, this time a scene on a video tape which the A and B pairs watch together, and, again, there is a controlled amount of disparate information, since each pair watches a further episode which the other pair does not see.
- Again, there is distribution of authority, in that each pair is authoritative with respect to its own privileged information. However

completion of the task this time rests equally with both pairs. It is not the case here that one pair is more motivated by the specification of the task, as was the case in the Map task.

– Again, there is a deliberate attempt to require the participants to distinguish between similar individuals/entities and similar types of location.

Thirty-two narrative episodes acted out by a group of amateur actors were recorded on a silent video film. These episodes were spliced together to create a number of different narratives. The narratives were made easier or more difficult by showing a longer or shorter shared episode to begin with, and by manipulating the complexity of the plot and the similarity of the characters – for instance one version of the narrative involved three potentially confusable female characters, whereas an easier version involved one male and two female characters.

The 'three women' version, which will be the topic of the discussion in this chapter, was constructed in the following manner. The first scene (which is simultaneously watched by all four participants) showed two young women, coming out of a lift and chatting in an institutional corridor. Each of them carries a wire stationery basket containing letters and packets. One of the women moves away towards a flight of stairs and the smaller of the two women walks off down a corridor. She enters an empty office which contains a desk under the window, with telephones on it, and a second desk jutting out into the room at right-angles to the first, with stacked stationery baskets and a computer on it. She takes an airmail letter from her tray and puts it down on the edge of the desk nearest to the door, and to the camera, where the desk juts out into the room. The camera zooms in to focus on the airmail letter. As she turns to leave, another woman with dark curly hair comes into the room, talking to the second woman who we saw outside the lift, who is considerably taller than both the other two women. The three women chat for a moment, and then the dark-haired woman gestures towards one of the telephones and, lifting it, begins to talk, apparently answering some enquiry, turning her back slightly to the others. The other two, still conversing, move towards the door.

The second episode (seen by one of the pairs) shows the tall woman from the first episode come back into the office where the dark-haired woman is still talking on the telephone with her back to the room. The tall woman walks up to the dark-haired woman and hands her a parcel from her basket of post. The dark-haired woman turns, smiles briefly, and begins to open her parcel as she turns back to her telephone call. Then, still carrying her basket of letters, the tall woman walks up to the desk with the airmail letter on it, and spills some of the letters and packets out of the tray on to the desk where the airmail letter is. She picks up the spilt mail, including the airmail letter, and goes out of the office.

The third scene (watched by the other pair) shows this same tall young woman entering a different office, sitting at the chair in front of the desk, and distributing the mail from her basket into a number of piles on the desk. She opens one of the letters, an airmail letter, from which she extracts some currency notes, which she conceals. Finally she re-seals the airmail envelope.

In this task, 14–16 year-old subjects worked as quartets. There was also, however, a successful pilot study in which six pairs of undergraduates worked together, one taking the A role and the other the B role. The data discussed in this chapter will be drawn from the discussions of eight quartets of 14–16 year-olds, all recorded at one Essex school, and the six undergraduate pairs. Each group worked separately. The A-role and B-role subjects in each group watched scene 1 together. Then one pair was taken to a different room where they watched scene 3, while the other pair stayed in the same room and watched scene 2. The quartet was then brought together again and asked to determine the order in which the two scenes which they had viewed independently must have happened. Quartets undertaking this task watched it under two different conditions. Four of the quartets were told that they were watching a video showing something being stolen (the 'title condition'). The remaining four quartets were not given this information (the 'no-title condition'). When the quartet had reached a conclusion to their discussion (and, in two cases of severely confused accounts by one of the pairs, at a rather earlier point), the quartet was shown the entire sequence of events in the correct order. Their comments on the sequence as it unrolled were also tape-recorded.

All the data discussed in this chapter derives from one or other version of the 'three women' narrative.

Detailed features of the Stolen letter task include the following:

- Pairs A and B shared some information (scene 1 which introduced the characters, the institutional setting and the baskets of mail), and each pair in addition had some information which the other lacked (either scene 2, or scene 3).
- The participating characters were three young women. The salient locations were two similar offices, furnished with similar desks, chairs, personal computers, etc. Two of the young women were handling similar wire stationery baskets with similar looking letters in them. The need for referential clarity in distinguishing between similar individuals and entities was established by the structure of the task.
- There were no external prompts for subjects as they tried to work out the order of the episodes. To complete the task successfully, subjects needed to be able to hold in memory the sequence of events in the scenes which they had watched, to interpret correctly the information given by the other pair on the events in the scene which they had separately watched, and to compare their mental representations of the two scenes. Their knowledge of the two scenes derived from different source modalities, one visual and one auditory.
- Successful performance on the task was likely to be at least partially dependent upon the title having been given, which motivated subjects to search for a criminal who, once located, could be referred to by a consistent form of referring expression (typically *the thief*). This individual then became the focus of attention, and was seen as the central protagonist. Intentionality was attributed to her tipping-out of the letters, picking up and concealing the airmail letter, opening the airmail letter, concealing the money, re-sealing the airmail envelope, and so on (Brown 1989).

As we have seen, in a number of ways this task resembles the Map task. In several important respects, however, it differs from the Map task. An obvious distinguishing feature is that the Stolen letter task is concerned with a narrative, and that the narrative involves familiar-looking people in a familiar type of environment, whereas the Map task concerns specially drawn features on a specially constructed landscape. In the Map task, subjects sat with a low screen between them so that neither of them could see what the other was looking at, and their visual attention was primarily focussed on their maps, although many pairs did look up and make eye contact from time to time, particularly when they encountered difficulties as they proceeded. The nature of the task constrained the manner in which they approached it, so they typically began at the point marked START and then A instructed B to move along the route, one feature at a time. Certainly there were occasional recapitulations, as we saw for instance in the long extract (3f), but the order of procedure was largely dictated by the structure of the task. The A-role speaker had the authoritative version of the map stably and visibly present. Answers to questions which A understood could be given without equivocation. The form of interaction could clearly be characterised as an exchange of information. In general, the interaction was managed by A, though as we saw in extract (3l), since B is the individual responsible for completing the task, if A falters, B may take over the management of the interaction.

During discussions over the Stolen letter task, subjects sat around a table with no artificial constraint on what they could see, and with no visual prompt to draw their attention away from what other members of the group were saying. In this task, they were asked to work out the order in which episodes 2 and 3 must have happened. Typically one member of each pair, sometimes with assistance or modification from the other member of the pair, would give an account of the episode which they had watched, and then the second pair would give an account of their episode. Sometimes these accounts were interrupted by questions from the other pair. Once the narrative accounts were completed, the discussion ranged freely with no predetermined structure, often with apparently random shifts of topic from one scene or part of a scene to another, as one participant who was particularly interested in some aspect of one of the scenes managed to secure a turn.

No single individual was responsible for completing the task, and in none of the interactions is there one participant who is obviously managing the entire interaction. Although the topic of all the conversations remained fixed on the content of the task, there is less similarity between the conversations of the quartets (or indeed between the conversations of the undergraduate pairs) than there was between the interactions of participants who undertook the Map task. The various groups of subjects spent strikingly different amounts of time on different aspects of the action, and some individuals would return persistently to one particular aspect of a character or action which is not mentioned by other groups.

A striking difference between the conversations of the pairs and those of the quartets is that a member of a pair may be sure that any utterance by the other speaker is intended for just that one addressee situated in that listener's current state of knowledge. In a quartet, the interactional structure is much more complex. Whereas the introductory narrative statements may be seen as primarily addressed to members of the other pair, they are necessarily uttered in the presence of the second member of the speaker's own pair, who frequently interjects additional statements and may take over the narrative for a while. Speakers in such a situation are necessarily looking over their shoulders, as it were, as they speak, since the narrative will be judged for its adequacy by this second, informed, member of their own pair. Such a situation arises, of course, quite frequently in everyday life in multi-party conversations. It provides basic material for caricature in television comedies, when a couple attempts to give a coherent account of a jointly shared experience to an audience, and each keeps correcting the other's version of events. (We return to this issue in 7.1.)

After the narrative stage, when each pair gives an account of its own scene, the interaction moves to the discussion stage. During this stage, speakers often appear to be addressing different subsets of the other three people present. Sometimes they reply directly to one individual's question, and these two may enter into a sub-conversation for a while. On other occasions, they address the other pair and also, from time to time, they check the accuracy of their memory of a particular incident with the other member of their own pair.

It is relevant here to draw upon a distinction discussed by Schober and Clark (1989), who suggest that direct addressees and indirect overhearers in multi-party conversations must go about the business of construing what the speaker says rather differently. The co-operative speaker constructs the utterance for the addressee, in what the speaker believes to be the addressee's current state of knowledge. Ideally, this should result in an utterance that is readily interpretable by the addressee. The overhearer, however, is in a different condition, even in the case of the fully licensed overhearers in the quartet groups of our subjects, since the utterance is not constructed with the overhearer's state of knowledge in mind. In the experimental conditions described by Clark and his associates, there is only one nominated speaker in any group, one addressee and one or more overhearers. The roles are clearly and permanently identified for the duration of the experiment.

In the quartets which I describe here, any of the four participants may take the role of speaker and address one, two or three addressees. Sometimes there are two parallel conversations, each with one speaker and one addressee at any given time, though the roles are switched around. In such a fluid condition, whereas it is usually possible to identify the prime addressee, particularly when one speaker attempts to answer a question asked by another speaker, it is difficult to know of each of the rest of the group whether their role *vis-à-vis* a particular utterance is that of included addressee or excluded overhearer. The lack of a visual record is much more significant in multi-party conversations than it is in conversations between two participants who directly address each other. It should be noted, though, that for the analyst to have access to all the information available to each participant about who had eye contact with whom, and at which points in the conversation, one would need as many cameras as there were participants, and each camera would need to be constantly re-directed into the area in which the relevant participant was currently looking – a difficult technical feat.

Whereas, in the Map task, the interactions consisted largely of descriptions or instructions, questions, challenges and recapitulations, the interactions in the Stolen letter task necessarily include not only those, but also speculation about what might have been the order of events. These speculations take various forms. Since none of the participants had access to a stable and external record of what they had seen, it was frequently the case that they were not able to produce clearly and authoritatively articulated replies to questions about what they had seen, which leads to a far more tentative, often modalised, form of discussion. Participants, especially in the stage of trying to work out the order of events, frequently pause and leave uncompleted utterances, apparently unsure how to complete them.

A further significant difference between the tasks is that in performing the Map task, participants were told explicitly that there were likely to be mismatches of information concerning the nature of the features and the location of the features on their maps. In the Stolen letter task, participants knew that each pair had watched a previously recorded episode which the other pair had not seen. What they did not know was that the actors who appeared in each of these later episodes were a subset of the three young women who had appeared in the first, shared, episode, and that the difference in information lay in what these actors had done and not in who they were. For quartets where speakers did not explicitly identify the actors who they had watched in their own episode with actors in the earlier shared episode, there was an obvious danger that the listening pair would assume that a further set of actors had been introduced into the narrative.

Taken together, these differences mean that it is often harder for the analyst to be sure what the speaker meant, and to be sure whether or not the listener(s) understood what the speaker said, than in analysing the recordings of the Map task. And even there, as I suggested in 2.1, the attribution of intention in uttering is always somewhat risky.

In section 5.3, I illustrate and briefly discuss some of the features of the Stolen letter task which make it so much more cognitively and linguistically complex than the Map task. Then, in later sections, I move on to consider what this task further reveals about how listeners understand what is said to them. The issue of the equivalent of the Map task's **search field** in a task like the Stolen letter task will be considered in chapter 6.

5.3 **Initial reference**

It is noteworthy that we encounter in this temporal task initial descriptions of a type which were absent from the spatially structured Map task. As we saw in 3.6, landscape features on the maps were typically introduced by noun phrases which identified the features as tokens of a particular type, often, particularly in the more complex maps, accompanied by a locational specification in the form of a prepositional phrase. In the Stolen letter task we occasionally, but rarely, find human participants introduced where they are specified as to type alone (*person, woman, secretary, somebody*). Typically the initial introduction is accompanied by information on their location as in the examples below. The notable departure here is that, typically, information about what the individual is doing is also supplied, as in (5b), (5c) (of two individuals), (5d), and (5e) (also of two individuals):

(5a)   (ug pair 6)
    A1. there was another person in the room

(5b)   (quartet 6)
    A1. there + was a woman + in the office + talking on the phone

(5c)   (ug pair 4)
    A1. the setting was an office + and + a secretary presumably + was
        on the telephone and + somebody came in bringing some mail

(5d)   (quartet 1)
    B1. there was erm – a lady came in the + office with + some documents

(5e)   (quartet 2)
    A1. there was this woman in the office on the telephone + and + then
        this lady walked in with erm – some letters and parcels + n'a box

The information provided can be summarised in Table 5.1.

Entities other than humans are all introduced in a quite minimal way without any detailed description, just as the Map task features were: *the room, the office, the phone, some mail, some documents, some letters and parcels, a box.* They are presumably assumed to have default characteristics within the office frame (Minsky 1975), just as the landscape features in the Map task were typically given no description, just a type label. The only non-human entity which receives a fuller description in the Stolen letter task from some, but not all, speakers, is the airmail letter. Most speakers simply identify it by its location on the desk as in (5h).

(5f)   (quartet 4)
    B1. a little airmail letter it looked like + the little letter

(5g)   (quartet 1)
    A1. and picked up the – erm – a wrong letter

(5h)   (quartet 2)
    B2. and there was a letter on the table

Table 5.1

	Individual	location	function
(5a)	person	in the room	–
(5b)	woman	in the office	on the phone
(5c)	secretary	an office	on the phone
	somebody	in (office)	bringing mail
(5d)	lady	in the office	with documents
(5e)	woman	in the office	on the phone
	lady	in (office)	with letters, etc.

It is the entry of human participants into the narrative which is primarily responsible for the introduction of the additional types of introductory expressions. These expressions include not only type information and locational information, but also a description of what the human participants have been observed to be doing. The sole inanimate entity which is further distinguished is selected for attention because human agents act upon it in a deliberate and focussed manner, themselves discriminating between this letter and other letters which are mentioned.

So far we have looked at how human participants are initially introduced in the absence of any contrastive individuals of the same general type. In the next section, we see an additional variation on the Map task referring expressions, where speakers explicitly discriminate between characters in the video.

5.4 Distinguishing between potential referents

In the Map task, landscape features were typically ignored by both speakers once they were mutually known to be established on B's map. In one version of the task, the route looped around and it was necessary to mention, for instance, 'the church' again, but such recurring mention was rare, and when it did occur, later reference was being made to a feature which was stably represented on each map and which formed part of the common ground for both participants.

An immediate problem for many listeners in the 'three women' version of the Stolen letter task was that there were three young women, at least one of whom was involved in each episode, all dressed casually and viewed on a black and white monitor. Speakers distinguished between them on the basis of a quite restricted range of physical attributes (**hair** – fair/dark, straight/curly and **height** – short/tall) or on the basis of their actions during the video. Extract (5i) illustrates a quartet who mix allusions to physical attributes and actions in attempting to secure reference. (The quartet consists of two pairs of subjects: A1 and A2, B1 and B2, who occasionally show some traces of Essex dialect.)

(5i)   (quartet 4)

1	A2.	you know you said someone spilled something on
2		the table + the letters
3	B1.	yes
4	A1.	who was that
5	B1.	that was the tall lady
6	A2.	the – tall – one
7	B1.	yes
8	B2.	who was carrying the letters with her + I think
9		she just done it so she could pick up this
10		letter
11	A2.	hm
12	B2.	so this other lady who was on the phone wouldn't
13		know
14	A1.	what colour hair did the girl – the lady with
15		the telephone + did she have
16	B1.	long brown hair
17	A1.	brownish sort of
18	A2.	she was the one on the phone before
19	A1.	'cos it was curly + dark – the one we saw
20	A2.	yeah it must be the same one
21	A1.	it was dark curly hair
22	B1.	what was it – longish
23	A1.	well yeah fairly + shoulder-length but a bit
24		longer than yours
25	B1.	yeah that's the same one

There are two women under discussion here. The first is described as:

> *the tall one/lady* (by A2/B1)
> *who was carrying the letters with her* (by B2)

and the second is described by B1 as having

> *long brown hair*
> *(hair) longish*

by B2 as

> *this other lady who was on the phone*

and by the A speakers as

> *the girl – the lady with the telephone*
> *the one on the phone before*
> *(hair) brownish sort of*
> *(hair) was curly + dark*
> *dark curly hair*
> *(hair) shoulder-length but a bit longer than yours*

It appears to be the combination of descriptions – *who was on the telephone* and having *long brown hair* which enables the A pair to recognise the figure (whom they met earlier in the first episode), and the detailed description of the hair colour, curliness and length which enable the B pair to be sure that they are all talking about the same individual. (The colour 'brown' is mentioned by B1 (line 16) and *brownish – sort of* is agreed, though with reservations, by A1 (line 17), where the term is presumably used to indicate dark tone rather than brown hue, since the speakers have only seen a black and white video of the hair colour.) The repetitive checking in lines 16–24 indicates that these participants are all aware of the risk they run of using what the speaker says wrongly and hence of mis-identifying the individual. Interestingly, their strategy, like that of other participants in this task, is to make the description of the physical feature that they have lighted on (in this case 'hair') more fine-grained, rather than look for other confirming features.

The range of features used to discriminate between the women in all the data of the Stolen letter task is quite narrow. It includes for instance:

hair
- colour   *dark-haired, with black hair, blonde, with brown hair, fair*
- length   *with long hair, long-haired, shoulder length, short-haired, with the shortest hair, with the bob*
- curliness *black curly hair*

size/height
- size   *the smaller of the two, the little one*
- height   *the taller, tall, shorter, the short one*

enumeration
- *the second, the first, the third, the other*
- *a different girl from the one who was there before*
- *the same, one of the two,*

action/place/time attributes
- *on the (tele)phone, the one with the telephone, the one who wasn't on the telephone*
- *with the post, that came in with the post, that put the letter on the desk, who had been looking through the letters, that had picked up the letter, that's carrying the basket*
- *the two that came out of the lift, the one coming out of the lift, the girl in the other office*
- *the woman that we saw in the third scene*
- *the one that came in first*

role/personality attributes
- *the one we don't think pinched*
- *the suspect, the thief*
- *that strange girl*
- *the secretive woman*

None of the subjects in this data mentions features of the face, the clothes which the actors are wearing, or the girth of an individual.

For subjects who introduced the individuals in the narrative with minimal differentiation, and who make no attempt to utilise the shared knowledge of the first episode, the later discussion, which involves their listeners in attempting to discriminate between these minimally specified individuals, is inevitably confused. Here is an example of an insufficiently specific set of introductory expressions, which the A-pair listeners fail to follow:

(5j)   (quartet 2)

B1. first – first of all a girl goes into a room + comes goes into the room and puts – puts a letter out of a basket and puts it down on a table + seconds later that – two girls come into the room and one of the girls picks up n'answers the phone – the two other girls then start talking + 'n + they decide that that – they go out the room while the other girl is still on the phone

(Later in the discussion B1 tries to explain, in answer to a question from A2, who it was who had taken the money):

A2. who took the money + the one on the telephone?

B1. no the one on the telephone had + was + was one of the second two girls that come after the first girl had gone in + the first girl that had gone into the room + took – went out with the other girl + that was the one that took the money

B1's language is not easy to follow here for a number of reasons. It seems that this low academic achiever experiences considerable stress in attempting to give a clear account of what he has watched on the video. This stress results in relatively incoherent language where, for instance, he replaces one verb form by another (*goes/comes/goes, decide/go out, had/was/was, took/went out*) or where, apparently having activated *put* too early, he uses it inappropriately in *puts – puts a letter out of a basket* before using it appropriately in the phrase *and puts it down on a table.*

In the first of the two extracts cited above, B1 introduces the participants in the episode as though they were seen in this episode for the first time. He makes no reference to their appearance in the first, shared, episode and perhaps has not realised that he himself has seen them before. B1's account, though certainly not fluent, is actually perfectly self-consistent, and essentially correct, as a detailed perusal of the transcription of what B1 says shows. Nonetheless the A pair evidently find it impossible to follow, or at least to put to use, what he has said, and they abandon the attempt to question him further on this issue. It is clear from A2's question that the characterisation *on the (tele)phone* has been adequate to identify one participant and to separate her from the others but the speaker apparently fails to permit the listeners to discriminate between the other two participants.

The problem for the A-role speakers appears to arise, at least in part, from B1's strategy of not attributing permanent identifying characteristics to any individual but introducing them all simply as 'girls'. It is then necessary for the listeners to discriminate in memory between these individuals by the order in which they were originally introduced and then to follow B1's strategy of pairing off couples in changing relationships. If we call the two girls outside the lift A and B, of whom A is the tall fair-haired girl who steals the letter, B the one who delivers the letter, and C the girl on the telephone, we can see the problem if we focus on B1's referring expressions together with their accompanying, non-distinguishing, predicates:

a girl goes into a room	B
two girls come into the room	A and C
one of the girls answers the phone	C
the two other girls then start talking	A and B
they go out the room	A and B
the other girl is still on the phone	C
the one on the telephone	C
was one of the second two girls	A and C
the first girl went out with	B and
the other girl	A
the one that took the money	A

An obvious problem for a listener is that no salient feature is attached to the first girl who enters the room (B) to distinguish her from the member of the pair who then enters the room and does not answer the telephone (A). These two can only be distinguished, in B1's account, by their order of appearance in the room. Immediately after B1 had offered his second explanation, the experimenter asked the rest of the group how many girls they thought there were altogether in the film. A2 suggested that there were *six girls*. If A2 is counting the three women in the first episode as distinct from those introduced by B1, then A2 has, at least, correctly understood that B1 has been talking about three individuals. Of these, A2 is able to distinguish 'the one on the phone' but is unable to distinguish between the other two, and appears not to relate 'the one on the phone' to the young woman who A2 had seen talking on the phone. The problem seems to lie first in B1's failure to relate the young women he is talking about to those seen earlier, and secondly in his trying to distinguish between them solely on the basis of temporally structured information.

A similar problem with using attributes which depend on temporary characteristics was found with a different task, this time showing a sequence of events in the mock-up of a vehicle crash (described in Brown, Anderson and Yule 1985). Where subjects reported an accident involving vehicles which were well differentiated by colour or by type – for instance 'a lorry', 'an ambulance' and 'a bus' – subjects had little difficulty in giving adequate descriptions of the accidents and hearers had little difficulty in following the description. However when the same structure of accident befell three similar looking grey cars, subjects were frequently forced to discriminate between the cars in terms of the previous history of each car, as in the following extract from the report of a 16 year-old who had been asked to give an account of what he had seen as if he had witnessed a real accident:

> *I was standing near a junction and there was a car coming across + and cars + two cars coming down ı well ı ı it should've stopped but it didn't ++ and the light coloured one which was in the right came on ++ and the other + which was going too fast crashed into it ++ but the one who caused + the accident got away*

This description is not immediately transparent for a listener (or for a reader). The three cars (A, B, and C) are differentiated in the following terms:

A. *a car coming across*
it (should've stopped)
the one who caused the accident
B. *cars – two cars*
the light coloured one which was in the right
(crashed into) it
C. *cars – two cars*
the other
which was going too fast

For some subjects in the Stolen letter task, the three individuals are primarily differentiated only by their temporal history, not by their stable physical characteristics, as we saw in extract (5j). Both in the Car crash task and the Stolen letter task, listeners found reports which offered such modes of description relatively hard to follow.

5.5 Tracking referents through anaphoric expressions

The discussion in this section will include not only consideration of the use and understanding of anaphoric pronouns but also, more generally, the use of noun phrases used anaphorically to refer back to individuals who have already been introduced into the discourse.

Many early writers on discoursal anaphora suggested that the use of an anaphoric expression must be taken as referring back to some earlier full lexical expression which occurs in the text (see for example Halliday and Hasan 1976; Tyler 1979). This pronominal surrogate hypothesis has been shown experimentally to fail to explain the fact that anaphoric expressions are often interpreted as containing different information from that contained by an initial full lexical noun phrase (McKay and Fulkerson 1979). In Brown and Yule (1983), we argued that change of state predicates must be incorporated into a developing discourse interpretation. Thus, to take a gruesome but apt example, consider the following recipe from Robert Carrier (1967:154):

> Split the live lobster down through the middle of the body and tail
> . . . Grill *it* for 8 to 10 minutes on the shell side; turn *it* over, spread
> ( ) with softened butter and grill ( ) for 6 to 8 minutes on the flesh
> side . . .

(my italics to indicate anaphoric pronouns; brackets indicate anaphoric elisions)

It would be an inadequate cook who, in the middle of cooking this recipe in which an actual individual lobster is involved, construes the anaphoric pronouns and anaphoric elisions as coreferential with the initial lexical expression *the live lobster*. Note also that the second *it* should be understood as denoting 'the lobster which has already been grilled for 8 to 10 minutes on the shell side'.

There was relatively little use of potentially ambiguous anaphoric expressions in the Map task data where, in most discussions, the landscape feature which is the current focus of interest is related explicitly to another, already agreed, feature. Moreover, in the Map task, there were few change-of-state predicates – the pronominal surrogate hypothesis would hold well enough in discourse which describes static relationships between features. The Stolen letter task evokes a much greater use of anaphoric expressions, since the genre at issue here is a narrative. Many of these involve changes of state, as characters and objects disappear and reappear, performing a range of different functions. The 'three women' version of the Stolen letter task offers particularly rich opportunities for studying how listeners understand language which contains anaphoric expressions which are potentially ambiguous. Sometimes the recourse to anaphoric *she* produces no problems for the listeners, since only one individual is in conceptual focus at the relevant point, as in extract (5k).

(5k)   (quartet 5)
1   B1. and so the dark-haired girl and the second girl
2   came into the office
3   A1. no – the one with the bob came into the office +
4   while the smaller one was in ⌈there
     B1.   ⌊the office
5   B1. and where was the dark-haired girl at this point
6   A1. she came in with the taller one
7   B2. when the phone rang?
8   A1. she answered the phone and the other two went out
9   B1. ++ she could have taken the money while the –
10   other + two were – out ++ couldn't she
11   A1. but she didn't 'cos we saw the other one put it
12   in her pocket
13   B1. hm + right
14   B2. mm
15   A2. so what happened when the other two went out?
16   B1. well she handed over there – the one with the bob
17   + um – came in with the tray – handed – erm –
18   sorted through the letters and handed one over to
19   the girl with dark curly hair + um – did that

20   strange girl look up

21   B2. no – she just opened the package – and – erm ++

22   there was a book inside so – she flicked through

23   it and er – it looked like one of our text-books

24   B1. did it

25   B2. yes it's important really

26   B1. and then she answered the telephone didn't she

27   B2. erm she just stood there and read the book –

28   flicked through the book while the other women

29   walked out and went – went back out

The opening lines of this excerpt show B1 and A1 apparently correctly understanding each other. The individual here characterised as *the dark-haired girl* is consistently more readily recognised and less confusable than the other two participants. This may be because her hair was strikingly darker than that of the other two, or because she is the only one who answers the telephone, or because she is distinctive in that she has no role in picking up or delivering letters, or some combination of these, perhaps together with other qualities. As we saw in extract (5i), it was the careful identification of the dark-haired girl on the telephone which enabled quartet 4 to determine that a character in two separate episodes was in fact one and the same person. This participant in the action is also referred to, apparently successfully, in line 20 of extract (5k) as *that strange girl*. There is no taped record of this expression having been used before by this pair or of any comment having been made on her 'strangeness'. Nonetheless B2 appears to answer the question appropriately. How does she achieve this?

B2 did, of course, watch the same episode as B1, so she is aware that only two girls are at risk of being referred to at this point. B1's use of the expression *that strange girl* may be used to avoid an underspecified anaphoric *she* following her carefully distinguished characterisation of the two relevant participants in her previous utterance – *the one with the bob came in with the tray . . . sorted through the letters and handed one over to the girl with dark curly hair*. However, her chosen expression *that strange girl* is not guaranteed to distinguish between the two just-mentioned referents unless she can rely on her listener sharing a notion of 'strangeness' – and perhaps she can. It may of course be that it is not the referring expression *that strange girl* which enables B2 to pick out the correct referent, but rather the whole of the utterance which includes a crucial predication: *did that strange girl look up*. If 'the tall girl with the bob' is handing over a letter, there may be a protypical expectation that she will look at the person she is handing it to, whereas the girl speaking on the telephone might continue to concentrate on her conversation, or, on the other hand, she might look up to acknowledge the presence of the giver of the parcel.

We have already noted that expressions such as *the second girl* are frequently confusing. One reason is, presumably, that these orderings are not salient in memory and, if this is so, reference to them will not enable the listener to identify the individual if he or she is later re-introduced into the narrative. In (5k) line 3, A1 is confident that the wrong girl is being referred to by this expression, and she now describes the same individual as *the smaller one*. This apparently makes sense to B1, who chimes in with *the office* at the end of A1's utterance, which also makes sense at this point. B1 then re-introduces the dark-haired girl in line 5, and by this question establishes her as B1's focus of interest. A string of anaphoric *shes* follows in lines 6–11, produced by A1 and by B1 herself. References to *the taller one* (line 6) and *the other two* (line 8) are clearly to subsidiary roles which are established in relation to the individual in primary focus, 'the dark-haired girl'.

In line 15, A2 moves the focus of interest to a later time in the episode by asking another direct question: *what happened when the other two went out?* B1 begins quickly to reply with an anaphoric pronoun *she,* which appears to refer back to the same dark-haired girl but, apparently realising that this will be the likely interpretation, she co-operatively corrects what she has said, showing that her focus of attention has now shifted, by inserting the expression *the one with the bob* as subject of the string of predicates *came in / sorted through / handed over*. From her current empathetic focus of attention, the tall girl with the bob, she can now look over to *the girl with dark curly hair* and, using the non-proximal deictic pronoun *that,* ask *did that strange girl look up*. By her question, she now shifts the focus of attention back again to the girl on the phone.

B2, who has presumably been listening carefully to what her partner says and has empathetically shifted her own focus of attention to 'the one with the bob' and then back to 'the girl with dark curly hair', immediately and correctly replies, using an anaphoric pronoun *she* to refer to 'the girl with dark curly hair'.

B2 is momentarily distracted by the similarity of the book to their school textbooks, and then B1 reverts to her own focus of attention, the girl with dark curly hair, once again simply referring to her by the expression *she*, and of course secure in the knowledge that the predicate *answered the telephone* will in any case uniquely identify her. B2 replies not altogether co-operatively. She echoes B1's form *she* to refer to the girl on the telephone, not responding directly to B1's request for a check on the behaviour of the girl answering the telephone, but paying attention again to what happened to her own entity of interest, the book.

We can see in this extract how predicates are accumulated by a particular referent. In line 5, B1 asks where the dark-haired girl was at this point, and A1 replies that she came in with the taller girl. After B2's next question, A1 replies *she answered the phone*. After this interchange A1 must have in memory at least the following information:

dark-haired girl
- had come in (to the office) (6)
- answered the phone (in the office) (8)

When, later, in line 20, B1 asks *did that strange girl look up*, B2 replies *she just opened the package . . . she flicked through it*. After this interchange B2, and the other three if they have been listening, should know of the dark-haired girl at least the following:

dark-haired girl
- had come in to the office (6)
- was answering the phone in the office (8)
- had been handed a letter by the girl with the bob (18–19)
- had not looked up when handed the letter (20–21)
- had opened the package which she had been handed by the girl with the bob while she was answering the phone in the office (21)
- she flicked through the book which was in the package which she had opened (22–23)

It must be the case that, once the dark-haired girl has been established as being in the office, that information carries through and is presumably retained in memory as a fact about her during the period of discussion, even if the listener were later to be told that she moved to another location. And, as other information comes in, it is presumably accumulated with the information about that person, at that location and during a series of events (though, as we shall see later, such information does occasionally appear to have been wrongly filed or, when retrieved, located inappropriately with material from another file).

A series of anaphoric references, which looks so underspecified as to be bound to be misleading, occurs at a later point in the same transcript, where B2 has offered to attempt to recapitulate the entire action of the narrative:

(5l)   (quartet 5)
 1   B2. she walks into the office with the mail tray ++
 2   sort of sneaks over ++ ⌈and pushes the letters
 3   A1.   ⌊just sort of moves some
 4   B2. on onto the table
 5   A1. oh – quite obvious isn't it
 6   B2. ++ pretends to be looking through and then picks
 7   that one up with the letters
 8   B1. puts them on the –
 9   B2. and gives the woman a parcel – who's on the
10   phone + says thank you + goes back to her
11   telephone call
12   A1. so she didn't notice that other letter being
13   picked up
14   B2. no – she sneaks back out again
15   A1. and the shorter one put it there in the first
16   place
17   B1. so she just goes in to hand over the letter ++
18   that's the one with the book in it
19   B2. yeah ++ she opens the parcel and looks inside ++
20   she flicks through it

The 'she' referred to in lines 1–9 is the tall girl with bobbed hair who picks up the airmail letter and is later seen abstracting money from an airmail letter. In line 9, B2 shifts from talking about this tall woman to talking about the woman on the phone. The only indication that her focus of attention has changed is the relative clause *who's on the phone*. The most obvious syntactic analysis, with an apparently conjoined empty subject of the verbs *gives, says* and *goes back* is revealed to be inadequate by the facts of the matter, which are that the girl with the bob gives the dark-haired woman a parcel, whereas the dark-haired woman is the one who says *thank you* and reverts to her telephone call. B2's syntax is misleading here, as is her intonation. There is no overall contour break in this sequence, just a series of relatively flat patterns on the same pitch level with prominence on the last lexical item in each contour – *parcel, phone, thank you, telephone call.*

In spite of the misleading nature of the formal cues, A1 apparently has no problem in understanding the utterance since she immediately replies in line 12 using an anaphoric pronoun *she* to refer to the girl on the telephone, picking up on B2's last focussed individual. In the next line, line 13, B2 answers *no*, presumably indicating that she has understood A1's question, which she answers appropriately, and then smoothly continues with another anaphoric pronoun *she*, which this time must refer once again to her original focus of interest, the girl with the bob, since the predicate *sneaks back out again* appropriately attaches to her and not to the girl on the phone. In line 15, A1 reintroduces the third member of the trio with a lexicalised expression, *the shorter one*. B1 immediately follows in line 17, by introducing a referent with *she*, which must refer back not to 'the shorter one' mentioned by A1 in line 15, but to the girl with a bob mentioned by B2 in line 14, since it is she who delivers the letter with the book in it. And to complete the reader's confusion, B2 responds in lines 19–20, again introducing her referent with an anaphoric *she*, but this time we must suppose that she is referring not to the just-mentioned girl with the bob, but to the girl on the telephone, since it is she who opens the parcel and looks inside it.

On a standard account of how anaphora is used, this quartet must be said to be using anaphoric expressions loosely and riskily. Indeed, to the reader coming cold to this data and reading it out of context, the anaphoric expressions may well be, at least momentarily, confusing. Yet it seems clear that

Table 5.2

line	speaker	focus	lexis
1–2	B2	girl with bob	*sneaks over / pushes letters*
3	A1	"	*moves some*
4–9	B2	"	*pretends / picks up that one with the letters gives . . . a parcel*
9–11	B2	girl on phone	*on the phone*
12–13	A1	"	*didn't notice . . . other letter*
14	B2	girl with bob	*sneaks back out again*
15–16	A1	shorter one	*put it there . . . first*
17–18	B1	girl with bob	*hand over letter . . . with book in*
19–20	B2	girl on phone	*opens the parcel / looks inside / flicks through*

these participants are adequately successful in communicating with each other, since their replies to each other make perfectly good sense. How do they achieve such harmonious understanding? It seems at least plausible that during a conversation about such an episode which has been witnessed by two participants and described to the other two, they mentally construct visual representations ('mental models', see Johnson-Laird 1983) of the scene. As they consider the imagined or remembered scene, they scan between the two major participants, recalling what they have seen or been told that each of them does. It is these actions which they have seen or been told about which most crucially identify and characterise the individual actors in their continually updated memory of the events. The linguistic identification here is regularly achieved not by distinctive noun phrases (except in the case of the third individual 'the shorter one' who is introduced later) but by the sequence of actions which each undertakes, which constitute crucial distinguishing characteristics. (Lyons 1977:209–10, argues that the role or function of objects appears to be more important in determining the denotation of lexemes than a description of the denotata.) I summarise this analysis in Table 5.2.

We shall return, in chapter 6, to a consideration of the effect of focus in constructing a plausible search field for interpretation, which seems in many ways to be equivalent to that constructed by listeners in the Map task.

There are rather few examples of obvious misunderstanding of specific linguistic expressions in this data. Those which do arise generally involve a failure to resolve an anaphoric expression. Extract (5m) illustrates this:

(5m)　　(quartet 7)
　　　A1. she gave her the bigger package + and − took out the letter with the other pa − letters in the basket
(The B pair now report the content of their episode)
　　　B2. right + the short one − you know − the one with the longish hair + right + she came in with − the basket of letters + looked at this one and then took it out + put it on a desk + and then
　　　B1. she looked at it a long while before she put it on the desk
　　　A1. what + she looked at what
　　　B1. the letter
　　　A1. the same letter?
　　　B1. she held it up and looked at it for quite a while

A1's difficulty may arise because the apparent antecedent of B2's *this one* is *the basket of letters*, and then B1 takes over the narrative from B2 simply continuing the string of anaphoric pronouns. But it seems at least plausible that A1's problem is compounded by the fact that she herself has just been talking about two letters, 'the bigger package' and the airmail letter, and that she realises that it is important to keep them distinct. After B1's reply *the letter*, A1 checks again *the same letter?*, receiving a rather unhelpful reply from B1.

A somewhat similar difficulty occurs in extract (5n) which involves repetition of lexical expressions as well as anaphoric pronouns (capitals indicate contrastive emphasis, marked by an extended intonation contour beginning on the primary stressed syllable of each word together with relatively slower and more explicit articulation):

(5n)　　(ug pair 1)
　　　B. the tall lady + came into the room and delivered another letter ++ accidentally − the letters which she was holding + probably in the

container fell out ++ and ++ she accidentally took the letter +
well probably it was an accident + or she did it on purpose ++
took the letter which was on the table + and replaced it + and she
put another letter + for the dark-haired lady ++ and the dark-
haired lady + unsealed the letter

A. that letter is not the second letter + is not ++ erm + another letter
+ I mean its + GENUINELY ANOTHER letter ++ erm it's not
that she replaced the letter then + she didn't + she did give her

B. she did give her another letter

It is not entirely clear what A's opening remarks mean, though her
problem may arise because B speaks initially of *the tall lady* 'delivering'
another letter. B's long account of how the letters were upset and picked up
separates this initial introduction from her later remark*s: took the letter
which was on the table + and replaced it + and she put another letter + for the
dark-haired lady.* It is not clear from B's account how many letters are at
issue, since she reiterates the expression *another letter* without it being clear
that these are repetitive accounts of the same event. A appears to see that too
many letters may have been introduced into the discourse. One source of
her difficulty may arise from B's use of the expression *replace,* which, as we
shall see in 5.6 extract (5r), seems to be an expression which is differently
interpreted in the context of this scene by different individuals.

5.6 Lexis and referential identity

In the Map task, we observed occasions where one speaker consistently used
a particular term to refer to a shared feature and the other consistently used a
different term. In such cases, it was suggested, it would be hard to claim that
the two speakers shared the same or even a very similar thought, though
they were apparently able to use the denotation of the other speaker's expression to identify the intended referent. An example of such an apparent
difference of view appears in extract (5l), above, where B2 regularly uses the
expression *the parcel* to refer to the package containing the book which is
handed to the woman on the telephone, whereas B1, in lines 17 and 18,
refers to the same object as *the letter – that's the one with the book in it.* This
different use of expressions to describe the package is common throughout

the Stolen letter data. If we recall Labov's experiment (1973), described in 1.1, it might suggest that the sort of small padded bag which a paperback book arrives in might indeed be caught in that indeterminate class which is neither a prototypical letter, which has relatively no thickness, nor a prototypical parcel, which has distinct thickness and is tied up with string. It is not the case that all subjects in this data constantly switch from using one term to another, sympathetically echoing a previous speaker, though at least two speakers do regularly switch terms in this way. Most subjects tend to stick with their own chosen term, even when there is a long stretch of conversation between the first and later use of the term.

The most striking variety of expression in the description of entities occurs in the range of terms used to characterise the three female participants. They are referred to as *secretaries, young women, women, ladies* and *girls*. As I have already noted, individuals tend to persist throughout the discussion with the term which they use initially. In Extract (5o), A2 uses the expressions *girl* and *girls*, whereas A1, B1 and B2 regularly use the expressions *lady* and *ladies* throughout the discussion, except for one occasion when A1 begins to use *girl* and then substitutes *lady:*

5o (quartet 4)
      B1. that was the tall lady
      A1. yeah
      A2. the – tall – one
      B1. yeah
      B2. who was carrying the letters with her + I think she just done it so she could pick up this letter
      A2. hm
      B2. so this other lady who was on the phone wouldn't know
      A1. what colour hair did the girl – the lady with the telephone + did she have

Are we to say here that A1 changes her mind about how to view the individual in mid-sentence, or are we to suggest rather that she believes that these are, in the context, synonymous in denotation but that the more formal term, *lady,* is the more appropriate in the context of this recorded discussion, or, perhaps, that she is modifying her own preferred expression to make it conform to the expression just used by B1 and B2? Or, again, might we argue that she is considering different aspects of the same individual and selecting one rather than another as relevant on this occasion? Rommetveit argues against assuming that reference to an individual must be 'to an unequivocally defined point in a monistic and epistemological transparent space . . . where the severe laws of truth values prescribe that the speaker must know (the referent) fully or not at all' (1974:48). My own guess is that those who use the term *lady* (and these include both some 14–16 year-olds and some undergraduates) are seeing the participants in the video as professional women, qualified secretaries, playing a grown-up role. Such women might appropriately be described by the term *lady* to distance them in status from the speaker. Those speakers who use the term *girl* might be supposed to be concentrating on the features of youth and informality of dress which characterise the participants and make them available for description in terms which the speakers would use of themselves and their peers.

It is clear that different aspects of multi-faceted human personalities are more or less salient for different individuals. Some people pay more attention to hair style or to hair colour, others pay attention to clothes or to characteristic patterns of behaviour. It seems likely that the three participants in the following extracts select different aspects as the crucial characterising features:

(5p)   (quartet 5)
    A1. the one with the bob
    B1. the taller girl
    B2. the taller one with the long shoulder length hair that came out of the lift

(5q)   (quartet 7)
    B1. the other woman came in + er + you know the one with + the tall one + the suspect
    B2. the one with brown hair
    A1. dark brown hair

In (5p), A1 has consistently referred to this character as *the one with the bob* as we saw in extract (5k). B1 has, in a co-operative, chameleon-like manner, tended to use whatever expression the immediately previous speaker has used, but when she introduces this character herself, she regularly comments on height. B2 appears to be attempting a summary of what has been said but rather than using the expression *with a bob* – she uses the expression *with the long shoulder length hair*, apparently assuming that hair which comes down to the shoulders is inappropriately described as *a bob*. However the character's hair is perhaps not quite so long as her description suggests, and it is possible that she is confusing this aspect of the character with the long dark hair of the woman who talks on the telephone. However, she does add a further detail which definitely excludes the woman on the telephone, and that is the fact that the relevant character *came out of the lift*. The expressions *the taller one . . . that came out of the lift* do uniquely characterise one individual, and the rest of the group now agree that they have in mind the same individual – *that's the one – yes*. Whether we would want to claim that they all see this individual in a totally similar way seems questionable. Certainly, they see her in a way which permits the listeners to secure identification on this occasion.

In (5q), B1 appears to identify the character she is speaking of quite adequately. B2 seems to be adding a confirming check, though the feature she adds is hardly distinctive. A's further modification of B2's utterance, *dark brown hair,* actually might have confused the issue since most speakers agree that the suspect's hair is light rather than dark. Indeed B2, near the beginning of this transcript, has described her as *the woman with + the tall one + with blonde hair.* Just as in the case of the implied equivocation between speakers on whether or not her haircut can be described as 'a bob', so we find here a difference of opinion about the relative lightness or darkness of her hair. Such variability in judgment seems perfectly familiar from everyday experience.

David Hockney outlines what seems a plausible account of what happens: 'When you walk into a room you don't notice everything at once and, depending on your taste, there is a descending order in which you observe things. I assume alcoholics notice the booze first, or claustrophobics the height of the ceiling, and so on' (Hockney 1976:92). A rather similar account is given by Bartlett, in considering the implications of such variable reactions to simple stimuli for the experimental psychologist. He writes:

'Uniformity and simplicity of structure of stimuli are no guarantee whatever of uniformity and simplicity of structure in organic response, particularly at the human level. We may consider the old and familiar illustration of the landscape artist, the naturalist and the geologist who walk in the country together. The one is said to notice and recall beauty of scenery, the other details of flora and fauna, and the third the formations of soils and rock. In this case, no doubt, the stimuli, being selected in each instance from what is present, are different for each observer, and obviously the records made in recall are different also' (Bartlett 1932:3–4).

I have suggested that variations in the lexis chosen in referring expressions may be held to reveal a difference in the view that different speakers adopt on the referent. To adopt such a view requires that speakers' utterances closely reflect their thoughts. It seems likely that, in taking a turn in a multi-party conversation, a speaker has the option of simply confirming the correctness of the previous speaker's view, or of adding further limiting but relevant dimensions. Consider extract (5r):

(5r)　　(quartet 3)
    B1. she muddles up the letters
    B2. she spilt all the letters
    A2. switches
    B2. yeah
    A2. switches the letter that was on the desk
    B1. no she ain't switched it
    B2. I said she spilt them all + and then + picked up the letter + which was already on top + and handed the lady the book
    A2. and replaces it with one which was ++ in the tray in the first place

Here B1 uses the expression *muddles,* which B2 obviously understands but apparently finds insufficiently explicit, since he proceeds to specify how this muddling was achieved, using again here the expression which he used two pages earlier in the transcript: *she spilt all the letters.* A2 now offers a further refinement, *switches,* a term which is rebutted by B1, who presumably understands 'switching' to involve replacing the letter taken from the desk by another letter put in its place. (A similar interpretation might account for A's difficulty in understanding B in extract (5n), where B uses the expression *and replaced it* of the letter.) The careful B2 again restates the sequence of events, omitting the suggestion of replacement, and then A2 repeats his view that 'switching' has indeed taken place, but now uses the term *replace* in his reformulation. It looks as though A2 interprets the expression *switch* in this context more loosely than B1 is prepared to do, just as, in extract 5n, B was happy to use the term *replace* of the relationship between the two letters, whereas A insisted that this was not the appropriate way to express the relationship between the stealing of the airmail letter from the table and the handing of the package containing a book to the dark-haired woman on the telephone. The denotation of the terms *switch* and *replace* apparently suggests for some participants (as it does for me) that item *a* should be replaced by item *b* in the same location, and with the intention that *b* should function as an alternative to *a*. Other participants appear to be content to use these terms far more loosely, simply to indicate a sequence of events which involves, in this case, two different items of mail, located in different places within the same room and with different functions.

5.7 Language and the world

I raised the issue in 3.5.2, and again in the section immediately preceding this one, of the problem of giving some account of the perceptions of individuals who interpret aspects of the visually presented world in a radically different manner from other participants (and from the analyst). The first case discussed was illustrated in extract (3e), where a B-role speaker apparently understood what was intended to be represented as a lake on her map as an island. Only after two attempts at reference to a lake by the A-role speaker was she enabled to see her 'island' as 'a lake'. While she was perceiving the lake as an island, no reference to the lake made sense to her.

The range of lexical expressions which can refer to participants in the action of the video (*secretary, woman, girl, lady,* etc.) are apparently all understood by the listeners as referring to appropriate individuals, even though they may, as I have suggested, be picking out different aspects of those individuals. This amount of variability appears not to block communication. However, where radically different interpretations of the world are made by speakers, communication is necessarily disrupted.

In the presentation to quartet 1, the sequence of episodes was shown without any title, that is without any indication that the action shown would represent something being stolen. When A2 gives an account of the third episode, he offers an account of what the tall fair-haired woman has done which suggests that he has not arrived at the intended interpretation of her actions:

(5s)   (quartet 1)

> A2. the lady walked in the room put the ++ post on the table and sat down and checked through – through the post and – as she + was checking through she + went into this other room and put this airmail post on this table + and then she went into this other room and sat on – at this desk and she was near a typewriter ++ she + opened one – one letter and she was doing up another letter ++ and an' she put a hanky in her pocket

This account is problematic in several respects. It is particularly disfluent, and it contains several expressions which suggest that the speaker has not wholly grasped the narrative. It appears to represent a juxtaposition of random events rather than an intentional series. First, there is the problem of location. According to A2's account it appears that 'the lady' went into at least two rooms (*walked in the room – went into this other room*) and possibly even three rooms (*and then she went into this other room*), whereas all the action takes place in a single room. No other speaker suggests that more than one room is entered during these events. Just as each phase of the action appears to be located in a separate room, so the relationship between opening an envelope and resealing the same envelope is represented as separate and unrelated actions, dealing apparently with different letters: *she opened one – one letter and she was doing up another letter.* More important for the interpretation of the thief's actions, A2 apparently interprets the act of concealing the money which the fair-haired woman has taken from the airmail letter, as the innocuous action of putting her handkerchief in her pocket. A1, who contributes rather little to the discussion in this quartet, makes no attempt to venture any correction to A2's report.

Since A2's account was so misleading, the experimenters immediately showed the episode which the A-role pair had watched to all the members of the quartet, and then invited them to comment on what they had just seen. The B-role pair began the narrative which continued in this manner:

(5t)   (quartet 1)
    B2. she picks up the letter
    B1. opens it
    B2. with her hanky
    B1. mmm? ++
    B2. weren't a hanky she put in her pocket
    A2. n' it was
    B2. it was – it was the + letters
    B1. yes – the the stuff that was inside the
        letter + then she re-sealed it

B2's initial interpretation of what he has seen is apparently influenced by what he had heard A2 say earlier, since he suggests that the thief picks up the letter together *with her hanky*. It is not until B1 offers a dubious long-drawn out *mmm?*, on rising intonation, that B2 feels able to produce a reassessment of what he had watched. The correctness of this reassessment is denied by A2, who adheres to his original interpretation of what he saw, as most of us tend to do (following the effect described by Wason 1960, mentioned in 3.3). B2 now suggests that what the thief put in her pocket was 'the letters', a formulation which is obviously understood by B1, who then sharpens it to suggest that it was the contents of the letter which were at issue (where the expression *the letter* seems to be intended as a synonym for *the envelope*). This is an instance where the misperception of actions in the world by one participant led to an initial breakdown of communication. The members of the B-role pair are eventually able to complete the task, but only when they have been shown what it was that the A-role pair were intended to communicate verbally.

We passed silently over another instance of an apparent misperception reported in extract (5e), where A1 reports *then this lady walked in with erm – some letters and parcels + n'a box*. None of the listeners queries A1's mysterious addition of 'a box' to a list of correctly reported items. We could speculate that the expression *n'a box* might be interpreted as meaning 'and a box', where A1 has misremembered a parcel as a box, or as meaning 'in a box', where A1 describes the wire stationery basket as a box.

A somewhat similar example of different perceptions of the action which is hard to explain, and which left at least one participant unsatisfied by the explanations given by other speakers, is shown in 5u:

(5u)　　(quartet 5)

　　A2. it's obviously come from overseas or something if it's airmail – so it's got to be sealed to come

　　B2. maybe she wrote the letter to ask for money

　　A1. yeah

　　B1. what did the little white letter have to do – 'cause did she take the money out of the little white envelope?

　　A2. +++ it's the airmail letter isn't it + on the side

　　B1. so what did the little – the little white envelope have to do with + nicking + the money in the airmail

　　A1. what env – what one

　　B1. the one that was – they left on the desk that she put the letters over to pick up

　　A2. that WAS the airmail letter

　　B2. that was the airmail letter that the money was in

　　B1. thought it was a big envelope though

　　B2. no

　　A1. no

B1 has taken an important role in the discussion of this active and highly-motivated group. It is not until they have, between them, worked out the order of the episodes and are speculating in a relaxed manner about possible events leading up to the action shown in the video, that B1 introduces a question about 'the little white envelope' which appears to leave the others bemused. This was the first time that this expression had been introduced into the discussion, and there had been no previous indication of B1 not having understood references to 'the airmail letter'. Indeed B1 gives evidence in this extract of having understood the description by the A-role pair of the 'nicking' of the money in the airmail letter. Her problem appears to be that she has not previously identified the envelope in the episode which she watched, which was left on the table *on the side* in the first office, as 'an airmail envelope', and has not realised that that letter was the same as the one from which the money was extracted by the thief. She uses the expressions *little white envelope/letter* three times, emphasising the relatively small size of the letter as it appeared to her, and she has apparently inferred that the airmail letter from which the money was extracted must have been in a large envelope. She seems eventually to accept that the two envelopes are one and the same and does not press her question further. However, the problem which surfaces here casts doubt on her full, correct, understanding of some of the earlier discussion which she appeared to participate in without any immediately striking problem. What, for instance, does B1 understand of this earlier interchange?

(5v)　　(quartet 5)

B2. and she didn't see her pick it up 'cause she would have said something wouldn't she

A2. mm

B1. yes – but there were a lot of other letters there as well weren't there – so put – so she – she wouldn't have noticed one going missing

A2. but why would it be on her desk if it wasn't hers ++ why would she have to reseal it?

A1. maybe that's the letter you saw

B1. well – probably – because she –

B2. it was an airmail letter – little airmail letter

A1. mm – saw it with something in it (*whispering*) she put the –

B1. well perhaps she's just a carrier – delivering different letters + between offices

A2. yet it seemed to be her desk she was sitting at didn't it

B1. yeah – but if she was a carrier she'd have a desk wouldn't she + and then she'd just (. . . letters?) ++ so if she knew there's none in there she'd seal it back up + give it to who it belonged to + and erm + it'd look like she hadn't opened the letter ++ what d'you think

A2. mm

B1's first contribution here is a rational response to B2's suggestion, so at this point she fully appreciates that she watched a letter 'going missing' in the scene that she saw, and she offers a plausible reason why the woman on the phone may not have observed this happening. A2's next remark appears to refer to the scene that the A-role pair watched, where the referent of A2's expressions *her, hers* and *she* seems to be 'the girl with the bob' who is the only person who sits at a desk. A1 does not reply directly to A2. Her next remark appears to be addressed to the B pair.

On an initial analysis, I had taken B1's *probably* to indicate that B1 had understood A1's proposal, which appears to suggest that the letter which the A pair saw the girl with a bob open, and then reseal, was the same as that picked up by the girl with a bob in the episode watched by the B pair. In the light of the later evidence that B1 has not appreciated that the letter in each of the two scenes is the same letter, I now suggest that B1 at this point is beginning to formulate an answer to A2's question and that she pays no (or little) attention to the (for her, peripheral) conversation between A1 and B2, which makes the significant proposal that only one letter is involved and that that letter is 'a little airmail letter'. In her next turns, B1 continues with her attempt to answer A2's question, an effort supported by A2's *mm*. If this reanalysis is correct, it demonstrates the problems for a listener in participating in a multi-party conversation where more than one exchange may be simultaneously in progress. The listener cannot simultaneously pay attention to both conversations.

It also demonstrates the problems that such data presents for analysts whose default assumption is that all participants pay full attention to everything that is said. A visual record of the conversation would be helpful here, if it were able to record the stance and eye contact of each of the four participants simultaneously.

In some instances, the different memories which participants construct of the action which they have seen or heard about lead to explicit contradictions between the speakers:

(5w)   (quartet 3)
   B1. the small one put it there + and the tall one muddles the letter up – she took it in the office – the one on the right
   B2. the tall one – was the one who spilt the letters

A2. the one on the left re-sealed the letter at the end
B1. no she didn't
A2. did
B2. ++ she didn't – it's the one – on the right
A1. it was the one on the right

The problem here is that B1 stops using a characterisation of the thief in terms of permanent attributes like height, and moves to using a temporary attribute, the spatial location of one individual relative to the other when they came out of the lift in the first episode. A2 apparently remembers 'the tall one' as having been on the left, whereas all the others remember her (correctly) as having been on the right. When the group eventually reverts to using the permanent height characteristics, A2 immediately says *oh it's the tall one,* abandoning the argument about whether the character stood on the left or the right.

There are not a great many instances of evidence of such radical differences of view of the events which the subjects watched in the data that I am discussing in this chapter – nine such overtly discussed instances occur in the fourteen transcripts. Nonetheless, they arise sufficiently frequently to underline the riskiness of communication. In particular, they draw attention not only to the risk of the misunderstanding of linguistic expressions but also to the risk of different individuals constructing different views of the world, even where the world is highly constrained. We are of course accustomed to supposing that in great issues of politics, history and philosophy it is possible to adopt different points of view. We are perhaps more likely to take for granted in small matters of everyday life of the type mirrored by the tasks which I have described, that the perceptions of different individuals will be very similar, if not identical. Consideration of this data suggests that we should adopt such an optimistic perspective only with caution.

5.8 Constitutive expressions in the Stolen letter task

Whereas the Map task ideally requires that the A-role speaker select a nominal expression which will distinguish one feature of the landscape from all the others within the relevant search area, the Stolen letter task makes quite different demands on speakers. The point here is that each of the actors in the drama is an individual of the same general type as the others – they are all young women. The locations (offices) and the props (mail) can similarly all be described by superordinate expressions. The same claim might have been made about the features on the landscape in the Map task – participants might have spoken about moving to *another feature*, *thing*, or *drawing*, but in fact no participant uses a superordinate term at this level of abstraction to refer to the landscape features in the Map task.

In the Stolen letter task, on the other hand, as we saw in 5.3 and 5.4, the characters and locations are, typically, initially introduced by nominal expressions which merely indicate general types. The level of type is usually, for the female characters, a superordinate term which simply indicates that they are human and female – *lady*, *woman*, *girl* – though occasionally they are identified as *secretaries*. Later expressions are sometimes used to differentiate between them. (The forms of interest are italicised.)

(5x)   (quartet 6)
    A1. +++erm ++ there was *a woman* + in *an office*

(5y)   (quartet 5)
    A1. *they* were in *an office it looks like* and there were *two secretaries*

(5z)   (quartet 1)
    B1. *a lady* came *through the door* – met *some other ladies in there* talking + an' *one of the ladies* picked up *a telephone*

(5aa)   (quartet 2)
    A1. there was *this woman* in *the office* on *the telephone* + and + then *this lady* walked in with erm *some letters and parcels*

(5ab)   (ug pair 4)
    A.   the setting was *an office* + and + *a secretary presumably* + was on *the telephone* and *somebody* came in bringing *some mail*

The initial introduction commits the speaker to very little – simply to the most abstract stereotype. In (5z) the speaker does not even bother to specify that what the lady came through the door of was an office. But, once again, it is important to remember that the speakers knew that their listeners were listening within a context of having themselves seen the first episode of the narrative which had, in the speaker's own experience, continued in very much the way it had begun – with more institutional surroundings, more young women carrying carrying baskets of mail and so on.

From the listener's point of view, we must suppose that they construct interpretations which are constrained by what they themselves have seen, both in the episode which they shared with the other pair and that which they watched by themselves. Presumably, if the speaker had watched an episode which strikingly contrasted with the initial episode – which was set in a rich eighteenth century salon, or where the actors were representing garden gnomes, characters from **Thunderbirds** or chimpanzees – the speaker would have mentioned this on the general communicative principle enunciated by Dahl (1976) 'mention that which changes'. The listeners, like the speaker, must surely assume that the women which the speaker speaks of must be of the same general sort – late twentieth-century, casually dressed, youngish – as those whom they had seen earlier. Similarly, they must expect that the office spoken of will be the sort of office which would appropriately open off a corridor of the sort they saw in the shared scene, and that the mail would look rather like the mail in the shared scene and be carried in similar wire baskets. The very generalised descriptions provided by the speakers presumably enable the listeners to construct very generalised mental representations of what occurred in the scene which they have not witnessed. The denotations of non-specific expressions can surely only be constitutive of rather non-specific mental representations, but the structure of these representations must be much more constrained when interpreted in the context provided here, than the denotation of the words alone would permit.

Certainly, those who listen and respond to such vague and underspecified accounts respond in a quite natural way, as though they have sufficient information, and as though it is sufficiently structured to talk about, as we see in the following extract:

(5ac)   (ug pair 2)
    A. the same lady comes into ++ into an office . . . she delivers the
        letter on the desk . . . but when she is coming out + two other
        ladies come in + and then the telephone rings + and one of them

> – goes to answer it . . . while she's talking + the other two go out of the room
>
> B. er + the same lady + do you mean the same smaller lady
> A. the same smaller lady + that one that was delivering mail at the beginning ++ . . . and she left a letter on the desk
> B. nothing happened to the letter
> A. ++ mm?
> B. something happened to the letter?
> A. + no nothing + we can see a + er ++ we can still see the letter at the end of the scene
> B. it's still on the desk
> A. it's on the desk
> B. you know that – the other two ladies ++ they seemed a little bit curious about the letter?

In this extract, one character is mentioned whom B apparently assumes that she has already met, 'the same smaller lady'. Apart from this character, everything is, as far as B knows at the moment, new to her – the other two ladies, the office, the desk, the letter. Yet as soon as they are introduced into the discourse, naturally she feels able to talk about them, just as we all do in everyday life, on the basis of minimal information about them.

Note that all of the expressions relating to these individuals and entities are presumably, for B, at the moment when they are introduced into the conversation, constitutive rather than referring. All she can initially do is establish 'a letter' in her discourse representation, together with the information that it was delivered by 'the same lady', and that it was placed on a desk in an office, and similarly establish headings of 'a desk', and 'an office' and associate each of these with inferences such as 'the desk is in an office' and 'the office has a desk in it'. Later in the discussion, she must realise that the letter on the desk is in fact the same letter as that which, she already knows, was picked up by the tall fair-haired secretary. The desk and office, as well as 'the other two ladies', are all, in fact, known to her already. What she had presumably first taken to be constitutive expressions, she must retrospectively understand as referring expressions. She must then assign all the information which has been filed under two separate addresses to a single address in memory, that which was established on the first occasion of mention.

This postulated process raises many interesting questions. Gernsbacher (1990:64) suggests that, typically, incoming information is mapped on to developing discoursal structures 'when that incoming information overlaps with previous information' but that changes in topic, point of view, location or temporal setting 'trigger comprehenders to shift and initiate new sub-structures'. For the moment, we will adopt this metaphor. We might then suppose that, in the type of discourse generated by the Stolen letter task, the listener lays the foundations of a narrative structure while watching the initial shared video episode and the following episode. This structure will presumably differentiate between individuals, locations, objects and the temporal sequences internal to each episode. When listeners hear the account of the episode which they have not witnessed, they can attempt to map the new (auditorily acquired) information onto the existing (visually acquired) discoursal structure, as B seems to do in extract (5ac), or, apparently, establish a separate structure as appears to happen in extract (5j). Presumably, an intermediate position would be that the listener sets up a new structure but tags it, to mark that it may turn out to be possible to amalgamate this new structure with the earlier structure. We might wonder whether it is some process such as this which gives rise to B's questioning of A about the letter in extract (5ac). Indeed some such process which is intermediate between instant amalgamation with existing structures and the establishment of separate structures may give rise to many of the checking questions which arise in this data (for example those which we noted in extract (5i)).

5.9 Conclusion

In this chapter, we have observed a range of problems which are introduced for the listener who is trying to understand a narrative, problems which did not emerge for listeners in the Map tasks. To begin with, we observed that in order to discriminate between characters in a narrative, listeners need access to identifying features which are stable with respect to the character and have a good chance of being fixed in memory, rather than temporary features like being the second person to enter a room or of standing to the left of another character. Among transient features, we saw that salient attributes like talking on the telephone may be successfully used as an identifying attribute if no other character has performed a similar action. Among stable features, we saw that there were sometimes different perceptions among subjects of attributes like the type of hair cut (*bob* versus *shoulder-length*) and hair colour (*dark* versus *fair*).

A further necessary condition for following a narrative successfully is to be able to keep track of each distinct individual participant and of entities which are salient in the narrative. We saw that in spite of what often appears to be ambiguous or misleading use of anaphoric expressions, listeners appeared, in general, to be able to keep track of individuals, though there were occasional difficulties arising from the use of insufficiently explicit expressions.

Finally, we began to consider the issue of how listeners may update an existing discourse model. In addition to establishing distinct characters and tracking them through a number of episodes, listeners need to be able to establish whereabouts events were located and how events followed each other in time. These issues will be considered in chapter 6.

6 · Understanding narratives

We have repeatedly raised the question of what, in the Stolen letter task, constitutes the equivalent of the search field in the Map task. In chapter 4, we noted that deictic expressions play a potentially crucial role in situating the listener so that the listener adopts the same perspective on the search field as the speaker. We saw in chapter 3 how listeners who failed to locate themselves in the same vantage point as the speaker failed to understand adequately what the speaker said. Does deixis perform the same central role in the narrative task as it did in the spatially structured task? If so, is temporal deixis the crucial element here?

This chapter begins by laying out the broad outlines of the temporal structures which are referred to by subjects who undertake the Stolen letter task. I move on to examine how temporal deixis plays a part in restricting the contextual search field for the listener and how this interrelates with person/entity deixis. I then consider the part played by spatial deixis and person/entity deixis. Finally, I discuss how the Map task search field, viewed from a particular anchor point, can be related to the Stolen letter task search field and in this context I examine the function of what Fauconnier (1985) calls 'space-builders'.

Before we turn to consider the use of deixis in the narrative Stolen letter task, we should briefly recall the use of deixis in the spatially structured Map task. In chapter 4, we noted the extensive use of spatial deictic expressions used to guide the listener through the landscape. We noted also, in considering person deixis, that definite expressions were widely used by speakers not only to refer to entities whose locations had been agreed and which had been established as in the common ground, but also in speaking of entities which the A-role speaker was introducing into the discourse for the first time, not knowing whether or not they were represented on B's map but assuming that, if they were, they would be visible from B's current anchor-point within the proximal search field.

We have made no explicit comment yet on the use of temporal deixis in the Map task. This is because there is little to say. The structure of the task largely constrains the order of instructions, though these are sometimes prefaced by *now*, or *and*. Occasionally a speaker suggests a series of moves where the first is supposed to be executed first and the presence of the second is marked by *then*, as in *you've got the bridge right + up towards the wood + then go between the two rivers – you've got the two rivers – right*. The predominating tense is the present tense, used to speak of the present time and of the immediate future action of B as in *that island's the lake, you go up + between a swamp and a the Palm Beach, you're going to have to cross the river now*. (A frequent verb form is of course the imperative, unmarked for tense.) Occasionally the past tense is used to speak of some event in the immediate shared past time of the participants, as in *wait a minute what did you say about woods*. If the Map task data were the only data available to us, we might suppose that there was a rather neat match between speaking of past time and the use of the past tense, and speaking of present and immediate future time and the use of the present tense.

I have used the term **present tense** in this discussion, and I shall continue to use it because it is familiar. There are, though, strong arguments for considering the tense opposition in English to be most satisfactorily categorised as a past/non-past distinction (see Lyons 1977:678 and discussion in 6.1.1).

6.1 The temporal structure of the Stolen letter task

One of the reasons for constructing the Stolen letter task was to explore the ways in which speakers and listeners coped with talking about individuals who were participating in events in a complex series of embedded time domains.

As we have noted, in the Stolen letter task, each pair of each quartet watched two video-recorded episodes. In each episode, they watched a sequence of events which, they must have assumed, had taken place and had been recorded at some period in the past. Let us call this period of the original action, Time A (we could, if necessary, add subscripts to Time A to distinguish between the time spans of each episode, and between the sequence of events in each episode).

Then there is the later time during which the pair watched the recording of each episode being shown. Call this watching period Time B (which again could be tagged to distinguish between the watching time of pair A and that of pair B).

Then at a slightly later time than Time B, each pair discusses with the other pair their memories of the events of Time A which they saw during Time B. This discussion period we shall call Time C. In their discussions, speakers refer to each of these time periods and, in doing so they necessarily use one of the English tense forms, either past or present.

6.1.1 Establishing Time A

Speakers refer to the time when the action took place, Time A, using both the simple past tense, as in (6a), and the simple present tense, referring to third person participants, as in (6b), or in a mixture of simple present and past tenses as in (6c) and (6d). (The forms of interest are italicised.)

(6a)   (quartet 4)
   B1.   the tall lady + she *went* into an office and *locked* the door behind her + and what *did* she *do* with the letter
   B2.   she *opened* it up

(6b)   (ug pair 5)
   A.   then the tall girl *drops* the mail on the desk
   B.   mm
   A.   where the airmail letter *is* – what I will call the airmail letter + I'm sure it was one
   B.   yes
   A.   and in the confusion and everything else she *picks up* all the mail – including the letter
   B.   yes
   A.   which I originally took to be an accident but subsequent events make me think it's quite deliberate

(6c)   (ug pair 6)

A.   *was* it ++ how *did* it get into her possession then ++ the secretive one

B.   she + actually *picks* + she *sorts* some out + when she *put* those on the desk + and probably *picked* it up ++ and *walked* out with it ++ maybe she *put down* loads on the desk + like + that ++ then she sort of *went through* some + and *puts* – some back in the tray again

(6d)   (quartet 5)

B2.   there *was* a letter on the desk + and there *was* a woman standing behind the desk – she *was* on the telephone ++ and she *saw* the woman with the long hair came in and so she *called* her and the woman with the long hair *walks* over to the desk and *takes* the post + and the woman – on the phone *takes* the parcel but the letter on the desk *has gone* ++ so that as she *puts* the phone down the woman *looks* inside the parcel ++ *saw* a book in it – and she *flicks* through it

The use of the present tense to refer to past time is not a feature of the narrative passages of all the speakers in this data, but it occurs with varying frequency in twelve of the fourteen transcripts.

The issue of the use of the present tense in the narration of events which have occurred in the past has long been discussed. Indeed this construction has sometimes been identified as a distinct tense, called the **historic present** whose forms just happen to be identical to those of the simple present in the third person singular (though they differ in the first person which does not occur in this data). Thus Jespersen writes: 'Among expressions for the simple past we must here also mention the so-called historic present, or, taking a hint thrown out by Brugmann, the *dramatic present*. The speaker in using it steps outside the frame of history, visualising and representing what happened in the past as if it were present before his eyes . . . it serves to produce an artistic illusion. But however artistic this trick is, it must not be imagined that it is not popular in its origin; one need only listen to the way in which people of the humblest ranks relate incidents which they have witnessed themselves to see how natural, nay inevitable, this form is' (Jespersen 1924:258).

It is widely held, as noted earlier, that the past tense is the marked tense in English, the present tense being unmarked (non-past). A range of arguments which have a certain family resemblance has been proposed in support of this suggestion. Bolinger (1947:436) suggests that the present tense is the base tense which expresses no more than the fact that the type of process denoted by the lexis of the verb is at issue. The present tense is sometimes seen as timeless, since it can express the widest possible temporal relations in English, speaking of the present, the past and the future, as well as expressing habitual aspect, and being used in generic and gnomic sentences (see Wolfson, 1979). Fleischmann (1990) remarks of our experience of time, that in everyday life it is the *now* in which the speaker is currently situated which is unmarked, the **past** (or **not-now**) which is marked, and she quotes the view of Schlicher (1931:48): 'Whereas present experience is largely a mere suggestion of events, the past is a pattern in which . . . details have found their place according to the significance to (the speaker)'.

If we follow this line of argument, we might propose that it would be natural to use the present tense to speak of any events, or aspects of events, which have not yet been sorted into a coherent mental representation. When we report an event in the present tense, it is as though it was directly perceived, still present on some mental retina. Whereas once we report the event in the past tense, we adopt a historian's stance, as though the event had now satisfactorily assumed its place in a matrix of past events, perhaps at this point being propositionally represented in memory rather than only being available in pictorial snatches. In the Stolen letter task, there are of course two sources of information for subjects. One is the visual source of information, provided by the video recordings. The second is the verbal, propositionalised, source provided by the other pair of speakers. Another possibility is that the directly experienced visual information might be more likely to be expressed in present tense terms than the verbal information provided by the other speakers.

It is indeed the case, in this data, that directly experienced visual information is more likely to be narrated in the present tense than data which the narrator has only heard about from another participant, though, as we shall see, some narrations of visually experienced information are, at least in part, narrated in the past tense. Whereas it is relatively rare for a subject to speak of information exclusively derived from another speaker in the present tense (even when it was originally narrated in the present tense), this does occur.

Another way to think about this issue might be to suppose that where information about past events has been verbally agreed between speakers, and is established as shared in their common ground, we might expect to find use of the past tense. On the other hand, we might expect the present tense to be used when a speaker is straining to remember a series of visual impressions which have not been spoken of before, and which are not yet fully assimilated into the speaker's view of the narrative.

If we now look again at extracts (6a)–(6d), we can observe whether or not there may be a pattern here. In (6a), B1 and B2 are telling the A-role pair the content of the episode which they have watched, hence directly experienced. B1 consistently uses past tense forms to report this visual experience, even when she is unsure of what happened and checks with B2 *what did she do with the letter*. In (6b), A is narrating to B an incident which neither speaker has spoken of before, which she herself directly experienced, and she uses present tense forms to refer to events in the narrative. In (6c), A asks B a (past tense) question about information only directly available to B. The question presupposes that the letter came into 'the secretive one's' possession. B replies in a way which suggests that she has not yet sorted out her ideas on this yet. She begins by using *picks*, present tense, and almost immediately replaces this with *sorts some out*, again using the present tense. Her past tensed expression *when she put those on the desk*, recapitulates what she has told A earlier. However, she then moves into a hypothesising mode, marked by the use of *probably*, *maybe* and *sort of* and in this mode, uses past tense forms: *picked – up*, *walked out*, *put down* and *went through*, and then she reverts to the present tense to mention an action which she has mentioned earlier, *puts – back*.

Similarly in (6d), where B2 is attempting a summary of material, all of which has been mentioned before in discussion by the quartet and which she has experienced visually, she begins in past tense mode (*was, was – standing, was, saw, called*) but then, for no obvious reason, switches into present tense mode (*walks over, takes, takes, has gone, puts, looks*), and, again for no obvious reason produces one past tense form, *saw*, before reverting to the present tense in *flicks*.

None of the possible explanations which we have mentioned seems to give a description of this data which is fully satisfactory, though I believe that each of these considerations may play a part. The analytic problem lies in trying to identify the individual, and differently combined, effects of such factors. It seems to me likely that we shall have to accept that there cannot be a determinate account of this phenomenon.

We should note that this switching between tenses is characteristic not only of narrative as normally construed, but also of a quite different genre, that of expository prose. Observant readers may have noticed that, through-out this book, whenever I have given an account of how the data which I discuss has been collected, I alternate between using past tense and present tense. There is no single feature of the text which I change, in re-reading the manuscript, more often than this, using the magic of the word-processor. I am aware that I am torn between two modes of discussion. In one, I give an account of a range of experiments which continued, in one form or another, over a period of ten years, whose data is not yet exhausted and whose format will almost certainly be used again. It seems appropriate to write of this in terms of an ongoing investigation, which seems in turn to imply writing in the present tense. In the second mode, I would give an account in terms of an achieved, completed, series of work, which implies writing in the past tense. The reader should not suppose that I am alone in this difficulty. Check through a dozen papers which give accounts of extended series of experiments and observe the variable usage of tense forms. Or, more generally, consult a dozen academic books and look at the variation of use in attributions to earlier writers: *Bloomfield (1933) wrote . . .* versus *Bloomfield (1933) writes*, or, even more strikingly because more current, *Chomsky (1988) suggested* versus *Chomsky (1988) suggests*. My own intuition is that I am more likely to use the present tense in referring to recent writing, or where the point made is one that I agree with and which I believe still holds true.

Wolfson (1979) suggests that the 'dramatic' account of present tense narrative in the past, which is espoused by writers as diverse as Sweet (1892), Jespersen (1924) and Quirk *et al.* (1972), is inadequate. However, it does appear to embody the aspect of immediacy which derives from the use of the present tense in the Stolen letter data. Sometimes, when speakers are embarked on trying to report what they have witnessed, it is as though they

are replaying their visual memory as if it were a video tape, aligning themselves temporally with the action as it is being acted out, rather than looking
back at a completed event. They give the impression of being able to view
the mentally represented tape, looking through it again, and noticing extra
details. Indeed some of their comments on the remembered detail might be
taken to imply that they are scanning such detail at the moment of speaking,
as in this extract from one of the pilot undergraduate pairs, where B appears
to be describing her memory of the letter, rather than the film, as *fuzzy*. Both
subjects watched this episode on video. (The film at this point zoomed into
sharp focus on the air-mail letter, a fact which is commented on by speakers
in some quartets.)

6(e)   (ug pair 5)
  A. you know the letter that was delivered + that that erm + 'd
     originally put on the desk
  B. yeh I remember it
  A. which I think was an airmail – I took it to be an airmail letter
     +++ anyway
  B. yes – it's a bit fuzzy
  A. right – we saw a close-up of that first

When information about narrative detail is exchanged in rapidly alternat-
ing short turns, the past tense form is most frequently used, especially when
a specific action or series of actions is being focussed on, which is rapidly
established as common ground between the speakers. Interspersed among
accounts of the narrative, we often find, as in (6b) and (6e), comment on the
experience of watching the film and/or the experience of recalling the detail
of what was watched. In support of the suggestion that B's remark in (6e)
relates to her current experience of trying to remember the pictorial detail of
the film, is her use of the present tense to describe her experience. As we shall
see in the next section, speakers generally refer to Time B, the time of watching the video, using past tense forms (as in (6b)).

6.1.2 Establishing Time B
Time B can conveniently be divided into Time B1, which is the time when
all members of the quartet watched the first scene together, and Time B2

when they split up into separate pairs. Speakers quite frequently refer to some part of an episode which they remember as having watched with members of the other pair, presumably to establish for the listeners that this is indeed part of what they have already shared, as in (6f) and (6g). Time B2 is the time when each pair was watching a further episode on its own. Speakers sometimes mark explicitly pieces of information which are not shared as in (6h). (The forms of interest are italicised.)

(6f)   (quartet 4)
     B1. em well – the tall lady *that we were looking at*

(6g)   (quartet 8)
     B2. she then ++ er + put them all back into a tray and left ++ and + walked + into a different office
     B1. *they saw that bit*

(6h)   (ug pair 5)
     A. and then – *the bit I then saw – was you got a close-up first of all* of the airmail letter on the desk

In speaking of their own past experience in watching, or of that of the other pair, speakers regularly use past tense forms to refer to past time.

6.1.3 Establishing Time C

Speakers use many expressions which relate to the here-and-now of the discussion of what they have been watching. They frequently employ the present simple tense in relation to the experiences or beliefs of first or second persons: *I think, you know, I remember* as in the examples below. Occasionally, as in (6l), we find a speaker referring to Time C using the present tense, *I can't see* followed by the past tense to refer to an event in Time A *how anything could be nicked.* She then comments on Time B using the present perfective, *I haven't seen any money* and backs off further within that to a counter-factual world relating to Time A *unless one of the other envelopes contain money.* In spite of this complexity, and the iteration of present tense verb forms, the speaker feels able again to use the present tense form of the verb, *contain,* to refer to the most distant past time.

(6i) (ug pair 5)

  B. well – *you start* – you were the one in first

(6j) (ug pair 5)

  A. well – *you know* – the letter that was delivered + that that erm – 'd originally put on the desk

  B. yeh – *I remember it*

(6k) (quartet 8)

  B2. but then she tips them all over to make – to mix them all up

  B1. + *do you reckon*

(6l) (quartet 5)

  B1. *I can't see* how anything could be nicked – *I haven't seen* any money unless one of the other envelopes *contain* money

The present tense is regularly used to refer to present time, the time of speaking.

Obviously each major time domain contains complex temporal structures within it. This is particularly true of Time A. It is notable that language referring to complexly related temporal structures of the kind exemplified in (6l), appears to be interpreted quite effortlessly by listeners. It is only with the obscure internal structure of Time A that participants sometimes have difficulties, a point we shall return to.

6.2 **Temporal deixis**

Just as spatial deixis is held to derive from the speaker's location in a particular point in space to which deictic expressions must be related in order to arrive at an interpretation, so temporal deixis is held to inhere in the speaker's location in time, at the time of speaking (see Fillmore 1975, Levinson 1983; Lyons 1977). These two variables together provide the here-and-now of the context of utterance. The major linguistic categories associated with the expression of deictic temporal relations are adverbs such as *now, soon, recently, today, next year,* etc., and the category of tense in the verb. The past tense is held to realise the non-proximal relation to the speaker, and the present tense, the proximal relation. In their most characteristic uses, the past tense is used in sentences concerning past time, whereas the present tense is used in sentences concerning present, future or putative time.

In the Map task, speakers were speaking of time *now* and place *here*, orienting themselves to the map visible in front of them as they were speaking. To interpret what they said, listeners needed to achieve the same orientation, the same perspective, on the map which they had in front of them. In the Stolen letter task, speakers are speaking of events which they have witnessed in the past. Bühler discusses the relationship of deixis used to refer to the here-and-now, at the time of speaking, with that used to refer to an earlier period, the there-and-then, when the spatial relationships mentioned are no longer present: 'The matter changes with one blow, it seems, when the narrator leads the hearer into the realm of what is absent and can be remembered . . . and treats him to the same deictic words as before so that he may see and hear what can be seen and heard there . . . Not with the external eye, ear, and so on, but with what is usually called the "mind's" eye or ear in everyday language' (Bühler [1934] 1990:141).

In English, we have available at least two modes of talking about past events. In one mode, we look back in memory, after the events have occurred, adopting a perspective which yields the outcome of the most recent events as closer and more salient to the speaker, whereas events which happened earlier in time are perceived as being most distant from the speaker. This is sometimes called the historical mode. It yields a relation of events from the point of view of an omniscient narrator, one who knows all of the relevant happenings and whose view of them may be coloured by the nature of the outcome. This can be modelled by constructing a time-line on which the sequence of events is represented, and where the speaker's moment of utterance is shown well to the right-hand side of this time-line, in an elevated position, so that he or she can survey the entire series of events. In this mode, the events may be conceptualised as being fixed in time, and they are called into prominence by having the speaker's moveable attention shifted, so that it is focussed on a particular point in the series of events, in the knowledge of what happened later. We might suppose that this mode is most naturally associated with narration in the past tense and associate it with Schlicher's remark about the past being a structure in which 'details have found their place' (1931:48).

Within this organised structure, we may assume that the speaker's stance in looking back constitutes the anchor-point which the listener is invited to adopt, and that the totality of past events constitutes the larger search field (the equivalent in the Map task of the complete map). We shall explore this suggestion in 6.6.

In the second mode, the speaker is put into a less elevated and detached position and sits, as it were, like a member of an audience in a cinema. The film of the sequence of events is run past the speaker, in the speaker's mind (past the mind's eye and ear, as Bühler suggested). The speaker's attention is (largely) determined by the event currently being shown on the film. This can be thought of as the experiential mode, where the speaker is not viewing a completed series of events from the vantage point of the outcome, but is re-experiencing a memory of the events as they happened, not necessarily being aware of how they fit into a larger picture. We may suppose that this mode is most naturally associated with narration in the present tense. In this mode, it is less obvious what constitutes the search field for the listener and how the listener is to identify the speaker's anchor-point.

6.3 Temporal deixis in the Stolen letter task

As discussion in the previous section indicated, often the only suggestion that a speaker may be shifting from one mode of description to another is a change in the selection of the tense forms of verbs which relate to Time A, to the world shown in the video. Similarly, whereas the listener will usually hear Time B being referred to consistently in the past tense, this is by no means obligatory, as we shall see in (6m). A better indication seems to be that it will normally be associated with first and second person pronominal subjects (though, this again, is not a completely reliable cue as we saw in (6g)). The listener may rely upon Time C being referred to consistently in the present tense, again characteristically associated with first and second person pronominal subjects, but that alone will not always be sufficient to differentiate Times B and C. To assess the contribution made by temporal deixis to the listener's interpretation, let us consider extract (6m).

The speakers here, having heard each other's accounts of the episodes they have watched, and having discussed the likely order of events, are now attempting to reconstruct the entire narrative.

(6m)   (quartet 5)
```
 1   A2.  well – the two blonde girls in the lift
 2   B1.  they came out – they sorted through the erm
 3        – sorted through the files + which they had in
 4        erm ·
 5   A2.  trays
 6   B2.  trays
 7   B1.  sorted – sort of looked casually through + and
 8        then
 9   B2.  and the shorter one walked off in another
10        direction and the one with the long hair walks
11        down a very long corridor ++ and you don't see
12        what she does after that ++ she's still got the
13        filing tray in her hands though
14   B1.  then Sarah's scene comes next
15   B2.  yeah
16   A1.  with the shorter one going into the office – c'so
17        they must have met up again to go back into the
18        office with with the dark-haired girl + or was
19        the dark-haired girl with the other two
20   B2.  no she wasn't
21   A1.  dark-haired one came in with the tall girl
22   B1.  so the shorter –
23   B2.  dark-haired girl came in with the shorter
24   A1.  both go – one's left
25   B2.  so an' she must have come back then mustn't she
26   B1.  so who was originally in the office before the
27        other two walked in
28   A2.  the shorter one
```

A2 establishes the opening shot, without specifying time in any way, in a tenseless phrase which identifies the two participants as blonde (not a judgment which I, or most other participants make, *fair* is the most widely used term in the data) and, crucially, 'in the lift'. The location is sufficient to specify the time uniquely, since there was only a brief initial moment when the two young women were in the lift and no later action is related to the lift location. B1 uses a tensed expression *they came out,* which is deictic not merely with respect to time, but also with respect to the persons spoken of by A2 in line 1, now referred to as *they,* as well as to the observer's viewpoint in watching the video: the two blonde girls (just spoken of) came out (at a time previous to my current report) from where they were (in the lift) to a space nearer to me (the observer/speaker).

In lines 2–8, B1 (with some lexical assistance from A2, who did of course watch this sequence together with the B pair) describes the actions of the girls in sorting through the files, which must be understood as happening subsequent to their emergence from the lift. There is no formal indication of this, but we must here take account of the principle of **ordo naturalis** in narrative, which may loosely be described as requiring that actions should be narrated in the order in which they occur unless the speaker gives some indication of a disruption of the natural order (see Levelt 1981 for discussion of the various effects of ordo naturalis). So we must suppose that when B1 says *they came out* in line 2, the action described here precedes the looking through the files. Since we are not told that the girls moved away from the lift, we must suppose that they stopped immediately outside the lift. The principle of ordo naturalis might suggest that *sorted through the files* (line 3) and *sort of looked casually through* (line 7) should be construed as sequential, but the meaning of the two expressions is so similar that it seems more likely that the second expression should be understood as synonymous with, or, at most, as slightly modifying, the meaning of the first expression and as referring to the same action.

In lines 9–11, B2 (who appears to indicate that she is keen to participate by her echo of A2's expression *trays* in line 6) takes over the narrative. She now discriminates between the two 'blonde' girls who have emerged from the lift and sorted through their files. Still using past tense forms, she describes how *the shorter one walked off in another direction,* where *off* appears to indicate that she disappears from the speaker/observer's view, and *another* suggests both that the direction of disappearance is different from that of the second girl, and that it is either unknown to the speaker or not worth specifying. The second girl is characterised as *the one with long hair* and her walking away is described using the present tense with what might be supposed to be an empathetic characterisation of the very long corridor which she walks down and which the observer can see down. It might be suggested that the choice of present tense shows a greater empathy with this character than the other, particularly as for this character a description of the corridor is provided.

However, there is a curious feature of this description and that is that the young woman who is shown on the film as walking away down the long corridor is not, as B2 suggests, the taller woman but, in fact, the shorter one. It appears that B2 has transferred this memory of the corridor to the more memorable character, a confusion which is not corrected by any of the other members of the quartet, all of whom have watched this episode.

Then in line 11, B2 introduces a reference to Time B1. This utterance, *and you don't see what she does after that* is in the present tense, and so are the immediately preceding and following utterances. The present tense may here refer back to past time when the quartet was watching the video, but it does not securely discriminate between a specific time period and a timeless generalisation, and it may well be that to insist upon such a discrimination in this casual speech is unnecessary. A more helpful indicator of the scope of the time period being referred to here is the pronoun *you*, here presumably to be interpreted as a generalised pronoun which includes the speaker, the listeners and anyone else who watches the video. In her final utterance (lines 12–13), B2 again uses the present tense, reinforced by *still*, to refer back to Time A. We infer this, not from the tense of the verb or from *still*, but rather from the content of what she says which relates to Time A.

In line 14, B1 produces an utterance with a verb in the present tense and two potentially deictic temporal expressions, *then, next*. The expression *Sarah's scene* refers to the scene watched by the A pair which includes Sarah (A1). *Then* is presumably non-deictic here, simply indicating that 'Sarah's scene' follows the scene which has just been described. *Next* seems to be interpretable either as non-deictic, simply indicating the sequence of scenes, or as deictic, indicating what should be described next, following the moment of speaking. Similarly the present tense may either be deictic, indicating what is about to follow the moment of utterance, or non-deictic, indicating that the correct form of the video sequence has a timeless structure, in the way that a novel or a play has. (The reader will have noted that, in this present discussion, I write of the data for the most part in the present tense, as it is preserved for us in a stable, interpreted and permanent form in transcription, rather than narrating it in the past tense as though it had happened once in a transitory manner, leaving no permanent record.)

A1 takes up the narrative with an untensed phrase in line 16. The meaning of what she says next (lines 17–18) is not immediately clear. The reader may find it easier to consider the dialogue which follows these lines if we summarise the relevant action here:

Episode 1
  outside the lift:
    shorter (fair) girl + taller (fair) girl
Episode 2
  in the office (first):
    shorter (fair) girl + letter
  in the office (later):
    taller (fair) girl + dark girl
  answers telephone:
    dark girl
  leave office:
    shorter (fair) girl + taller (fair) girl

A1 has just declared that the shorter girl goes into the office (line16) – with the implication that, since she is the only person mentioned, she is the only person who goes into the office at this time. But then who constitute the 'they' who must have *met up again*? The implication of A1's last utterance (line 19) is that she has been speaking of the two outside the lift, *the other two,* since she goes on to enquire about the dark-haired girl. And she shows, in line 21, that she knows that it was the dark-haired girl who came in with the tall girl – was it these two who 'must have met up again'? Perhaps the problem simply arises because she cannot remember the point at which she first encountered the dark-haired girl.

The problem is now compounded by the remark of B2 (line 23), who asserts (falsely) that the dark-haired girl came in with the shorter girl. Her remark here appears to be a partial echo to that of A1 in line 21 – *dark-haired one came in with the tall girl* – which correctly describes what occurred. B2's remark retains the same neutral intonation as A1's, with no indication of an intention of making a contradictory remark. However, B1 has begun a fragment which includes the word *shorter* in line 22, which B2 may have heard, since as she cuts B1's intervention off, she substitutes the expression *the shorter* for A1's expression *the tall girl*. This echo, with one single but crucial expression substituted for another, may be the source of B2's own confusion (though we recall her earlier remark about the taller woman walking down the corridor which may indicate a more fundamental and enduring confusion). Her remark in line 25, *she must have come back then mustn't she* is presumably trying to reconcile two entrances to the office by the shorter fair girl, one alone, and one in company with the dark-haired girl. (Remember that B2 did not watch this scene in the office, but has constructed an interpretation from the earlier narrative of the A pair, together with A1's confusing remark about 'meeting up'.)

At this point (lines 26–27), B1 tries to clarify the problem, using the quasi-deictic term *originally* to establish the time domain which she wishes to concentrate on with respect to the office location. It appears that all the participants understand that, at the beginning of this episode, one girl entered the room alone and was later joined by two other girls. A1, however, despite her clear and correct account (*with the shorter one going into the office)* in line 16, has, by her later remarks, confused the issue. A2 now gives a clear and correct response (line 28).

In extract (6m), we see confusion arising over the sequence of events during Time A, presumably due in part at least to the inadequate verbal characterisation of the three actors, who our subjects quite frequently fail to keep sufficiently close track of, and to the use of vague expressions of the type that we noted in the Map task data. It seems clear that temporal deixis is not playing a central role in identifying events or in indicating the sequence of events, certainly not a role as crucial as that played by spatial deixis in the Map task. Indeed in this data, indication of location seems more central to the identification of events, or to the identification of relative time and, as we remarked earlier, the order of telling seems to be relied upon to indicate the order of happening, with the participants indicating when they are departing from that order as in line 26, where B1 asks *who was originally in the office*.

6.4 **Ordo naturalis in the Spoken letter task**

In (6n), one of two undergraduates attempts to narrate the entire narrative, beginning with the same incident as that described in (6m), showing the same reliance on **ordo naturalis** to convey sequence of events and a similar paucity of reliance on temporal deictic expressions:

(6n)   (ug pair 6)

 1 A. well + the two people arrive + they've both got +
 2   mail to deliver – they've both got – erm- trays of
 3   it ++ both go in different directions – presumably
 4   they've both got different areas to cover + in
 5   their mail delivery
 6 B. they go out together in your scene
 7 A. er no + the scene + was + just this room ++ er ++
 8   so they go off in different directions anyway +
 9   with their m' – respective mails ++ presumably that
10   + the + the other woman – the secretive woman ++
11   wants a letter that's in the shorter one's tray ++
12   so ++ erm – the shorter one goes into that room –
13   delivers a letter + then the other woman + she'll
14   know where the letter is + she'll see it +
15 B. doesn't she see the letter there
16 A. (*mutters*) mm – anyway – she comes in later +
17   (*aloud*) but there's that other woman with the – by
18   the telephone

The speaker here intersperses her narrative with speculation on why the characters acted as they did, relying, presumably, on knowledge of the world to draw inferences about the procedures of the secretaries in delivering mail, and on having heard from B that the tall woman secreted money which she had taken from a letter in the episode which B watched. This speaker opens with a description in the present tense which does not indicate location. Her characters *arrive* and then they *both go in different directions*. The expressions *arrive* and *go* are presumably both to be interpreted deictically, 'arrive where I can see them' and 'go from where I can see them to where I cannot see them'.

B, who has watched this scene, comments at this point (line 6), maintaining the present tense, *they go out together in your scene* perhaps simply meaning 'they left at the same time' which would be descriptively true. What is odd here is the expression *in your scene*. B may here be remembering that A has reported that during the delivery of the mail scene, the two fair girls went out of the room together, leaving the dark-haired woman talking on the telephone, in which case she may be comparing the two occasions on which these two leave together. But if the expression *in your scene* is ignored, this utterance could also be understood as suggesting that the two women leave the area outside the lift which A has just been describing, accompanying each other, which would directly contradict what A said in line 3. A, presumably understanding what B says in this sense, gives a disjointed response which does not immediately (in line 7) appear to address B's comment. In line 8, she appears to locate the outside-the-lift scene inappropriately in 'this room'. However, she may have intended this as the beginning of the narration of the scene in the office, which she then interrupts to address B's question, repeating her original description of the two having gone *in different directions*, and then following this up with a speculation as to why they might do this, thus very effectively denying the possibility that they left 'together' in the sense of having departed in the same direction at the point in the narrative which she has now reached.

A then ventures the speculation that 'the secretive woman' wants a letter which is in the shorter woman's tray. She picks up the narrative again in line 12, still in the present tense, *the shorter woman goes into that room – delivers a letter*. The spatial deictic expression *that room*, appears to be contrastive with the location described as *this room* in line 7 (though, as we suggested in the previous paragraph, it may be the same room, referred to by the anaphoric expression *that room*). The sequencing of *goes into that room* and *delivers a letter* suggests, appropriately, that the first-mentioned action preceded the second-mentioned action. She then predicts that the secretive woman, *the other woman*, will see where the letter has been put (lines 13–14).

B appears to be somewhat bewildered by the intertwining of direct narrative and speculation, and asks *doesn't she see the letter there*, apparently supposing that the other woman is present while the letter is being delivered (and in fact later in the discussion it becomes clear that B has understood that both the other two women are present while the letter is being delivered). A again does not reply directly to B's question. Her *mm*, short, and uttered quite high in her voice range with fairly flat intonation, sounds more like a brief acknowledgement that a question has been asked than an affirmative response. Her *anyway*, spoken quickly, low in her voice range and again with rather flat intonation, seems to suggest that whatever B has just said does not address a relevant point in the narrative, and, still low in her voice range, she mutters *she comes in later*, as if in parenthesis.

She then (lines 17–18) reverts to a pitch higher in her voice range, speaking louder and with greater intonational movement, as she says *but there's that other woman with the – by the telephone* with contrastive emphasis on *other*. She gives no indication that this 'other woman' has not been present in the room throughout the time that the shorter woman was in it. B, as it later turns out, has failed to understand correctly the order in which the three women entered the office. The sense she appears to have made of this account is that all of the women were present throughout this action, that the dark-haired woman was exclusively occupied with the telephone throughout, and that the tall woman was watching the actions of the shorter woman.

We should note that A has used the expression *other woman* three times in the sequence of expressions referring to the three women:

A. line 8 *they* go off in different directions
  9 and 10 presumably that *the other woman* ++ the secretive woman –
      wants a letter
    11 (the shorter one's tray
    12 the shorter one goes into that room)
    13 *the other woman* + she'll know where the
    14 letter is
B. 15 doesn't *she* see the letter
A. 16 *she* comes in later
    17 *that other woman* by the telephone

There is no mention, in her summary, of an initial individual woman who can be differentiated from 'the other woman' mentioned in line 10. She must presumably be supposed to be the non-salient member of the pair of people referred to in line 8 as *they*, the shorter woman. Whether or not B grasps this is not clear. A relates both mentions of 'the other woman' in lines 10 and 13 to the letter, and B continues this relation in her question in line 15, though, since she uses the pronominal form *she*, we cannot be certain that she is referring to the tall fair girl who steals the letter, though it seems reasonable to suppose that she is. In line 16, A must certainly be referring to the tall fair girl because she almost immediately contrasts her with the other woman by the telephone, using a *that* here which may be deictic, since the woman by the telephone is always seen as more distant from the camera, hence further away from the viewers, than the other characters.

We have no reason to suppose that it is simply the non-specific expressions which A uses to refer to the three women which cause difficulty for B, since in each case these non-specific expressions are associated with predicates which could pick out one character uniquely. The problem for B, apparently, does not lie in being unable to distinguish between the participants appropriately but, rather, in not grasping the order in which each of them entered the office to which the airmail letter was delivered by the short fair woman. It seems likely that it is A's mingling of speculation about the characters' motives with her narrative which leads B to suppose that all the characters are present throughout the scene. What little temporal deixis A produces is not particularly helpful. A tells the story in the present tense throughout, except for the scene-setting sentence in line 7: *the scene was just this room.* The sole potentially deictic temporal adverb *then* (line 13) is misleadingly ambiguous, in that it suggests a close link between the delivery of the letter and the tall fair woman's knowledge of where it is: *delivers a letter + then the other woman + she'll know where the letter is.*

6.5 Achieving a shared perspective in the Stolen letter task

The last extract we shall examine while we are looking for the effect of temporal deixis is one of the few narratives in the data which suggests that the speaker has fully understood all the action that she has watched on the video in the way intended by the makers of the video. Her account of events is produced in a manner which is unlikely to mislead a careful listener, though this is not a particularly fluent account. It is produced by an undergraduate subject who is not interrupted at all by her partner during her initial narration. The partner simply sits and constantly nods supportively, but without saying anything at all. This leaves the A-role speaker, during the brief period of narration, with the possibility of planning without being side-tracked into having to confront issues which interest B.

(60) (ug pair 1)
```
 1   in this scene the – erm ++ shows the smaller –
 2   secretary + who was talking in the first scene +
 3   erm + she went to deliver a letter + in one of the
 4   offices ++ erm + as she was ++ putting a letter on
 5   the table she started looking + trying to peep what
 6   was inside the letter + the – she relu- she
 7   reluctantly put the letter on the table ++ as she was
 8   about to go out the other woman came in – the taller
 9   one and another dark-haired lady ++ erm ++ then they
10   have + they exchange a few words erm ++ then both of
11   them went out + both of the clerks + erm + leaving
12   the dark-haired lady in the office and + she was on
13   the telephone
```

Speaker A frames her narrative with the expression *in this scene* which commits her to finding a new subject for the verb, which she appears to think about but then abandons the attempt. She opens in the present tense, setting the scene, and identifies 'the smaller secretary' as one of the two *secretaries* who A and B had watched together as they were talking in the first scene. She then (line 3) shifts to the past tense to describe the series of actions *she went, she started, she . . . put, the other woman came in,* where the principle of **ordo naturalis** leads us to expect that these actions happened in the related order. She shifts into the present tense in line 10 (*have, exchange*) still describing Time A.

It is clear that the switch between present and past tense forms does not reliably indicate a switch between Times A, B and C. Rather it appears to indicate a move from the narrative to the experiential mode. Apart from tensed expressions, two occurrences of potentially deictic *then*, and the deictic expressions *in this scene/ in the first scene,* there is no obvious marking of temporal deixis in this narrative. There are helpful adverbial clauses and

Table 6.1

	6m	6n	6o
outside the lift			
(secs. A & B emerge from lift)	*came out*	*arrive*	*coming out*
(short sec. A leaves)	*walked off*	*go*	*went away*
(tall sec. B leaves)	*walks down*	*go*	*walked along*
into the office			
(A enters office)	*going into*	*goes into*	*went to*
(B enters, with C)	*came in / walked in*	*comes in*	*came in*
(A leaves with B)	*walked out / went back out*	*left*	*went out*

phrases which specify the temporal relations holding between actions: *as she was putting a letter on the table, as she was about to go out, leaving the woman on the telephone.* Apart from this, A relies on ordo naturalis. The use of location-describing expressions is sparse. We are told that the smaller secretary went to deliver a letter 'in one of the offices' with the unspoken assumption that the listener should locate the succeeding action in that office.

In the three excerpts which I have just been discussing, the most striking deictic usage occurs in the selection of verbs such as *come/arrive* versus *go/leave* which indicate a consistent point of view for the observer/speaker in each location, and hence provides a consistent anchor-point for the listener, as shown in Table 6.1.

The picture is quite consistent for the speakers in extracts (6m), (6n) and (6o) – that *come, arrive, walk in* are used of entry into the space (corridor, room or office) which is nearest to the observer in each episode, whereas *go, walked off/out* and *leave* are used as characters leave that space and go out from it to where they can no longer be observed. The only exception, and it is a remarkably consistent exception across the transcripts in this task, is in the case of A entering the office. A possible explanation of this is that in the previous episode outside the lift, A is briefly tracked to a nearby door which she opens, with the apparent intention of entering. In the next episode, she is seen from a viewpoint on the right hand side of the room, where she is already inside the room having come through the door in the right-hand wall, and advancing further in towards the desk on which she will deposit the letter, which means that her left profile and back are presented to the observer. *Go* appears to be the default verb of human motion, which is used when the *go/come* opposition is inoperative (just as the non-proximal forms *that, there, then* are used as the default terms where there is no opposition with *this, here, now*). In the case of A going into the office, where there is a possibility of using the default term, this appears to be preferred.

In the Map tasks, we observed the importance of assuming a deictic construal of *come/go* and related verbs, and interpreting them with respect to a fixed and agreed point of departure (the anchor-point) from which the search field could be viewed. We might suggest here that these verbs perform a similar function in the Stolen letter task, offering the listener a stable vantage point, hence a shared perspective, from which events are to be viewed in each episode. Thus, *come* in this data must be interpreted here as 'come from where they were away from me to where I can (or could) see them' and *go* as 'go from where I could see them to somewhere else'. We shall return to this issue in 6.6.

6.6 How is context constrained in temporally structured tasks?

Hitherto in this chapter, we have explored the role of temporal deixis in constructing a context within which discourse is to be interpreted in a temporally complex task. We have seen that the role of tense appears not to be central with respect to this particular aspect of discourse interpretation, since the choice of past and present tense does not reliably indicate that a speaker is talking about past or present time (though we might propose that it does indicate whether the speaker is talking about past or present *experience*). Similarly we have seen that potentially deictic adverbial expressions, like *now* and *then*, are frequently used quite generally to relate to the structure of the discourse, rather than specifically to progress through a particular time-domain. Speakers then, have to rely heavily on the principle of ordo naturalis to permit their listeners to structure the order of events which they describe.

Whereas temporal deixis plays, as we have seen, a rather restricted role in structuring the narrative for the listener, spatial deixis seems to play a more important role, especially in the sense of indicating what is proximal and what is non-proximal to the observer of the video, when he or she attempts to narrate the observed sequence of events. Just as, in the Map task, expressions which implicitly encode a particular perspective on a location play a very important role, so here, once again, a crucial role appears to be played by formal indicators of perspective on what is being narrated. In the Map task, we developed the idea of a search field which listeners appeared to construct to constrain their searches of the maps. We have so far failed to identify an exact equivalent in the Stolen letter task. We have, however, hypothesised that here, too, the perspective adopted by the speaker plays a role in offering the listener linguistic cues which help to construct a perspectivally structured mental model seen from a point of view from which the listener should be reluctant to move unless there is clear evidence in the speaker's utterance that the time has come to shift.

In this section, we shall consider what cues speakers offer to their listeners that the time has come to shift their current vantage point and survey some fresh aspect of the field. Here I shall borrow the term 'space-builder' from Fauconnier (1985) who proposes that there are some linguistic expressions which function to open up new mental spaces in a discourse representation: 'Language . . . is involved in constructions of its own. It builds up mental spaces, relations between them, and relations between elements within them' (Fanconnier 1985:2). I shall assume that such expressions can act, *inter alia*, as cues to the listener to move to a new vantage point and to survey a new search field.

The features of the Stolen letter video which are significantly liable to change over time are the same features which we have considered in examining the function of deixis – persons (and things), locations and times. We shall examine transcripts of four dialogues, all dealing with the same event. In this event, the tall fair secretary picks up the airmail letter from the desk in the office where the dark woman is talking on the telephone. We shall look in some detail at the first extract and then go on to see how far the account developed for that is generalisable to the three further extracts.

(6p)   (ug pair 1)
1   A. erm + the dark-haired lady + is still on the phone +
2   and – then the taller – clerk came in ++ erm + she –
3   she wanted to deliver a letter as well ++ erm + as
4   she was putting her ++ erm – container – er sort of
5   carrier – on the table + erm + some of the letters
6   accidentally fell + fell out from the container and
7   er + it was ++ she accidentally collected the letter
8   that was originally on the table + and put it inside
9   the container – erm ++ at the same time she also had
10   another letter + for the dark-haired lady ++ erm +
11   but the letter that was on the table had been put
12   back – in the container + erm + the last scene was
13   the lady opening the second letter
14   B. erm the second letter + is that the letter –
15   A. it's not the letter
16   B. it's not the one which we saw on the table

A begins by setting the scene, picking up from the initial episode which A and B had watched together. She might simply have assumed that what is unchanged need not be spoken of, following the principle articulated by Dahl in the following terms: 'Indicate only things that have changed and omit those which are as they were before' (1976:46). However, A states explicitly that things are as they were before, using *still* (what we might call a **space-maintainer**): *the dark-haired lady + is still on the phone*. She goes on to introduce a series of temporal shifts with the space builders: *and* (lines 2, 6, 8) *then* (line 2), *as she was putting her . . . container . . .* (line 4), *that was originally on the table* (line 8), *at the same time* (line 9), *also* (line 9), *that was on the table* (line 11), *had been put back* (lines 11–12), *the last scene was* (line 12).

Just as she indicates temporal shifts, so this A-role speaker regularly indicates spatial shifts (or spatial maintenance), dealing first with the characterisation of the location in which the action occurs, where the dark-haired lady is *on the phone*, and, since she does not indicate any change, we understand that the taller clerk *came in* to the same location where the dark-haired woman was on the phone. A also indicates the location of each salient action and object in a sequence of space builders: *on the table* (lines 5, 8, 11), *out from the container* (line 6), *in(side) the container* (lines 8–9, 12). Once *the container* is located *on the table* (*line 5*), the listener should assume that it remains there until there is some indication that it has moved.

Similarly, this A-role speaker clearly indicates a shift of focus of interest from one character to another by relexicalising after a string of anaphoric pronouns: *the (dark-haired) lady* (lines 1, 10, 13), *the taller clerk* (line 2), *she* (lines 2, 3, 4, 7, 9). And she distinguishes between the two letters in terms of their spatial and temporal history: the first letter is described as *the letter that was (originally) on the table* (lines 7–8, 11), and the second is described as *a letter* (line 3), *another letter* (line 10) and *the second letter* (line 13). In spite of A's attempt to distinguish between the two letters, B is evidently still unsure of whether the second letter is the one she saw on the table (line 14), and she checks this again in defiance of A's pre-emptive denial (line 15), that this is the relevant letter. We may speculate that the problem for B is one that we have identified before, namely that it is difficult to distinguish between entities described by the same expressions simply in terms of their temporal history. Where A-role speakers distinguish between an airmail *letter* on the table and a *package* containing a book which is handed to the dark-haired woman, listeners do not appear to confuse the items.

Having seen how carefully the A-role speaker, in extract (6p), offers cues to the listener as to when to shift the parameters of person, place and time, we shall now turn to look at three further extracts. Note that whereas in extract (6p), the A-role speaker was interacting only with one B-role speaker, in the extracts which follow, each of the main speakers is addressing a second member of the same pair, who watched the same video scenes, as well as the two members of the second pair. In these narratives within quartets, the account often emerges as a duet rather than as a solo turn, since the second member of the pair frequently participates, on some occasions contradicting the first speaker.

(6q)   (quartet 7)
1   A2. we saw the dark-haired lady talking on the phone
2   A1. she was the only one in the office at the time

3	A2.	yeah – there was only her ++ and as we came closer
4		to her + we saw a letter – sitting on the – what
5		was it
6	A1.	it was like a desk + an airmail + it looked like
7		an airmail letter
8	A2.	right + and then the tall lady + came in with a
9		tray ++ and she like + put the tray down + and
10		like all the bits on it like fell off + as if
11		she'd done it on purpose
12	A1.	deliberately + like + she deliberately tips them
13		on all off
14	A2.	yeah + and so as she was picking up all these bits
15		again ++ she took the letter ++ and put it with
16		all the bits ++ and she gave the dark-haired lady
17		+ like + a big package or something didn't she
18	A1.	yeah
19	B1.	there might have been something in the letter or
20		something

(6r)		(quartet 8)
1	B2.	well + after the two – ladies entered – walked –
2		came out of the lift + er + the tall one waited
3		for her friend to go down the corridor + then she
4		turned into a d- into an – office + and walked up
5		to a desk which + with a lady who was talking on
6		the phone
7	B1.	and there was an envelope on the desk
8	B2.	yeah + she then put the + tray which which she was
9		carrying onto ++ the desk + and tipped a load of
10		letters over ++ and ++ picked up + the letter
11		which was already on there ++ she then put all the
12		letters back onto – into the tray including the
13		one which ++ was mm to be on the desk ++
14	B1.	yeah ++ that's what we saw + but the lady went
15		into the office + and gave another lady a letter

16		++ just ++
17	B2.	when she was on the phone
18	B1.	a business letter letter I suppose
19	B2.	and ++ the lady who was on the phone er – opened
20		it up + and found a book + and started reading
21		through the book

(6s)		(quartet 6)
1	A2.	there was ++ the dark haired woman was on the
2		phone + and erm + the letter was on the desk +
3		and the shorter of the two girls erm + came into
4		the office
5	A1.	no it was the taller one
6	A2.	++ no I think she
7	A1.	no – the taller one came in + and she picked up
8		all the letters didn't she
9	A2.	well – she had some letters + and she picked up
10		the letter on the desk anyway
11	A1.	yes + that one that had been put on there + she
12		picked that up as well
13	A2.	and she gave the woman a letter and then went out
14	B2.	what + she picked it up by accident?
15	A2.	yeah – where the woman was on the phone ++ she
16		picked it up by accident
17	A1.	because she was picking up some letters + and +
18		she picked that one up as well

Now let us consider how the speakers provide cues to shifts in the parameters of person, place and time in order that the listener can construct an
appropriate interpretation for these narratives. First of all, the *location* of the
action needs to be identified and to be held constant, unless and until there
is a change in location. Most speakers (a) identify the continued location by
reference to the woman *on the phone* and then (b) they describe the tall secretary as *entering* the same location, the office where the woman on the
phone is talking:

(6p) (a) the dark-haired lady + is still on the phone
    (b) the taller – clerk came in

(6q) (a) the dark-haired lady talking on the phone
    (b) the tall lady + came in with a tray

(6r) (a) (a desk . . .) a lady who was talking on the phone
    (b) the tall one . . . turned into a d- into an office

(6s) (a) the dark-haired woman was on the phone
    (b) the shorter/taller of the two girls – came into the office

Most speakers go on to identify (c) a more constrained location for the letter, using a space-builder which implicitly places it within the office where the dark-haired woman was on the phone, (d) a change of location for the letter, again using a space builder and (e) they relate a second letter (or package) to the dark-haired woman:

(6p) (c) the letter that was originally on the table
    (d) collected the letter . . . and put it inside the container
    (e) she also had another letter + for the dark-haired lady

(6q) (c) (closer to the dark-haired lady) a letter – sitting on the . . . like a desk
    (d) she took the letter ++ and put it with all the bits
    (e) she gave the dark-haired lady + like + a big package

(6r) (c) an envelope on the desk
    (d) picked up the letter . . . put all the letters back . . . into the tray including the one . . .
    (e) into the office + and gave another lady a letter

(6s) (c) she (picked up) the letter on the desk
    (d) she picked up the letter
    (e) she gave the woman a letter

The temporal structure in these extracts is mostly dependent upon the principle of ordo naturalis, where the order of tellings reflects the order of events. Speakers differ in the degree to which they use explicit space-builders like *and* and *then* to shift the event time. However, speakers do generally explicitly indicate durative events or overlapping events, and they generally mark any departure from telling about the order of events as they occurred:

(6p) (a) is still on the phone
    (b) as she was putting her container on the table . . .
    (c) at the same time she also had another letter
    (d) the lady opening the the second letter

(6q) (a) the dark-haired lady talking on the phone
    (b) as we came closer to her
    (c) sitting on the . . . desk
    (d) as she was picking up all these bits again

(6r) (a) a lady who was talking on the phone
    (b) after the two – ladies entered . . .
    (c) the tray which she was carrying
    (d) the letter which was already on there
    (e) when she was on the phone

(6s) (a) the dark-haired woman was on the phone and the letter was on the desk
    (b) that one that had been put on there

In general, a shift in attention from one character to another is marked by relexicalisation:

(6p) (a) the dark-haired lady
    (b) the taller clerk . . . she . . . she . . . she . . . she . . .
    (c) the dark-haired lady . . . the lady

(6q) (a) the dark-haired lady . . . she . . . her . . . her
    (b) the tall lady . . . she . . . she . . . she she . . . she . . . she
    (c) the dark-haired lady

(6r) (a) the two ladies . . . the tall one . . . (her friend) . . . she
    (b) a lady who was talking on the phone
    (c) she . . . she . . . she . . . the lady
    (d) another lady . . . she

(6s) (a) the dark-haired woman
      (b) the shorter of the two girls / the taller one . . . she . . . the taller
          one . . . she . . . she . . . she . . . she . . . she . . . she
      (c) the woman

The only drastically misleading information here is given in extract (6r), where B1 adds at the end of the account of the letter being picked up what appears to be a further example of *ordo naturalis*, (lines 14–15). B1 says *but the lady went into the office + and gave another lady a letter.* This utterance appears to suggest that this was a separate, and later, event of going into the office – an office which is no longer reliably the one previously mentioned, since this appears to be an unrelated event. An interpretation of the incident as a separate event is further supported by the indefinite expressions *another lady* and *a letter.* It seems likely that B1's *but* here is an objection intended to indicate that there has been an omission in B2's account, an omission that B1 wishes to rectify. We might suppose that the other pair might have found it difficult to interpret this passage, but in fact a later attempt by A2 to put together the narrative suggests that he has adequately understood the B narrative, at least in so far as it relates to the tall secretary having given the woman on the telephone a package with a book in it:

(6t)   (quartet 8)
      A2. because the lady in the last + scene opening the letter + and it –
          sealing it again – looked suspicious . . . + as she was putting the
          letter + which you said had a book in it + which the woman was
          reading on the telephone ++ so I think probably + the woman
          with the filing tray + stole something from the letter at the end

6.7 Conclusion

It seems that, if speakers are reasonably careful to use linguistic markers to indicate any shift in focus of attention in terms of person, place or time, listeners can set about achieving an interpretation, in a temporally structured task such as this, in a way that is quite similar to the mode of procedure that we hypothesised to account for the remarkable degree of success achieved by listeners in the Map task, (remarkable given the vagueness of the language produced by the speakers).

Listeners to narratives can, like listeners in procedural tasks, make use of deictic expressions, notably those verbs which relate to the proximal/non-proximal distinction, particularly *come* and *go,* to align their perspective with that of the speaker from the same vantage point, very much in the way that listeners in the Map task identified the anchor-point that the speaker had in mind, and remained there while they searched in the proximate search field until they were confident of the the next move. Listeners to narratives can also make use of personal, temporal and spatial indicators of any shift in the speaker's focus of interest to build a new mental space, related as closely as possible to the previous scenario. We might suggest that it is the alignment of perspective on situations and events which permits the listener to form an interpretation which does, indeed, frequently yield a thought which is sufficiently similar to that of the speaker to permit communication to be largely successful.

Finally, we should note that these listeners, like listeners in the everyday world, were not simply gleaning information from a single source, from a series of spoken utterances. They were engaged in trying to make sense of what was said in the light of their own independent knowledge. Problems for listeners arise not just from the relative vagueness or complexity of linguistic expressions, but of how what is said relates to the listener's perception, or memory, of states of affairs in the world.

7 · The listener and discourse comprehension

7.1 Listener roles

7.1.1 Accounts of listener roles

The standard account of the communicative situation, as I remarked in 1.6, envisages a single speaker addressing a single listener, where the role of the listener is seen as understanding what the speaker says, and the listener's full attention is given to what is being said (see Goffman 1981:129 for a characterisation of such a traditional view). We have seen, in the Map task data, that listeners may have intentions and goals in listening which are, to a greater or lesser degree, independent of those of the speaker. We have observed the same phenomenon in the Stolen letter task data, but here we noted as well that different listeners in a group listen in different ways.

Goffman draws our attention to three different types of listener: 'those who *over*hear, whether or not their unratified participation is inadvertent and whether or not it has been encouraged; those (in the case of more than two-person talk) who are ratified participants but are not specifically addressed by the speaker; and those ratified participants who *are* addressed'(1981:9–10). Addressees are particularly oriented to by the speaker and will be the persons designated to respond in an appropriate manner to what the speaker says. Later in the same volume, Goffman writes 'the relation(s) among speaker, addressed recipient and unaddressed recipient(s) are complicated, significant, and not much explored' (1981:133).

In an attempt to explore some of these relations, Clark, together with various associates, mounted a series of experiments, reported in Clark and Carlson (1982), Clark and Schaefer (1987), and Schober and Clark (1989). In the last of these papers, Schober and Clark report an experiment in which they constructed a task where a speaker (A) instructed a listener (B) to lay out a series of twelve figures on a sorting frame in the order in which they were presented on A's frame. (The figures were black cut-out figures (Tangram figures), capable of being interpreted metaphorically in many different ways, rather as ink-blots can be interpreted metaphorically in many ways.) A and B were so arranged that they could not see each other. Also present in the room was an overhearer (C), concealed behind a further screen, who A and B were told was present to reduce experimental bias. In fact, the task C had been given was exactly the same as that of B – in both cases, they were supposed to match the order of the figures on A's frame. B and C had identical sets of figures, and both of them heard everything that A and B said, as it was said. Neither B nor C could see A, as A spoke. The difference in their situations was that B spoke to A, and was directly addressed by A, whereas C did not speak at all, and was never directly addressed by either of the other two participants.

In this experiment, the B subjects completed the task significantly more accurately than the C subjects. Over a series of trials, the B subjects placed their figures correctly with increasing speed, as they succeeded in establishing each referent in conversation with A, whereas the overhearers showed a significantly larger range of variation in the timing of the placing of the figures. Schober and Clark conclude that addressees understand faster and more accurately than overhearers. Why should this be?

Schober and Clark suggest that the traditional view of how listeners process is what they call **the autonomous view**, where each listener decodes each utterance and interprets it against what they take to be the common ground, or mutual knowledge, of the participants in the conversation. Against this view, they propose another, which they call **the collaborative view**. In this view, speakers and listeners do more than simply process autonomously. They actively collaborate with each other to ensure that understanding takes place, and they do not proceed with the conversation unless they feel secure in having achieved mutual understanding up to that point. These authors suggest that, if the autonomous view were correct, addressees and overhearers should both interpret utterances in the same manner, since they have access to exactly the same information. They explain the difference in the performance of the B and C subjects in the experiment by suggesting that it is the collaboration between A and B, a collaboration which is denied to C, which enables the B subjects, the addressees, to perform so much better on this task than the overhearers.

Schober and Clark draw attention to three differences in the conversational opportunities available to the B subjects (addressees) but not to the C subjects (overhearers). I summarise my reading of these below:

(1) **monitoring of understanding**: B can indicate to A what is obscure or uninterpretable in what A has said, or B can indicate with expressions such as *yes* or *right*, that B has interpreted A's expression. C has no opportunity to comment on difficulties which may be different from B's, or to indicate that what has been said can now be treated as agreed.

(2) **criterion of understanding**: B can determine the moment at which B's understanding of what A has said is adequate, depending on B's judgment of what is adequate in this context, which may of course be different from C's. Schober and Clark report that the overhearers complained that the conversations between A and B *went too fast*, and that the pacing of the conversation was inappropriate for C, who was *forced to rush on to the next figure whether or not I'd gotten the previous one*, or, in another case, *would fall behind and forget what needed to be filled in*.

(3) **perspective**: A and B can search for a common perspective, a shared way of conceiving of each figure. B can introduce a perspective as long as A agrees with it. C is denied any input to the process of establishing a perspective as shared, and may simply fail to perceive a likeness which A and B agree on.

Those subjects who took the role of overhearer frequently complained, after the experiment, that they felt frustrated at not being in control of the pacing of the input of new information, and at not being able to contribute to the discussion of the way the figures might be interpreted. Schober and Clark propose that the results of this experiment suggest that the social process of interaction, which is manifested in the behaviour summarised above, plays a central role in the cognitive process of understanding.

It is important to be clear that Schober and Clark, in opposing the autonomous processing view to the collaborative processing view, are concerned only with distinguishing between what the two approaches assume as input to the process of understanding. There is no suggestion that the resultant understanding is somehow located in a publicly available mutual space, rather than in the individual mind of each participant (a view often apparently associated with the expression **negotiation of meaning**, see, for instance, Varonis and Gass 1985). As Locke remarked: 'Man, though he have great variety of thoughts, and such from which others as well as himself might receive profit and delight; yet they are all within his own breast, invisible and hidden from others, nor can of themselves be made to appear' ([1689] 1971:259).

7.1.2 Listener roles in the Map task

The structure of interaction in the Map task may be characterised in terms of the traditional speaker-listener interaction, where there are only two significant participants, each of whom takes turns at speaking and at listening. Of course, there is also an overhearer present, the experimenter. However, this brand of ratified overhearer is not obliged to complete an interpretation of what is said then and there, as the discourse unrolls, in the way that Schober and Clark's overhearers had to, because the fact that the discourse is recorded permits the experimenter, *qua* analyst, to listen and re-listen to the taped conversation, to transcribe the conversation, to compare it with other similar conversations and to consider it as often as necessary on later occasions (a repetitive process which almost certainly leads to an awareness of detail which would not have been available to the original participants). The analyst of the Map task data also has the advantage of knowing what the facts-of-the-matter were that each speaker had been presented with, though not how, or how far, the speaker had perceived and understood that information. As Schutz remarks: 'The observer's scheme of interpretation cannot be identical with the interpretive scheme of either partner in the social relation observed. The modifications of attention which characterise the attitude of the observer cannot coincide with those of a participant in an ongoing social relation . . . what he finds relevant is not identical with what they find relevant' (1964:36).

We can perceive traces of the collaborative procedures identified by Schober and Clark in much of the Map task data. Extract (7a) will serve as a reminder. This is an extract which exemplifies the processes referred to by Schober and Clark with remarkable clarity:

(7a)   (TR & MP)

1   A. go down a little bit – past the tree
2   B. hang on + hang on + (*mutters*) go down
3   A. no – just go across + and past the tree
4   B. across what side
5   A. right
6   B. hang on
7   A. past the tree
8   B. hang on
9   A. round – the
10 B. hang on ++ past the tree
11 A. yeah
12 B. yeah
13 A. round the – lake
14 B. round the little thing
15 A. yeah
16 B. (*mutters*) round it
17 A. yeah
18 B. yeah

Monitoring of understanding: Both members of this pair constantly indicate whether or not they have understood what was said by the other speaker. B indicates that she has understood what A has said by explicitly repeating A's words (on two occasions muttering as if to herself, but by this expedient informing A that she has heard what A said): *go down* (line 2), *across* (line 4), *past the tree* (line 10), and by apparently paraphrasing A's expression in *round the little thing* (line 14) and *round it* (line 16). Her repetition, in line 2, of *go down*, provokes A into a modification of her first instruction, a modification which she might well not have made in the absence of B's response. When each speaker supposes that they are both now in possession of the same information, they say *yeah* (lines 11, 12, 15, 17 18).

Criterion of understanding: It is helpful here to recall the distinction drawn by Clark and Clark between 'constructing an interpretation' and 'utilising an interpretation' which was introduced in 2.2 (Clark and Clark 1977:45). It is not sufficient for B, in this task, simply to understand the content of A's utterances, she must be able to put them to use in the world, as represented here by the map in front of her. Her **criterion of understanding** will require that she complete the putting to use, the drawing of the route on her map, before she can acknowledge that she believes that her information is sufficiently congruent with that of A for her to continue with the next step on the route. Thus, although A, in the extract here, is merely reiterating what she has said twice already when, in line 7, she says *past the tree,* B nonetheless repeats *hang on* in line 8 because she has not yet finished drawing her route. Only when she has, to her own satisfaction, completed the drawing of her route, does she echo A's *yeah* in line 12. It is clear that it is the listener here who controls the amount of information which A can effectively deliver at one time, just as we saw in extract (3f), where the undergraduate listener, on five occasions, did not pay attention to A's mention of 'the woods', but waited until she had completed her drawing to her own satisfaction before saying *wait a minute what did you say about woods?* It is the listener who controls the timing and flow of uptake of what A says. The co-operative A speaker, like the A-role speakers in (3f) and (7a), adjusts the amount of information provided in each utterance to the amount that B can accommodate, and waits to hear that B has finished putting the most recent set of information to use, before adding new information.

Perspective: Even in this short extract we can see how A and B work together to achieve a shared **perspective** on the information they are discussing. A adjusts her direction in line 3, *just go across + and past the tree,* and B immediately checks the side of the tree she should go past. A replies with a deictic *right,* which enables B to approach the tree from the appropriate direction. When A, in line 13, says *round the lake,* B must see that she could go round the nearest feature which could be characterised as 'a lake' (though most subjects refer to this feature using the expression *a pond*), or the more distant and much larger lake which has a yacht on it. She presumably sees that A's instruction is potentially ambiguous and offers *round the little thing* as a way of achieving disambiguation, which yields a shared perspective on the nature of the referent.

It is certainly the case that those pairs who behaved in such a collaborative manner in undertaking the Map task were much more likely to achieve a map drawn by B which in most respects resembled A's original map, than those pairs who did not collaborate in this way (see, for instance, the discussion in 3.5.4 of extracts (3h) – (3k), where the A-role participant in particular behaved in an uncollaborative manner, and the resulting route-drawing by B was relatively less successful).

7.1.3 Listener roles in the Stolen letter task

The six versions of the Stolen letter task which derive from two undergraduates working together, in many ways resemble the patterns of interaction in the Map task. Once again, there are two people talking to each other, exchanging information, each taking turns as speaker and listener, and once again, there is an experimenter who sits to one side and does not participate in the conversation, who may be classified as a ratified overhearer in Goffman's terms. The pair interaction in this task does contain an additional element, missing from the Map task, and that is the joint attempt to reconstitute the entire narrative, once each member of the pair has recounted what he or she has watched. Since this joint attempt resembles, in many of its crucial features, the joint attempt in the quartet groups, it will not be discussed separately.

Much more interesting from the point of view of interaction, and much more complex than the pair interactions, are those versions of the task which were undertaken by members of quartets working co-operatively together. An initial characterisation of the different participant roles was introduced in 5.2. Here we shall concentrate on the various listener roles, ignoring that of the experimenter, since we have already commented on that in 5.2.

The listener roles vary at different points of the discourse. In the initial phase, one pair is responsible for narrating to the other pair the content of the episode which they alone have seen. This phase is followed by an equivalent narration by the second pair informing the first pair about what they have seen. After this narration phase comes a discernible shift in format, as the participants move into a discussion stage. In this stage, all four members of the quartet typically participate, asking and answering questions, and speculating about the possible order of the scenes which they have witnessed. This stage generally merges imperceptibly with a final stage where one individual attempts to narrate the entire sequence of events, assisted by the other members of the quartet. However this final narration is typically interspersed with questions and checks, and interpolations from other speakers, all of whom may wish to add their mite to the narrative. This phase, where all the participants have now seen, or heard about, the entire narrative, differs rather little from the main discussion phase in terms of manner of interaction. The major difference lies between the initial narration stage and what follows.

7.1.3.1 *The initial narration phase*

Our expectation might be that, in the initial narration stage, one member of a pair is nominated, or self-selected, to undertake the narration of that pair's episode to the members of the second pair, who appear likely to be the primary addressees. The second member of the pair must be, necessarily, a ratified listener, but not obviously a primary addressee. The role of the second member appears to be conceptualised by some participants simply as **observer**, since they play no part in the narration and make no comment upon its accuracy. By the majority of second members, however, it appears to be conceptualised as **critical listener plus potential side-narrator** or even as **co-narrator**. If we consider again part of extract (6q), now renumbered as (7b), we can observe how A1 listens to what A2 says, evaluates it against her own memory of the episode, and supplements it:

7b   (quartet 7)
1   A2. we saw the dark-haired lady talking on the phone
2   A1. she was the only one in the office at the time
3   A2. yeah – there was only her ++ and as we came closer

4		to her + we saw a letter – sitting on the – what
5		was it
6	A1.	it was like a desk ++ an airmail + it looked
7		like an airmail letter
8	A2.	right + and then the tall lady + came in with a
9		tray ++ and she like + put the tray down + and
10		like all the bits on it like fell off + as if
11		she'd done it on purpose
12	A1.	deliberately + like

A1 knows as much as any other person could about what A2 is trying to express, and her first utterance in line 2 shows that she has understood A2's opening statement. A2, having in her turn as listener heard A1's additional information, confirms its correctness in line 3 by paraphrasing what A1 said, echoing the use of *only*. It seems reasonable to suggest that, at this point, A2 is directly addressing A1, and confirming the correctness of her addition, and simultaneously informing the B pair of the correctness of A1's addition. A2 continues the narrative in lines 3–4, but then turns directly to A1, as primary addressee, for help, which A1 appropriately provides, *it was like a desk*, seeming to indicate, by her use of *like*, a sympathy with A2's problem in identifying the piece of furniture. She addresses A2 directly, but simultaneously informs the B pair how the piece of furniture could be characterised. At this point the dialogue appears to be a publicly enacted conversation where A2 and A1 are, in turn, speaker and the intended primary addressee, and the B pair are the intended secondary addressees for whose benefit the performance is being put on. A1 immediately continues with an additional piece of information, that the letter was an airmail letter, presumably primarily addressed to the B pair. A2 apparently acknowledges to A1, and confirms to the B pair, the correctness of this observation, saying *right*, and then again resumes the narrative, apparently now encouraged by A1's use of *like* in line 7 to modify descriptions which she feels are inexact in a similar manner, a use echoed again by A1 in line 12, where she appears to reinforce A2's *on purpose* by adding *deliberately* + *like*, this time, presumably, primarily addressing the B pair.

Each of these participants, in her turn as speaker, indicates that she has fully understood what the previous speaker has said. Each is thoroughly co-operative as a listener and as a speaker, maintaining her appropriate role. A2, in her speaking turns, maintains the role of principal narrator, in charge of introducing the next event into the narration, whereas A1 in her speaking turns maintains the role of side-narrator, helping when appealed to, and adding further detail to what A2 has already said, but not introducing new events into the discourse.

It is noticeable that between these two speakers, each of whom, we may suppose, knows pretty well what the other knows about the events, in broad terms at least, there is not a great deal of the overt collaborative work of the sort that we saw so amply illustrated in extract (7a). A2 does occasionally acknowledge the correctness of what A1 says (lines 3 and 8), but there is otherwise no apparent checking of correctness here. A1 presumably has some standard of adequacy of information as empathetically seen from the B pair's point of view, which is perhaps why she adds additional information, but this is a very different enterprise from that which the addressee B was embarked on in extract (7a), where B's own level of information was at issue. There seems to be no attempt by either A2 or A1 to control the pacing of information in this conversation – that would appropriately come, if at all, from the B pair. So far as perspective is involved, A1 seems anxious only to refine what A2 says for the B pair's benefit, rather than to agree with A2 about the appropriacy of what A2 says.

Compare the behaviour of this A-role pair with that of a similar pair in part of extract (6s), here renumbered (7c).

```
7c      (quartet 6)
 1  A2. there was ++ the dark-haired woman was on the
 2      phone + and erm + the letter was on the desk +
 3      and the shorter of the two girls erm + came into
 4      the office
 5  A1. no – it was the taller one
 6  A2. ++ no I think she
 7  A1. no + the taller one came in + and she picked up all
 8      the letters didn't she
 9  A2. well – she had some letters + and she picked up the
```

10   letter on the desk anyway
11   A1. yes + that one that had been put on there + she
12   picked that up as well

A2 begins the narration (lines 1–4) but then A1, in line 5, contradicts what A2 has just said. Here A1 directly addresses A2, while simultaneously informing the B pair that A2 has made an error. A2, in line 6, begins to deny the correctness of what A1 said, presumably similarly addressing A1 and informing the B pair, but is cut off by A1 reiterating the point that it was *the taller one* who came in. A1 then introduces the next piece of action, apparently now acting as co-narrator and informing the B pair what happened, but then, in line 8, turns to A2 and, directly addressing A2, asks him to confirm the correctness of this report. In asking A2 for confirmation in this way, A1 may be acknowledging A2's right to be principal narrator, a right which A1 has transgressed, or tacitly apologising for overtly contradicting what A2 said earlier, or both of these, or neither. A1's intentions are necessarily opaque, and there seems no good reason to suppose that A2 has privileged access to them. A2 replies directly to A1 in line 9, not fully supporting A1's report, and making this lack of support known to the B pair, and then resumes the narrative. A1 in 11–12, enthusiastically confirms the correctness of A2's description, now playing the role of side-narrator and simply adding further detail, perhaps still trying to placate A2, and presumably intending the B pair to benefit from his additional information.

In this extract too, there is little indication of the listeners collaboratively indicating clarity or lack of clarity in what the other speaker says, and there does not appear to be an issue of the pacing of the delivery of information. The problem which arises here is one of perspective, where the correctness, rather than the amount, of information is at issue, since each of the two members of the pair believes that a different individual came into the room at the relevant moment. This difference of view is indicated by *no*, uttered in each of lines 5, 6 and 7, as well as by the different characterisations provided by the two speakers. It is not clear whether A2 actually changes his mind and believes A1's view of events, or whether he is simply overborne at this point in the conversation (a problem which was discussed in 5.6 and 5.7).

On the basis of this initial narration data, we can see that it is not possible to draw a simple distinction between direct addressee and overhearer which will hold throughout a conversation. The question of the identity of the addressee of a particular utterance is not a simple one, as Goffman (1981:133, cited in 7.1.1) suggested. We can see also that the roles of each listener, particularly those of the members of the A pair, appear to change, to some degree, almost on an utterance by utterance basis. Most strikingly, we observe the difference in the role adopted by the listener who is experiencing the information for the first time, as the B role listener was in extract (7a), (and see also many further examples of this in extracts in chapters 3 and 4) where the discourse is relatively dense with collaborative markers of the type discussed by Schober and Clark (1989), as against listeners who are critically attending to accounts of an episode which they themselves independently know about (illustrated in extracts (7b) and (7c), and further examples in chapters 5 and 6). Here the listeners are apparently more concerned that the details of the narration should accord with their own memories of events and that the details should be adequate, in their empathetic judgment, for the purposes of the B pair.

A further point should be made here. It frequently seems impossible, in this data, to determine just what the speaker's intention in uttering is. This is particularly the case when members of the A pair conduct a side conversation during the course of the narrative. Are they, in fact, simply concerned with checking the details of the episode with each other at that moment, with the other member of the pair as sole intended addressee, or are they in fact (or simultaneously) intending to address the members of the B pair, and to inform them of the status of the information under discussion? This is an issue which we shall return to in 7.3.

7.1.3.2 *The discussion (and final narration) phase*

During the discussion phase, all four members of the quartet converse as long as they like, to check up on what they have not understood and to try to make sense of the series of events. In extract (7d), B2 has just completed an initial narration, having already heard the A pair's narration. (This quartet had been told in advance that somebody would be stealing something.)

(7d)   (quartet 7)
 A2. what happened to the + letter + the airmail letter thing
 B2. the letter + she put on the desk
 A1. the short hair – so the short-haired lady had the letter ++ or + or
   the letter was already there
 B2. no + she had the letter
 A2. she had the letter + she had a good look at that
 B2. she came in with a letter in the basket
 A2. and then put it down
 B2. yeah + before anyone else entered + she put it on the desk

The A pair is checking their understanding of the B pair's narration. A2 begins by relating her first question back to the airmail letter, presumably wondering whether this might be the airmail letter which was picked up by the tall fair woman in the episode which the A pair had watched. Her question seems to be directly addressed to B2. B2 certainly assumes that she is addressed, echoing part of the expression *the letter* and then answering A2's question. A1 then addresses B2 and checks her impression that the short-haired lady had the letter but she goes on to propose an alternative possibility. B2 collaboratively replies, again echoing part of what A1 said, and explicitly rejects A1's proposed alternative *no – she had the letter*. A2 now echoes B2's utterance, presumably indicating that this point is now established as common ground for them all, and adds a new inference of her own. It is not clear whether she is addressing B2 or the entire group at this moment, since no-one appears to be expected to reply to this utterance and no-one does so. B2 speaks again, still sticking to the original point, and making it clear that the fair-haired girl had come in *with a letter in the basket* (using an indefinite expression, rather oddly, to characterise this much discussed letter, as though reverting to an earlier point in the narrative). A2 collaboratively repeats an appropriate detail from B2's earlier narrative, which B2 assents to, and then adds the information that no-one else was present at this point.

During this part of the discussion, B1 remains a silent overhearer of the transaction, who may or may not be paying attention to all of what is said. Each of the A speakers directly addresses B2 when she speaks, while informing her own partner (if she is listening) of the content of her current question or speculation. When B2 replies, she replies to the question she has been asked and her addressee then becomes the person who asked the question. In answering the question, B2 also informs the other member of the A pair of the information contained in her answer.

In an earlier section, in extract (7b), we saw the co-operative behaviour of the A pair in this quartet, which involved rather little explicitly collaborative language. We see now, in extract (7d), how the participants carefully secure their understanding of each important detail of the plot when, as listeners, they are trying to understand something which someone else knows, but which they themselves have no first-hand knowledge of. Their informant, B2, is strikingly collaborative in meshing her replies to their questions, repeatedly using the same expressions as those used by the A pair, thus making it very clear that she has listened to and understood the question, and is prepared to adopt the same perspective on the incident as the questioner. In this discussion, the participants seem to be behaving more like the participants in the Map task, extract (7a), than they themselves behaved in the earlier narration phase of this task.

Finally, in this section, let us consider part of a final narration section which, typically, includes some discussion. A2 has volunteered to attempt a complete account of the narrative.

```
(7e)     (quartet 3)
 1  A2.  right + there's two women – one with a tray ++
 2       and the other one was carrying a folder ++ the
 3       one with the tray walked slowly down to the +
 4       room + where you saw her walk in ++ 'n she put
 5       a letter on the desk +++ at that time + the –
 6       taller blonde lady – seen in the last scene +
 7       and a dark-haired lady ++ came in +++ the
 8       dark-haired lady went straight to the telephone
 9       + started talking on – the on the telephone +++
10       I don't think – it had anything to do with finding
11       her there + or or anything ++ it was just
12       something she had to do ++ whilst the tall
```

13		blonde lady was + talking + to the woman with the
14		tray ++ at that point they both left + and then ++
15	B1.	she went back in there
16	B2.	the tall one + the tall one returned
17	A2.	yeah ++ the tall one returned and they made the
18		switch with the letter
19	B2.	she didn't actually switch it did she ++
20		what she did was + she spilt the letters on top
21		of the one –
22	B1.	yeah
23	B2.	– that was already on there + and gave the woman
24		+ a different letter back
25	A2.	and gave the woman a bigger letter with a book in
26		it
27	B1.	yeah
28	A2.	so anyway ++ she's switched them over hasn't she
29	B2.	well ++ she gave the woman on the phone a book to
30		probably + keep her occupied + while she took the
31		other one

A2 is telling the narrative to three listeners all of whom, in principle at least, know all of it, having either experienced it directly or been told about it. He incorporates, as many narrators do in this data, his own view of why the dark-haired lady went directly to the telephone (lines 10–12), in what seems to be a persistent search for causality and intention in human affairs. (Presumably his comment may be understood as meaning that the dark-haired woman was not telephoning the police or security officers in alarm at finding somebody in her room.) His listeners do not comment on his account but, as soon as he appears to be in doubt about how to continue, B1 offers a prompt (line 15) *she went back in there*, which makes good sense at this point, suggesting that B1 has adequately followed what A2 said. B2 then offers an explicit gloss on B1's formulation *the tall one + the tall one returned*, specifying which of the two women who had left the office had returned to it. It seems clear that, at this point, B2's remark adds little to the information which ought to be generally available to the quartet. It is not clear whether or not he has a specific addressee in mind, or whether he is simply anxious to keep the record straight in the public domain of the discussion, since there have already been disagreements earlier in the discussion about which woman did what.

A2 explictly agrees with what B2 suggested in line 17, echoing the same expression, *the tall one returned,* – and then adds the point about *the switch* of the letters. Earlier in the discussion, A2 introduced the term *switch* and the B pair had cavilled at this usage (transcribed in extract (5r)), and B2 again here, as he did earlier, suggests that the woman *spilt* the letters from the basket on top of the letter on the desk, and gave a different letter to the woman on the telephone. B1 (who in (5r) was the first to object to the term *switch)* supports this description. A2 agrees with the second part of B2's suggestion (lines 25–6) but then in line 28 resumes the use of the divisive term *switch.* B2, in line 29, appears to concede this description of events rather reluctantly, *well,* and goes on to make a new suggestion about the intention of the fair-haired woman in offering the (package with the) book to the dark-haired woman. The perspective on this action is clearly not fully shared, but each of the three speakers at this point must be fairly clear about what the other speakers' preferred terms mean with respect to this moment in the action – the action itself is apparently agreed.

Even in data as simple as this, we can begin to see how complex the listener's role may be in multi-party conversations. The listener may choose to take no active part in the conversation, simply playing the part of ratified non-participating observer. The listener may, more or less often, be selected by the speaker as the direct addressee who is invited to take the role of next speaker. The listener may be directly addressed as one of a plurality of addressees, who will self-select among themselves for the next turn of speaking, or take a role as one who is indirectly addressed while some other participant is directly addressed.

As someone who needs to know the information being expressed in the speaker's utterance, the active and collaborative listener must ensure that any reference to some crucial person or event is understood. To this end, the listener may, in the next turn of speaking, check with the previous speaker, either by reiterating what the speaker said (sometimes, but rarely in this data, with rising intonation – more often by adding a tag question), sometimes by reformulating what the previous speaker said in a manner which the current speaker prefers, sometimes by asking a direct question. In this narrative and discussion data, where the notion of the 'putting to use' of information can only relate to mental reflection, there is no sign of the control of pacing of the input of information of the sort which we saw in (7a), the extract from the Map task, where 'putting to use' involved applying the information out in the world, on the map. (It may be noted that it is the Map task data which most closely resembles the data described by Schober and Clark 1989.)

It seems clear that the striking change in the behaviour of listeners in terms of the amount of explicit agreement, checking, control of pacing and so on which we have observed in this chapter, depends upon how much of the information being spoken of is already known to the listener. This brings us to the vexed issue of common ground, mutual beliefs, or shared context which we shall address in the next section.

7.2 Shared context and shared information

7.2.1 Mutual knowledge and mutual beliefs
One of the many reasons why people talk to each other is to exchange information. The data discussed in this book exemplifies some aspects of this kind of communication. In a rational account of the exchange of information, we might suggest that a speaker, A, would construct an utterance to inform a listener, B, of some information which A knew, and believed would be interesting or useful to B, but believed that B did not know. It is, presumably, rarely the case in adult life that A simply frames an informative utterance and utters it, without giving any thought at all to the listener's state of information. The problem for A (of which A may be more, or less, aware) is how to construct the utterance so that the relevant information is made accessible to B, and can fit into B's existing structures of knowledge and belief. To do this, an ideal speaker will consider what B might already know which relates to this supposedly new information. In turn, an ideal listener will interpret what A says, not only in the light of what B already knows, but also in the light of what B knows, or believes, about A's own state of knowledge and belief.

The value for the listener, in considering what the speaker is likely to know while framing an interpretation of the utterance, is that this consideration may constrain the potential interpretation. Thus, for instance, the listener may know three people named Sarah and the speaker may refer to someone called Sarah without, in the predicate, indicating information which would allow the listener to select between the potential referents. If the listener takes no account of what the listener believes the speaker knows, the listener would now be forced to ask the speaker which Sarah is being referred to, or take a risk in assuming it is a particular one of the three. However, if the listener believes that the speaker only knows one of the three Sarahs whom the listener knows, and takes this into account while constructing the interpretation, the expression *Sarah* should unequivocally refer to that single Sarah who, the listener believes, is known to both speaker and listener.

We have seen, in 7.1, that participants in a conversation in which information is being exchanged, do not simply swap utterance tokens which contain new information. They spend a good deal of time ensuring that the other speaker is made aware of their own relevant information state, in checking the other speaker's information state, in trying to ensure that the other speaker adopts the same perspective on information and in attempting to relate the new information which they have just been made aware of to existing information.

What I want the informal term **existing information** to imply is, in part at least, equivalent to Sperber and Wilson's notion of **total cognitive environment**: 'An individual's total cognitive environment is the set of all the facts that he can perceive or infer . . . An individual's total cognitive environment is a function of his physical environment and his cognitive abilities. It consists of not only all the facts that he is aware of, but also all the facts that he is capable of becoming aware of' (1986:39). I would want to suggest, however, that knowledge of 'facts' (of the thoroughly secure 2+2=4 kind) probably constitutes a rather minor part of an individual's cognitive environment. Much more significant, surely, are **beliefs**, which may, of course, be mistaken, or partial, or biased because, for instance, they are founded on prejudice, but in all cases they represent what we believe we know as filtered through our individual intelligence, experience, and more-or-less adequate sense organs.

The issue of whether or not some form of mutual knowledge or mutual belief is necessary to communication, and, in particular, to the interpretation of utterances, has been warmly debated over the last twenty years (see papers in Smith (ed.) 1982). Proponents of the necessity of some form of mutual knowledge include Lewis 1969, Clark and Marshall 1981, and Schiffer 1972; opponents include Johnson-Laird 1983, and Sperber and Wilson 1986. I shall assume that mutual **knowledge** is too strong a requirement in any case (see arguments in chapter 1, and *passim*). Mutual knowledge is sometimes equated with common ground (see Clark and Marshall 1981), and/or with the notion of shared context as discussed by Downes (1984). Given the position I laid out in chapter 1, I assume that the strongest requirement that might be of interest is that of assumed mutual **belief**, a position which is quite close to that of Clark and Carlson 1982. However, I think they still hope to lay a foundation for a relatively risk-free account of communication, whereas I have argued throughout this book that communication is, in principle, risky, once we move beyond regular and familiar utterances of the type *did you lock the front door?* Kasher helpfully suggests that we should consider mutual belief as being hypothesised by participants in a conversation 'in the sense that it involves evidence and support rather than proof and certainty' (1991:573).

The notion of context typically brings in large-scale social/ethnographic issues such as knowledge of use of a particular language, knowledge of how to participate in a conversation, knowledge of how to be polite, knowledge of what to expect from a particular speaker (or type of speaker), knowledge of genres, etc. The general context must also include the encyclopaedic knowledge expected of all the participants, what Venneman (1975:314) calls the **presupposition pool**. Such features, taken together, it is often claimed, permit the listener to predict the type of language, the type of topic, the type of comment to expect. And, indeed, it seems likely that any of us confronted with a 4 year-old child would expect a given range of language and interests which would be different from those of a 14 year-old and, again, from those of a 40 year-old. Kasher points out that commands are performed 'within a certain hierarchy, whether formal or not, which grants certain speakers some authority with respect to others' (1991:579). The more knowledge we have of the speaker, the more confidently we feel able to interpret what the speaker says appropriately. Note that here I speak both of prediction of what the listener may expect before any utterance, and of interpretation, which is bound to follow (at least part of) the utterance. I mean by prediction only expectation of a very general kind, what you brace yourself for, the mental set that you adopt towards this particular addresser on this occasion, rather than specification of the detail of the form or content of the immediately following utterance – though with some thoroughly familiar speakers even this, in some contexts, is possible, as when one is able to complete an utterance which a stuttering speaker has barely begun.

It seems clear that the notion of mutual beliefs, or of the shared context, must apply rather differently to different participant roles in an interaction. When Bennett (1976:181) writes 'there may be many hearers, but there is only one hearer's *role*' he ignores not only the various intentions in listening which may be attributed to the different ratified participants, hearers directly addressed, hearers indirectly addressed and overhearers, but also just what the speaker may expect these diverse listeners to know. Most writers would agree that the speaker, in constructing the message for the listener, must take into account what may be expected to be shared, since it would be, in principle, quite impossible for a speaker to be explicit about all possible details of background information. The standard view, for instance, suggests that information which the listener is not expected to know should be fully specified, whereas information which the listener is expected to know about can be minimally specified. (See discussion in 1.6.1 about appropriate ways of referring to individuals mentioned for the first time in a conversation, and in 3.4 about the use of indefinite expressions.)

From the listener's point of view, there are scholars who suppose that there are some types of knowledge of the context which will predispose the listener to limit expectations of what an utterance might contain before it is uttered (most importantly, knowledge of who the speaker is, mentioned above). Others, for instance Sperber and Wilson (1986), insist that the listener does not need to have any access to knowledge of the context before interpreting the utterance, but will construct whatever context is necessary after the utterance, during the process of interpretation.

We must be careful to distinguish that set of knowledge and beliefs which alone makes possible the interpretation of an utterance, and the interpretation itself.

7.2.2 What the listener knows in the Map task

The striking feature of many claims made in the literature on mutual knowledge and beliefs, is that they are based on data invented to support a particular line of argument. One advantage of the Map task is that it offers us data (albeit, as I repetitively point out, of a restricted kind) which allows us to explore, at least for this data, how far mutual beliefs appear to be relevant to the processes of a listener understanding what the speaker said. We can examine what information is plausibly available to the listener before hearing an utterance, and what the hearer might plausibly be held to know after having interpreted the utterance.

In 2.3, I introduced a Map task transcript with an annotation which was intended to indicate what information about the task in hand was available to each participant at the end of each turn of speaking. I shall introduce part of this transcript again now, renumbered as (7f).

(7f)   (R and H)

	A.	(A/B)	B	(B/A)
A. do you have the start marked	+	?	+	+
B. yes	+	+	+	+
A. all right	+	+	+	+
+ do you have palm trees?	+	?	+	+
B. + yes	+	+	+	+
A. right	+	+	+	+
+ the swamp?	+	?	?	+
B. ++ what swamp	+	?	?	+
A. + to the – left of the palm trees	+	?	–	+
B. no	+	–	–	+

The columns under A and B represent what A and B could each see (or not) on his own map. The columns under A/B and B/A represent what each could have learned in the previous utterance from what the other speaker said about what the other speaker has on his map. Thus B could (and apparently does) infer from the fact that A asks whether B has 'the start', 'palm trees' and 'the swamp' that A has those features marked on his map. When B replies *yes* to the questions about the start and the palm trees, A apparently understands that B has those features on his map (and overtly indicates that he has understood this – or perhaps that this is a satisfactory outcome – by saying *all right* and *right*). At the point when B replies *yes,* we could say that A and B have good grounds for mutually believing that they have now established that both of them have 'the start' and 'the palm trees' or, put differently that the start and the palm trees are now part of their common ground or shared context. Of course, their beliefs may be ill-placed – the makers of the maps may have played them false and located the relevant features in different positions on the two maps. They appear to assume, no doubt riskily, that the maps are identical in these respects, so much so that in trying to fix the location of 'the swamp', A feels able to refer to 'the left of the palm trees', as though this were indeed a mutually shared location. Note that it is not until B has looked in this specified location that he himself knows the answer to A's question, and feels able to reply to the question about whether or not he has the swamp with a definite *no.*

In this, restricted, type of data, information from the spoken discourse is combined with information from the map in front of each speaker to constitute the context which can be called upon if necessary to locate later features. There is of course, as we noted in chapters 2 and 4, a wider context which is also shared. Both participants have heard the instructions pertaining to the Map task. Hence, they should both believe that there will be occasions when B's map does not have a feature that is on A's map (and vice-versa) and that 'the same feature' can be differently located on the two maps. However, this second warning is rarely obviously taken into account, except where some mismatch of features occurs as in the case of the swamp in extract (7f). Both speakers also know that it is A's job to describe the route to B, and that they should not show each other their maps.

The two participants also both know about an even wider context, such as that they should both speak English, that they should concentrate on the task rather than on some other occupation, that they should speak loudly enough to be heard by their interlocutor, that they should tell the truth about what is represented on their maps, that they should allow each other time to take a turn, and so on. We shall simply assume this wider context without further discussion, as we shall assume the construction of the limited search field, discussed in 3.7 and 4.3.

Even in the first few moves of the task, A demonstrates to B that he is starting from the beginning of the route, at 'the start', and that he is then moving to the nearest feature on the map, 'the palm trees'. From this behaviour, B could infer (and apparently does) that A will proceed in what might be thought to be the spatial equivalent of ordo naturalis, by moving on each occasion to the most proximate feature on the route. B might infer that A will follow such a procedure even before A begins, since it is almost certainly the tactic that B would have adopted if he had been allotted the A-role, since all A-role speakers adopt this tactic without any prior instruction to do so.

Note that, as the task begins, B is looking at what must seem to be an unstructured map, with no route marked upon it. Given that the map is quite rich in drawings, B may not even have noticed that there is a cross near the bottom. A's first utterance *do you have the start marked* may signal to B that he needs to search the relevant environment, the map, or may simply indicate to him that 'the start' which he has already noticed is also shared by A. In either case, the outcome of this utterance appears to be that B now knows that he has the start, and must be safe in assuming that A has it, since A's utterance presupposes its existence. He knows, however, that A has not yet been informed of B's own state of knowledge. After having said *yes*, and heard A's reply *all right*, B must now have achieved the following steps in the positive mutual beliefs mode, with respect to 'the start'.

(1) know that he himself has the start,
(2) believe that A has the start,
(3) know that A now has reason to believe that B has the start, and
(4) know that A now has reason to believe that B has reason to believe that A has the start.

Similarly, after the interchange with respect to 'the swamp', in the negative mutual beliefs mode, B must now

(1) know that he himself has no swamp to the left of the palm trees
(2) believe that A has a swamp to the left of the palm trees

(3) know that A now has reason to believe that B has no swamp to the left of the palm trees
(4) know that A now has reason to believe that B has reason to believe that A has a swamp to the left of the palm trees.

We can find plenty of evidence of the relevance of steps 1–3, in the way that listeners, when their turn comes, refer to entities which they have learned about. It is less obvious though, that step 4 actually affects what participants say. The relevance of steps 1–3 can be seen in analysing a less immediately successful interaction, seen from the point of view of both A and B in their roles as listener, (7g). (These are Scottish subjects.)

(7g)		(J & L)
1	A.	you start below the palm beach right
2	B.	+ right
3	A.	you go over to quite a bit below the bottom of the
4		swamp + in a big bend
5	B.	what swamp?
6	A.	swamp swamp
7	B.	how far is it away from palm beach?
8	A.	about forty miles (*giggles*) ++ it's quite a big bit
9		away
10	B.	is it near the crocodiles bit?
11	A.	++ no ++ haven't got crocodiles on this ++ have you
12		got the bit with the swamp no?
13	B.	no
14	A.	have you not got the swamp bit yet?
15	B.	no
16	A.	well I just telt you where it was + along from the
17		palm beach right ++ you start at palm beach
18	B.	right
19	A.	you – go ++ left ++ to the swamp
20	B.	++ right
21	A.	have you got the swamp now?
22	B.	no

Once B has interpreted A's first utterance and located the palm beach, he has presumably accomplished steps 1 and 2 in the positive mutual beliefs mode: he knows that he himself has the palm beach and has reason to believe that A has. Once he has said *right*, in confirmation that he has understood A's instruction, he can reasonably suppose that step 3 is now achieved. There is, after all, no reason for him to say *right*, other than to inform A of his own state of information. When B uses the referring expression *it* to refer to the swamp, in lines 7 and 10, this is licensed, not by what B knows directly of the swamp from his own map, but by step 2 in the negative mutual beliefs mode (perhaps also by step 4).

Now consider A's role as listener, interpreting B's utterances. By the end of B's reply in line 2, A can reasonably suppose, in a positive mode, the complementary set of assumptions to those available to B. A should

(1) know that he himself has the palm beach
(2) have reason to believe that B has the palm beach
(3) know that B now has reason to believe that A has the palm beach
(4) know that B now has reason to believe that A has reason to believe that B has the palm beach

There seems to be no significant difference between A and B in their roles as listener. However, this extract, (7g), provides us with an example of misinterpretation of a negative reply, when we come to the issue of the swamp, where A has not properly interpreted what B has said. A must, by the end of line 4:

(1) know that he himself has the swamp (from before line 3 when he refers to it)
(2) believe (mistakenly) that B has the swamp (in lines 3–4, A presupposes in his instruction that B has the swamp)
(3) know that B now has reason to believe that A has the swamp (since A has mentioned it). This belief may well be reinforced by B's mention of the swamp in lines 7 and 10 as *it*, as though he knows about it.

In his interchange with B, in lines 5–13, where B tries to identify the location of the swamp so that he can find it on his map, A appears to assume that B is simply not looking in the right place when he replies *no* in lines 13 and

15. He seems to interpret B's replies as meaning 'I can't see the swamp in the location I am looking at' rather than 'I haven't got the swamp at all'. Such an analysis is justified by the fact that, in lines 16–19, A re-describes the location of the swamp, speaking slowly and clearly, and then asks again in line 21 *have you got the swamp now?* only to receive, once again, B's disappointing reply.

So far, we have demonstrated that participants do appear to be using at least steps 1–3 of mutual belief in constructing replies to the other speaker about information which they have learnt about. Are there any occasions where we can see evidence that the embedded step 4 is required to give an account of a form produced by one of the speakers? Consider again part of extract (3m), now renumbered as (7h), from the point of view of B as listener:

			B	B/A	B/A/B	B/A/B/A
1	A.	you got the church	?	+		
2	B.	+++ no	–	+		–
3	A.	right + there's a				
4		church there	–	+	–	+
5	B.	. . . is it northeast . . .	–	+	–	+

(7h)   (DC & LC)

After A's remark in lines 3–4, B has reason to believe that A (who B believes has a church B/A) has understood that B has no church (B/A/B) and has also understood that B understands that A has a church, since B was able to answer *no* to a question which presupposed that A knows about a church and assumes that B knows about it too. In extract (7g), the A-role speaker at no point gave B evidence that A had grasped that B understood that A had a swamp, even though B himself had no swamp. In that extract, the A-role speaker seemed to be incapable of disengaging his own knowledge of the swamp and A's appreciation of B's knowledge of A's swamp, from B's own direct knowledge of a swamp. In the extract we are now considering, A shows, by shifting (lines 3–4) to an indefinite expression, *a church*, that he has managed to disentangle these issues. B may well be able to use this as evidence for supposing that A has understood how much B has understood, and indeed, B moves confidently in line 5 to refer to the church that he knows that A knows he knows that A has, by the expression *it*, assuming it to be fully shared.

Those who argue that step 4 is necessary to mutual understanding, should demonstrate that it has some effect in real-life conversation, rather than in constructed examples where a third party, an omniscient observer, constructs paradigms of mutual knowledge shared by both invented participants in a dialogue. As Searle remarks: 'By adopting a God's eye view we think we can see what Ralph's real beliefs are even if he can't. But what we forget when we try to construct a belief that is not entirely in Ralph's head is that we have only constructed it in our head' (1983:230). It is clear, from analysis of the forms of expression used in the simple Map task data, that participants do constantly use steps 1–3 in their interpretations. It is harder to find secure examples of the utilisation of step 4, and it seems quite impossible, in this data, to find evidence that speakers are utilising any further depth of recursion.

It is clear that there is evidence here both that speakers regularly take account of their judgment of who knows what, at least to a depth of step 3, in constructing their utterances, and that those who have just been listeners manifest, in their turn as speakers, that they have taken what they assume to be mutual beliefs into account in constructing their utterances. We see in the extracts we have just discussed how comprehensively the structure of these conversations is determined by the need to establish an adequate structure of mutual beliefs.

7.3 Expression meaning and speaker intentions

In 3.6.2, we began to discuss the issue of the gap which may appear between what an expression might conventionally be held to mean, if interpreted out of any context, and what it is used to mean by a speaker on a given occasion of use. The particular examples we were discussing (3n) – (3r), were ones in which speakers used a variety of expressions other than *a pylon* to refer to a pylon, and where the listeners, with some additional information, were nonetheless able to work out what type of referent the speaker was attempting to identify. In the case of (3q), where the descriptive expression used by the speaker was *a colon*, the listener was able to understand the speaker intended to refer to a pylon. I suggested there that we might fruitfully call upon Chomsky's (1988) distinction between **I-language**, a language internalised by a particular individual, constituting all the relevant linguistic (and contextual) experience of that individual, and **E-language**, the language externally available within a speech community, whose conventions are (in part) encoded in descriptive grammars, dictionaries and manuals of prescribed usage. We could, then, suggest that, while the expressions produced by the speakers might not conform to manuals of prescribed usage, the expressions used may adequately represent the speaker's intentions, in that all but one of the listeners was able to divine the speaker's intentions in spite of the speaker's use of an apparently misleading expression.

How can the listener have access to the speaker's intentions, and how informative can those intentions be?

Since Grice's influential 1956 paper, *Meaning*, speaker intention has been embraced by many philosophers and linguists as offering a way to distinguish between what is expressed in a sentence by virtue of its syntax and the words that it contains, and what a speaker intends to convey by uttering that sentence in a particular context. The performance of a linguistic utterance is offered by A, the speaker, to B, the listener, as evidence from which B can infer what A intended to convey. It is necessary for B not only to decode the linguistic utterance (to unwrap and assess the parcel of evidence), but also to consider why A produced this particular form of utterance, in order for B to arrive at an interpretation. Decoding the linguistic forms alone will only produce a parsed string of forms, not the interpretation of an utterance. D.M. Armstrong gives an account of what a listener, B, might understand from an utterance by a speaker, A, in a private communication quoted by Bennett: 'The utterance of "there is a snake behind you" is a *first-class* sign that A wants B to believe that A believes there is a snake behind B, a *rather good* sign that A believes there is a snake behind B, and a *fairly good* sign that there is a snake behind B.' (Bennett 1976: 151, original emphases, but Armstrong's symbols U, A are here replaced by A, B)

The position adopted by many scholars (particularly those committed to some form of cognitive science approach) is clearly expressed by Dennett: 'the interpretation of a bit of *outer*, public communication – a spoken or written utterance in natural language for instance – *depends on* the interpretation of the utterer's beliefs and desires' (Dennett 1990:191). Others who share, to some degree at least, this approach, include Fodor ('good old commonsense belief/desire psychology . . . tells us, for example, how to infer people's intentions from the sounds they make' 1988:3) and Sperber and Wilson (1986:25). Readers may remember from discussion in chapters 1 and 3, Evans' requirement that, to properly understand a referring expression, a hearer must proceed to 'the *right* (i.e. intended) interpretation. And if he is to be credited with understanding, he must *know* that it is the right interpretation' (1982:310, original emphases). (Those who see insoluble technical problems with the intention-based approach include Quine 1960 and Schiffer 1987.)

A problem for the discourse analyst is to determine just how intentions get into the public domain and become manifest to the listener. Many writers seem to view this issue as quite unproblematical. Davidson, for example, writes 'A better way to distinguish . . . meaning is through the intentions of the speaker. The intentions with which an act is performed are usually unambiguously ordered by the relation of means to ends' (1986:435). Clark and Schaefer suggest that addressees 'are intended to *recognise* what speakers mean – that is, infer it from conclusive evidence' ([1987] 1992:260). Similarly Sperber and Wilson, in constructing an account of ostensive-inferential communication, write that the ostensive stimulus must at least 'attract attention and focus it on the communicator's intentions. How can it do this? . . . Ostensive stimuli arouse definite expectations of relevance' (1986:154–5).

What is the term **intention** to embrace? Recognition of the speaker's intention is considered necessary not only so that the hearer should understand the meaning of the words uttered, but also so that the hearer should understand the kind of illocutionary act which the listener is attempting to perform. Strawson (1974) offers an account which suggests that interpreting the speaker's meaning, and interpreting what the speaker is doing in saying what he says, require a rather similar analysis of how the listener must interpret the speaker's intention in each case.

It is clearly the case that the speaker may simultaneously have any number of what we would normally describe as 'intentions' in uttering, such as:

- the speaker intends to address a given addressee (or addressees) and intends that the addressee should recognise this intention
- the speaker intends to inform, or to instruct the addressee, or to emphasise (e.g. by repeating), or question a belief or attitude of the speaker or of the addressee and intends that the addressee should recognise this intention
- the speaker intends to construct an utterance which will appropriately take account of the existing knowledge or beliefs or attitudes which the speaker attributes to the hearer
- the speaker intends that the addressee should recognise that the speaker intends to inform (etc.) the addressee *that P* (i.e. of the content of the proposition expressed in the utterance) and that the recognition of A's intention by B should be part of B's reason for believing *that P.*
- the speaker **may** intend to inform other ratified participants, while addressing the addressee and may intend that they should recognise the speaker's intention to inform them
- the speaker **may** intend to arouse, by uttering, a particular emotion (anger, pleasure, amusement, etc.) in the addressee (or other participants or overhearers) and may, or may not, intend that these intentions are recognised by the addressee. (Strawson notes that when we show off, we are intending to produce an effect on the audience, but in this case 'it is no part of our total intention to secure recognition of the intention to produce the effect at all. On the contrary recognition of the intention might militate against securing the effect' ([1974] 1991:297).)

We must recognise, then, the likelihood of a speaker having a complex set of intentions on each occasion of utterance, none of which can always be simply matched to the nature of the form of the utterance. There are extrovert speakers who wear their hearts on their sleeves, and appear to be passionately committed to whatever they are engaged in saying, enriching each utterance with a manipulation of phonological features of stress, loudness, exaggerated duration, variation in voice quality and expanded intonation patterns which can serve either to amplify or to modify the verbal message (see Brown 1990 for discussion of these phenomena). There are, however, other speakers who maintain a stiff upper lip in their self-presentation, whose phonological range in uttering is far more narrow, and who offer fewer overt facial and postural clues to the addressee about their attitude to what they are saying. Strawson makes a remark which rather obviously applies to some participants in the Map task: 'A speaker . . . may offer information, instructions, or even advice and yet be overtly indifferent as to whether or not the information is accepted as such . . . His wholly overt intention may amount to no more than that of making available – in a "take it or leave it spirit" – to his audience the information or instructions or opinion in question' ([1974] 1991:301).

How, then, are a speaker's intentions brought into the public domain so that a listener may have access to them? Anscombe ([1957] 1976), in a general discussion of intention, suggests that a good indication of what somebody's intentions are is what that person does. Most of the things that somebody does, that we pay attention to and would be capable of reporting, would be things that the person did intentionally (1957:8). She suggests that we should be capable of questioning intentional actions, and that the appropriate form of question will be *why* questions (1957:80). In the case of language used intentionally, we would suppose that what the speaker says should be (at least) one indication of what the speaker intends to achieve by speaking. The speaker offers the utterance as evidence for what the speaker wants the listener to understand, assuming of course that the listener will interpret the utterance in the relevant context. The nature of the performance of the utterance (which will include how it is said, whether for instance the speaker mutters as if to himself, or giggles while speaking) may offer a further clue to the speaker's intention in uttering.

If we now revisit part of the Map task extract which we have already discussed ((7f), now renumbered as (7i)), we can see how far we can proceed with the attribution of intentions:

(7i)　　(R & H)
　　A. do you have the start marked
　　B. yes
　　A. all right
　　　　do you have palm trees?

In two-party conversations of this type, there is rarely doubt about who is the intended addressee, or that the speaker intends to address the other party. When we discussed extract (7i) in 2.3, I pointed out that the form of A's utterances, interrogatives – direct questions, might be intended simply to request information for A's own use about B's information or might simultaneously be intended to inform B, indirectly, that A was in possession of 'the start' and 'palm trees'. There is no way, short of B directly asking A, for B to distinguish between these sets of intentions. The fact that no listener in the Map task data ever asks what the speaker meant by such an utterance, suggests that the listeners in this highly circumscribed situation are content to take each utterance at its face value as far as the dialogue is concerned, and to understand interrogatives simply as questions to be answered (humorously on occasions as the A-role speaker demonstrates in extract (7g) where in response to B's question *how far is it away from palm beach*, he replies *about forty miles*). Whereas the listener takes the interrogative at its face value vis-a-vis the speaker who put the question, the listener can also, independently, put to use the information about A's state of knowledge gleaned from the presuppositions expressed in A's question.

This independent putting-to-use may, or may not, have been intended by the speaker, but it hardly matters to the listener whether it was, or was not, deliberately and knowingly intended. In this information driven exchange, it appears to be, as we have noted now on many occasions, the listener's own immediate goals which will determine how the speaker's utterance is interpreted. It may be that for this type of genre, where the A-role speaker is the repository of information which B needs, that all that is necessary for B is to assume that A is addressing B, is speaking of the matter in hand, and is speaking of it truthfully and in an orderly manner.

7.4 Conclusion

In chapter 1, we noted that, in everyday life, adequate communication is regularly achieved, despite the pervasive underspecification of the meanings of utterances. We have observed in this chapter one of the mechanisms which appears to permit an adequate exchange of information – this is the establishment of a structure of mutual beliefs which, we have seen, enables participants to make rational and confident interpretations of the other's utterances.

We also noted in chapter 1, that a distinction is often drawn between sentence meaning and speaker meaning, a distinction which is based on an appeal to the speaker's intentions in uttering. We have noted that the evidence for the speaker's intentions in uttering appears in general to consist of no more than the form of utterance offered at a particular point in a conversational exchange. On the narrow basis of this evidence, it seems unlikely that the listener could attain to the correct ascription of intentions to the speaker in any very detailed manner. Appeal to intentions will not offer us an easy route to that chimera, universally correct interpretation. Certainly, listeners will ascribe intentions to speakers, but unless the speaker offers overwhelming linguistic or paralinguistic evidence of a specific intention, the intentions ascribed seem likely to be those which listeners would expect to experience themselves in uttering the utterance just heard in that particular context. That listeners do behave in this way, attributing to speakers what they believe that they themselves would mean by speaking in such a manner at that particular point in conversation, seems indisputable. As Cicourel remarks: 'It is the **presumption** that everyday participants in social life are operating under the same principles, "playing the same game", that is critical' (Cicourel 1973:87).

Epilogue

We have explored a range of basic questions in communication, examining the notions of communication, reference and context, and emphasising the role of the listener in communication rather than concentrating on that of the speaker.

We have seen, in the data presented here, examples of apparently fully correct interpretation by listeners, as well as a wide range of examples of apparently adequate and apparently inadequate interpretation, and we have speculated on the reasons for this variation. The Map task method has permitted us to address the points raised in 2.1 as possible reasons for a listener failing to respond adequately to what a speaker has said. It allows us to distinguish between occasions when a listener has apparently not heard what the speaker said, has heard but not interpreted what was said, has heard but not interpreted until later on what a speaker said, or has heard but not understood (all of) what a speaker said. We have seen many occasions when a listener selects just some part of the speaker's utterance to pay attention to, because only that part was relevant to the listener's current intentions, since for the listener, understanding what the speaker said is only a means to an end – and for the listener, it is the listener's end which is at issue.

In both the Map task and the Stolen letter task, we saw evidence that it is not only language which subjects interpret in different ways. In the Map task, we saw occasions of gross differences in interpretation (lake/island) and many occasions of minor differences of perspective on a given feature, as for instance, where different speakers had apparently paid attention to different aspects of the pylon. Similarly in the Stolen letter task there was a wide range of differences of interpretation, and/or of differences in what speakers remembered, of what they had witnessed in watching the filmed episodes. Using such fully contextualised tasks enabled us to see that misunderstandings frequently arise not directly from the linguistic form of the utterance but because of the listener's difficulty in relating what the speaker has said to the listener's own perception, or memory, of the nature of features or events in the world.

We have been able to see which configurations of information give rise to most problems for listeners. The different formats of the Map task and the Stolen letter task have enabled us to study differences in listener roles, and to appreciate how the establishment of mutual beliefs dominates the structure of conversation which is concerned with the exchange of information.

The differences between the spatially structured Map task and the temporally structured Stolen letter task have indicated the range of demands upon the listener which are thrown up by different genres. We may confidently expect that further genres would make more extended demands upon the listener. For example, the expository argumentative genre, which not only does not permit a stable externally provided model like a map, but also does not permit a visual mental representation in the way that a narrative apparently does, but, rather, depends uniquely upon logically ordered propositional sequences, must make a rather different set of cognitive demands upon the listener.

The data has permitted us to examine ways in which the making of reference was achieved, using fully specific lexical referring expressions, vague and underdetermined lexical expressions and bleached or anaphoric expressions. We noted that listeners appear to take a much wider range of expressions than those standardly accepted as referring expressions as expressions intended to refer. We have considered the variety of expressions used by speakers to refer, and we have explored the degree to which, in order to achieve reference, it appears to be necessary for speakers and listeners to think of referents in 'a pretty similar way' (Evans 1982), and we have concluded that, as long as they adopt the same perspective on the referent, look at it from the same viewpoint and take it generally as the same sort of thing, reference can be achieved. (Thus whatever is denoted by the expression *a yacht* is compatible, in the relevant context, with whatever is denoted by the expression *a boat*, whereas the denotations of the expressions *a lake* and *an island*, at least in the context we considered, are not compatible, and so communication breaks down.) We have explored some of the mechanisms by which listeners construct a mutually agreed anchor-point from which they can attempt to adopt the speaker's perspective within a constrained search field, and we have examined the role which deictic expressions, ordo naturalis and space-builders play in this process.

We have seen that listeners in these simple tasks apparently make only the most general appeal to speaker intentions in interpreting what speakers say. They assume that speakers intend to address them, that what the speaker says relates to the task in hand and they assume (with one or two exceptions which we noted) that the speaker is endeavouring to speak the truth. Other than that, they appear simply to take whatever the speaker says as evidence for what the speaker intended. The criterion I have suggested here is that suggested by many other scholars, for instance by Cicourel (1973); that is that the listener takes the speaker to intend an utterance to mean whatever the listener, had the listener been the speaker, would have intended it to mean. This conclusion suggests that an individual can only understand what that individual is capable of understanding in a particular context at a given moment of time (which raises again the problems of 'me and my friends' psychology (Stich 1983) which were discussed in chapters 1 and 2). The data I present here supports such a conclusion.

References

Allan, K. (1971) A note on the source of 'there' in existential sentences. *Foundations of Language* 7, 1–18

Allan, K. (1972) In reply to 'there I, there II'. Journal of Linguistics 8, 119–124

Allan, K. (1986) *Linguistic Meaning*. Vols. I and II. London: Routledge and Kegan Paul

Anscombe, G.E.M. ([1957] 1976) *Intention.* Oxford: Basil Blackwell

Barsalou, L.W. (1989) The instability of graded structure: implications for the nature of concepts. In (ed.) U. Neisser *Concepts and Conceptual Development.* Cambridge University Press (141–75)

Bartlett, F.C. (1932) *Remembering.* Cambridge University Press

Bechtel, W. and Abrahamsen, A. (1991) *Connectionism and the Mind.* Oxford: Basil Blackwell

Bennett, J. (1976) *Linguistic Behaviour.* Cambridge University Press

Bolinger, D. (1947) More on the present tense in English. *Language 23,* (434–36)

Brown, G. (1986) Investigating listening comprehension in context. *Applied Linguistics 7,* (284–303)

Brown, G. (1987) Modelling discourse participants' knowledge. In J. Monaghan (ed.) *Grammar in the Construction of Texts.* London: Frances Pinter (89–99)

Brown, G. (1989) Making sense: the interaction of linguistic expression and contextual information. *Applied Linguistics 10/1,* 97–109.

Brown, G. (1990) (2nd edition) *Listening to Spoken English.* London: Longman

Brown, G., Anderson, A.H. and Yule, G. (1985) Hearer effects on speaker performance: the influence of the hearer on speakers' effectiveness in oral communication tasks. *First Language 5,* (156–69)

Brown, G., Currie K. and Kenworthy, J. (1980) *Questions of Intonation.* London: Croom Helm

Brown, G. and Markman, S. (1991) Discourse Processing and Preferred Information. *Linguistics and Education 3,* (47–63)

Brown, G. & Yule, G. (1983) *Discourse Analysis.* Cambridge University Press

Brown, P. & Levinson, S. (1978) Universals in language usage: politeness phenomena. In E. Goody (ed.) *Questions and Politeness: Strategies in Social Interaction.* Cambridge University Press (41–189)

Brown, P. and Levinson, S.C. (1988) *Politeness.* Cambridge University Press

Brown, R. and Gilman, A. (1960) The pronouns of power and solidarity. In T.A. Sebeok (ed.) *Style in Language.* Cambridge Mass. John Wiley and Sons (253–77)

Bühler, K. ([1934] 1963) *Theory of Language.* (translated into English by D. Fraser Goodwin) Amsterdam/ Philadelphia: John Benjamins Publishing

Carrier, R. (1967) *Great Dishes of the World.* London: Thomas Nelson

Chomsky, N. (1988) *Language and the Problem of Knowledge: the Managua Lectures.* Cambridge, Mass.: MIT Press

Cicourel, A.V. (1973) *Cognitive Sociology.* Harmondsworth: Penguin Books

Clark, H.H. (1976) *The Semantics of Comprehension.* The Hague: Mouton

Clark, H.H. (1983) Making sense of Nonce Sense. In G.B. Flores d'Arcais & R.J. Jarvella (eds.), *The Process of Language Understanding.* Chichester: John Wiley (297–333)

Clark, H.H. (1992) *Arenas of Language Use.* The University of Chicago Press

Clark, H.H. and Carlson, T.B. (1982) Context for Comprehension. In J. Long and A. Baddeley (eds.) *Attention and Performance 1X.* Hillsdale (NJ): Lawrence Erlbaum Associates (313–30)

Clark, H.H. and Clark, E.V. (1977) *Psychology and Language.* New York: Harcourt,Brace Jovanovich

Clark, H.H. and Marshall, C.R. (1981) Definite reference and mutual knowledge. In A.K. Joshi, B. Webber and I. Sag (eds.) *Elements of Discourse Understanding.* Cambridge University Press (10–64)

Clark, H.H. and Schaefer, E.F. (1987) Concealing one's meaning from overhearers. *Journal of Memory and Language 26,* (209–25). Reprinted in Clark, H.H (1992)

Dahl, O. (1976) What is new information? In N.E. Enkvist and V. Kohonen (eds.) *Reports on Text Linguistics: Approaches to Word Order.* Abo, Finland: Abo Akademi Foundation (37–51)

Damasio, A.R., and Damasio, H. (1992) Brain and Language. *Scientific American,* September, (89–95)

Davidson, D. (1974) On the Very Idea of a Conceptual Scheme. In *Proceedings and Addresses of the American Philosophical Association,* (5–20)

Davidson, D. ([1977] 1986) A Nice Derangement of Epitaphs. In E. LePore (ed.) *Truth and Interpretation.* Oxford: Basil Blackwell (433–47)

Davis, S. (ed.) (1991) *Pragmatics: A Reader.* Oxford University Press

Dennett, D.C. (1990) Making sense of ourselves. In W.G. Lycan (ed.) *Mind and Cognition.* Oxford: Basil Blackwell (184–99)

van Dijk, T.A. and Kintsch, W. (1983) *Strategies of Discourse Comprehension.* New York: Academic Press

Donnellan, K. (1966) Reference and Definite Descriptions. *Philosophical Review* 75 (281–304)

Downes, W. (1984) *Language and Society.* London: Fontana

Dummett, M. (1986) 'A Nice Derangement of Epitaphs': Some Comments on Davidson and Hacking. In E. LePore (ed.) *Truth and Interpretation.* Oxford: Basil Blackwell (459–77)

Evans, G. (1982) J. McDowell (ed.) *The Varieties of Reference.* Oxford: Oxford University Press

Fauconnier, G. (1985) *Mental Spaces.* Cambridge, Mass.: The MIT Press

Fillmore, C.J. (1975) *Santa Cruz Lectures on Deixis.* Reproduced by the Indiana University Linguistics Club

Fillmore, C.J. (1977) Topics in lexical semantics. In R.W. Cole (ed.) *Current Issues in Linguistic Theory*. Bloomington: Indiana University Press (57–83)

Fillmore, C.J. (1981) Pragmatics and the description of discourse. In P. Cole (ed.) *Radical Pragmatics*. New York: Academic Press

Fillmore, C.J. (1982) Towards a Descriptive Framework for Spatial Deixis. In R.J. Jarvella and W. Klein (eds.) *Speech, Place and Action*. London: John Wiley (31–59)

Fleischman, S. (1990) *Tense and Narrativity*. London: Routledge

Fodor, J.A. (1986) Banish DisContent. Reprinted in W.G. Lycan (ed.) (1990) *Mind and Cognition*. Oxford: Basil Blackwell (420–39)

Fodor, J.A. (1988) *Psychosemantics*. Cambridge, Mass.: The MIT Press

Frazier, L. (1987) The study of linguistic complexity. In A. Davison and G.M. Green (eds.) *Linguistic Complexity and Text Comprehension*. Hillsdale, N.J.: Lawrence Erlbaum Associates (193–223)

Garnham, A. (1985) *Psycholinguistics*. London: Methuen

Gernsbacher, M.A. (1990) *Language Comprehension as Structure Building*. Hillsdale, New Jersey: Lawrence Erlbaum Associates

Gibson, J.J. (1966) *The Senses considered as Perceptual Systems*. Boston: Houghton Mifflin

Goffman, E. (1967) *Interaction Ritual*. London: Allen Lane, The Penguin Press

Goffman, E. (1981) *Forms of Talk*. Oxford: Basil Blackwell

Graesser, A.C. (1981) *Prose Comprehension beyond the Word*. New York: Springer-Verlag

Grice, H.P. (1956) Meaning. *Philosophical Review, 67*.

Grice, H.P. ([1967] 1975) Logic and Conversation. Unpublished ms of the William James Lectures, Harvard University, in part reprinted in P. Cole and J. Morgan (eds.) *Syntax and Semantics 3: Pragmatics*. New York: Academic Press (41–59)

Grice, H.P .([1975] 1991) Utterer's Meaning, Sentence Meaning and Word Meaning. In S. Davis (ed.) *Pragmatics: a Reader*. Oxford University Press. (305–16)

Halliday, M.A.K. and Hasan, R. (1976) *Cohesion in English*. London: Longman

Hanks, W.F. (1987) Markedness and category interactions in the
Malagasy deictic system. *University of Chicago Working Papers in
Linguistics, vol.3*

Haugeland, J. (1979) Understanding Natural Language. Reprinted in
W.G. Lycan (ed.) (1990) *Mind and Cognition.* Oxford: Basil
Blackwell (660–71)

Hawkins, J.A. (1978) *Definiteness and Indefiniteness.* London: Croom
Helm

Heeschen, V. (1982) Some systems of spatial deixis in Papuan language.
In J. Weissenborn and W. Klein (eds.) *Cross-linguistic Studies on
Deixis and Demonstration.* Amsterdam: John Benjamins

Herskovitz, A. (1986) *Language and Spatial Cognition.* Cambridge
University Press

Hockney, D. (1976) *David Hockney by David Hockney.* London: Thames
and Hudson

Hofstadter, D.R. (1980) *Godel, Escher, Bach: an eternal Golden Braid.*
Harmondsworth: Penguin Books

Jackendoff, J. (1983) *Semantics and Cognition.* Cambridge, Mass.: The
MIT Press

James, H. (1884) *The Art of Fiction.* Reprinted in M. Shapira (ed.) (1963)
Henry James: Selected Literary Criticism. Harmondsworth: Penguin
Books (78–98)

James, W. ([1890] 1981) *The Principles of Psychology.* Vols. I and II. New
York: Dover Publications

Jarvella, R.J. and Engelkamp, J. (1983) Pragmatic influences in producing
and perceiving language. In G.B. Flores d'Arcais & R.J. Jarvella
(eds.) *The Process of Language Understanding.* Chichester: John Wiley
(225–71)

Jesperson, O. (1924) *The Philosophy of Grammar.* London: George Allen
& Unwin

Johnson-Laird, P.N. (1983) *Mental Models.* Cambridge University Press

Johnson-Laird, P.N. (1990) What is communication? In D.H. Mellor
(ed.) *Ways of Communicating.* Cambridge University Press (1–14)

Kasher, A. (1991) Pragmatics and the modularity of mind. In S. Davis
(ed.) *Pragmatics: a Reader.* Oxford University Press (567–83)

Kiparsky, P .(1968) Linguistic Universals and Linguistic Change. In E. Bach and R.T. Harms (eds.) *Universals in Linguistic Theory.* New York: Holt, Rinehart and Winston (171–205)

Labov, W. (1973) The boundaries of words and their meanings. In C-J.N. Bailey and R.W. Shuy (eds.), *New Ways of Analyzing Variation in English.* Washington: Georgetown University Press

Lakoff, G. (1987) *Women, Fire and Dangerous Things.* The University of Chicago Press

Levinson, S.C. (1980) Speech Act Theory: the State of the Art. *Language and Linguistics Teaching Abstracts 13.1* (5–24)

Levinson, S.C. (1983) *Pragmatics.* Cambridge University Press

Levinson, S.C. (1992) Language and Cognition: The Cognitive Consequences of Spatial Description in Guugu Yithimir. Cognitive Anthropology Research Group, Max Planck Institute, Nijmegen, *Working Paper* 13

Levy, D.M. (1979) Communicative goals and strategies: between discourse and syntax. In T. Givon (ed.) *Syntax and Semantics* vol. 12: *Discourse and Syntax.* New York: Academic Press (70–9)

Lewis, D. (1969) *Convention.* Cambridge, Mass.: Harvard University Press

Linde, C. and Labov, W. (1975) Spatial networks as a site for the study of language and thought. *Language 51,* (924–40)

Locke, J. ([1689] 1971) *An Essay concerning Human Understanding.* London and Glasgow: Fontana

Lodge, D. (1990) The novel as communication. In D.H. Mellor (ed.) *Ways of Communicating.* Cambridge University Press (96–113)

Lycan, W.G. (1990) Introduction to 'The Status of Folk Psychology' In W.G. Lycan (ed.) (339–41)

Lycan, W.G. (ed) (1990) *Mind and Cognition.* Oxford: Basil Blackwell

Lyons, J. (1977) *Semantics.* vols. I and II, Cambridge University Press

Lyons, J. (1991) *Natural Language and Universal Grammar.* Cambridge University Press

McCarthy, R.A. and Warrington, E.K. (1990) *Cognitive Neuropsychology.* San Diego: Academic Press

McKay, D.G. and Fulkerson, D.C. (1979) On the comprehension and production of pronouns. *Journal of Verbal Learning and Verbal Behaviour 18*, (662–73)

Markman, E.M. (1981) Comprehension Monitoring. In W.P. Dickson (ed.) *Children's Oral Communication Skills.* New York: Academic Press (61–85)

Marslen-Wilson, W.D. and Tyler, L.K. (1980) The temporal structure of spoken language understanding. *Cognition 8.* (1–71)

Mellor, D.H. (ed.) (1990) *Ways of Communicating.* Cambridge University Press

Minsky, M. (1975) A framework for representing knowledge. In P.H. Winston (ed.) *The Psychology of Computer Vision.* New York: McGraw Hill

Morton, J. (1969) Interaction of information in word recognition. *Psychological Review 76,* (165–78)

Neisser, U. (1976) *Cognition and Reality.* New York: W.H. Freeman

Neisser, U. (ed.) (1987) *Concepts and Conceptual Development.* Cambridge University Press

Pateman, T. (1987) *Language in Mind and Language in Society.* Oxford: Clarendon Press

Popper, K.R. (1972) *Objective Knowledge.* Oxford: The Clarendon Press

Putnam, H. (1975) The Meaning of 'Meaning'. In K. Gunderson (ed) *Language, Mind and Knowledge.* Minneapolis: University of Minnesota Press

Putnam, H. (1978) *Meaning and the Moral Sciences.* London: Routledge and Kegan Paul

Quine, W. van O. (1960) *Word and Object.* Cambridge, Mass.: The MIT Press

Quirk, R. and Wrenn, C.L. (1955) *An Old English Grammar.* London: Methuen

Quirk, R., Greenbaum, S., Leech, G. and Svartvik, J. (1972) *A Grammar of Contemporary English.* London: Longmans

Reddy, M.J. (1979) The Conduit Metaphor. In A. Ortony (ed.) *Metaphor and Thought.* Cambridge University Press

Rommetveit, R. (1974) *On Message Structure*. London: John Wiley

Rosch, E. (1975) Cognitive representation of semantic categories. *Journal of Experimental Psychology* 104, (12–23)

Ryle, G. (1949) *The Concept of Mind*. Harmondsworth: Penguin Books

Sanford, A. and Garrod, S. (1981) *Understanding Written Language*. Chichester: John Wiley.

Schiffer, S. (1972) *Meaning*. Oxford University Press

Schiffer, S. (1987) *Remnants of Meaning*. A Bradford Book. Cambridge, Mass.: The MIT Press

Schiffrin, D. (1987) *Discourse Markers*. Cambridge University Press

Schlicher, J. (1931) Historical tenses and their functions in Latin. *Classical Philology 26*, (46–59)

Schober, M.F. and Clark, H.H. (1989) Understanding by addressees and overhearers. *Cognitive Psychology 21*, (211–32)

Schutz, A. (1964) *Collected Papers* II: *Studies in Social Theory*. A. Briderson (ed.), The Hague, Nijhoff.

Searle, J.R. (1979) Indirect Speech Acts. In P. Cole and J.L. Morgan (eds.) *Syntax and Semantics 3: Speech Acts*. New York: Academic Press (59–83)

Searle, J.R. (1983) *Intentionality*. Cambridge University Press

Senft, G. (1992) Everything we always thought we knew about space but did not bother to question. Cognitive Anthropology Research Group, Max Planck Institute, Nijmegen: *Working Paper 10*

Shannon, C.E. and Weaver, W. (1949) *The Mathematical Theory of Communication*. Urbana: University of Illinois Press

Smith, N.V. (ed.) (1982) *Mutual Knowledge*. London: Academic Press

Sperber, D. and Wilson, D. (1986) *Relevance*. Oxford: Basil Blackwell

Stevenson, R.J. (1993) *Language, Thought and Representation*. Chichester: John Wiley

Stich, S. (1983) *From Folk Psychology to Cognitive Science: the Case against Belief*. Cambridge, Mass.: Bradford Books, The MIT Press

Strawson, P.F. ([1974] 1991) Intention and Convention in Speech Acts. In S. Davis (ed.) *Pragmatics: a Reader*. Oxford University Press (290–305)

Sweet, H. (1892) *A New English Grammar*. Oxford: The Clarendon Press

Swift, J. ([1726] 1960) *Gulliver's Travels.* Oxford University Press
Swinney, D.A. (1979) Lexical access during sentence comprehension.
    Journal of Verbal Learning and Verbal Behaviour 18, (545–69)
Tannen, D. (1991) *You Just Don't Understand.* London: Virago Press
Tyler, S.A. (1979) *The Said and the Unsaid.* New York: Academic Press
Varonis, E.M. and Gass, S. (1985) Non-native/non-native conversations:
    a model for negotiation of meaning. *Applied Linguistics 6* (71–91)
Venneman, T. (1975) Topic, sentence accent and ellipsis: a proposal for
    their formal treatment. In E.L. Keenan (ed) *Formal Semantics of
    Natural Language.* Cambridge University Press
Wason, P.C. (1960) On the failure to eliminate hypotheses in a
    conceptual task. *Quarterly Journal of Experimental Psychology 12,*
    (129–40)
Wason, P.C. (1977) Self-contradictions. In P.N. Johnson-Laird and P.C.
    Wason (eds.) *Thinking.* Cambridge University Press
Wittgenstein, L. ([1953] 1978) *Philosophical Investigations.* Oxford: Basil
    Blackwell
Wolfson, N. (1979) The conversational historical present alternation.
    Language 55. (168–83)
Wright, P. (1990) Using constraints and making reference in task-oriented
    dialogue. *Journal of Semantics 7,* (53–65)
Ziff, P. (1969) Natural and Formal Language. In S. Hook (ed.), *Language
    and Philosophy.* New York: New York University Press (223–241)

Index